The Wealth of (Some) Nations

The Wealth of (Some) Nations

Imperialism and the Mechanics of Value Transfer

Zak Cope

PLUTO  PRESS

First published 2019 by Pluto Press
345 Archway Road, London N6 5AA

www.plutobooks.com

British Library Cataloguing in Publication Data
A catalogue record for this book is available from the British Library

ISBN   978 0 7453 3886 6   Hardback
ISBN   978 0 7453 3885 9   Paperback
ISBN   978 1 7868 0417 4   PDF eBook
ISBN   978 1 7868 0419 8   Kindle eBook
ISBN   978 1 7868 0418 1   EPUB eBook

Typeset by Stanford DTP Services, Northampton, England
Printed and bound by CPI Group (UK) Ltd, Croydon, CR0 4YY

Contents

List of Figures and Tables

FIGURES

TABLES

Acknowledgements

I would like to acknowledge the late Malcolm Caldwell as the author of a brilliant 1977 book with (almost) the same title as the present work. I would like to thank Immanuel Ness of City University New York for his personal and professional support, and Timothy Kerswell of the University of Macau and Gerry McAleavy of the University of Ulster for the opportunities and encouragement they have given me. I would also like to thank David Shulman of Pluto Press for his insights and his constructive comments on the draft manuscript of the present work, and Elaine Ross of Pluto Press for her careful work on the manuscript. Last but not least, I would like to thank my wife Brona, and my young daughter, Aoibhe, for always being there for me. This book is dedicated to them with love.

Introduction

The Wealth of (Some) Nations builds on the analysis presented in my earlier work examining the segmentation and stratification of the labour market in the capitalist world system and its effects on the dynamics of the global class structure. It explains the hierarchical division of labour internationally as the product of imperialism and relates this to the present crisis of capitalism. The book argues that for a century at least the Western left has largely repudiated labour internationalism in favour of struggles to procure for itself a larger share of value extracted from oppressed nations. The book aims to establish a durable strategic orientation for the labour movement in the contemporary era as based on consistent anti-imperialism and opposition to the sectional privileges enjoyed by metropolitan, settler and 'native' labour aristocratic workers over their counterparts in and from oppressed nations. The book develops a clear and detailed theoretical account of the mechanics of value transfer from the global South to the global North, and presents recent data providing empirical evidence to support its theoretical claims.

The book presents a taxonomy of the 'labour aristocracy' raising the concept to new prominence by documenting in detail the ways in which a bourgeois section of the working class is established in and through imperialism. Hitherto, there has been a variety of theories of the 'labour aristocracy'.[1] Thus Chartist leader Ernest Jones (1819–1869) considered that skilled artisans earning relatively high wages and organised in trades unions constituted the core of the labour aristocracy, and postulated that their activities had weakened the democratic movement by placing barriers in the way of working class unity.[2] Jones' contemporary, and Marx's friend and collaborator Friedrich Engels (1820–1895) had argued that the 'labour aristocracy' in England consisted of the entire national working class which relied on colonialism and industrial monopoly for its livelihood.[3] Later, Russian Marxist and Bolshevik leader Vladimir Ilyich Lenin built upon Engels' insights to argue that imperialism was the underlying basis for the social democratic reformism advanced by the mainstream of the working class movement in the industrial countries. British Marxist historian Eric Hobsbawm developed Lenin's views by arguing that the influx of imperialist superprofits and technological dynamism in the last quarter of the nineteenth century had reshaped Europe's occupational structures so as to ensure that the labour aristocracy possessing skills in short supply, occupying strategic positions in the economy, earning higher wages, and having considerable organisational strength was a much broader social layer than it had been in the earlier colonial period.[4] English historian John Foster stressed workplace authority and supervisory employment as the key determinant of labour aristocratic status.[5] He emphasised the 'bribery' aspect of labour aristocratic privilege which saw the elite stratum of the working class in the United Kingdom as the more or less conscious creation of the establishment in its attempt to defuse and divaricate workers' struggles along a conservative path. British historian Robert Gray, meanwhile, has examined how the labour aristocracy as distinct from the mass of the working class came to define the political outlook of the labour movement in the Victorian era.[6]

Considering these views, and especially those of writers such as H. W. Edwards, Arghiri Emmanuel, Samir Amin, Hosea Jaffe, Torkil Lauesen and Henry Park, the present work defines the labour aristocracy as that section of the international working class whose relatively high incomes, more comfortable occupations and greater social security are dependent upon the expropriation of value from the exploited nations. Even within the imperialist countries, the lower wages, job opportunities, housing conditions, health care provision and labour market precarity of the poorest sections of the metropolitan working class cannot be properly understood without acknowledgement of the legacy and ongoing reality of imperialism and labour aristocratic privilege.

The book argues that capitalism is inherently a system of imperialist international political economy. Imperialism is conceived as a historical and ongoing transfer of wealth from the poorest to the richest countries in the world economy through the mechanisms of colonial tribute, monopoly rent and unequal exchange. Imperialism produces an international class structure characterised by the unequal occupational division of labour and the unequal remuneration of labour internationally such that mass *embourgeoisement* may be observed in the leading imperialist countries. As such, *The Wealth of (Some) Nations* examines a subject that is virtually taboo on the left, namely, the connection between imperialism and the massive disparity in living standards between workers in the First World and workers in the Third World. It thereby fills a necessary gap in the established fields of dependency theory, world systems theory and imperialism theory. While these schools of thought tend to concentrate on the impoverishment of the global South and the enrichment of the global North, they do not usually examine how the attendant processes transfigure the class structure internationally. In particular, the extent to which ever larger transfers of value from abroad produce processes of de-proletarianisation and *embourgeoisement* in the major imperialist countries is largely unaccounted for in much left analysis. Likewise, the problems that enduring imperialist relations pose for socialist struggle internationally remain unclear. This work is intended to contribute to the labour movement's understanding of international solidarity, emphasising that this means much more than distinct subsections of the global working class winning a larger share of the 'national' income. Building on the anti-imperialist writings of a wide plethora of scholars and political activists, both historical and contemporary, the book argues that the ostensibly 'socialist' struggles waged by the metropolitan working class extend its incorporation into imperialist institutions insofar as much of the material wealth to be made available for redistribution is the product of the exploitation of nations. Whereas even the most insightful critics of imperialism tend to reduce the phenomenon to the capture of additional profits by monopolies, the book argues that imperialism affords the mass 'labour aristocracy' of the developed countries high wages, abundant leisure time and white-collar employment at the expense of labour in the underdeveloped countries.

Part I of the book articulates in depth and with reference to the large body of scholarly literature key concepts in the political economy of imperialism, namely, value transfer, colonial tribute, monopoly rent and unequal exchange. These are the key mechanisms by which imperialism operates, ensuring the transfer of value from the global South to the global North. Chapter 1 presents the theory of economic imperialism as the unrequited transfer of value between countries, and examines the extent to which international exploitation is the product of specifically capitalist imperatives in the modern era. Chapter 2 develops an analysis that emphasises the centrality of colonial oppression and exploitation to historical capitalist development, shifting the focus of anti-capitalist critique from the allegedly 'revolutionary' conflict between capital and labour in Europe and North America to the liberation struggles of the colonial world, the 'cutting edge' of class conflict in the imperialist era. Chapter 3 explores the various ways in which the development of monopoly capitalism as a global mode of production facilitates value transfer from the exploited to the exploiting nations. Chapter 4 describes the unequal exchange of embodied labour whereby divergent sums of productive labour are exchanged in international commodities trade, leading to a huge drain of value and capital from the global South and affording a concomitant economic advantage to both capitalists and workers in the global North.

Part II of the work presents various empirical calculations and findings on international value transfer, providing an evidence base in favour of the existence of the labour aristocracy. I attempt to calculate the quantum of value extracted from the global South by means of the mechanisms of value transfer identified in earlier chapters of the book, and by providing current data on the material position of the labour aristocracy itself. Chapter 5 attempts to refute several commonly raised objections against theories of economic imperialism, particularly those which are hegemonic on the metropolitan left. Chapter 6 sets forth estimates of the value transferred from the exploited countries to the imperialist countries in the world economy by means of the mechanisms described above, and sub-varieties of the same. Chapter 7 discusses the ways in which colonialism transferred the wealth of America, Africa and Asia to Europe and to European-descended colonial elites. Chapter 8 compares the foregoing estimates of transfer value to the value of profits, wages and fixed capital in the global North. It also compares transfer value to the costs of various social and economic goods in the global South (including the costs of poverty reduction and the elimination of hunger, as well as the value of savings and capital investment therein). In describing how divergent rates of exploitation internationally have profound consequences in terms of the wealth that workers in different countries consume, I compare total contribution to global production to share of total working class and middle class household consumption for the world's population, ranked in order of income deciles.

Part III of the book explores the concept of the 'labour aristocracy', or what may be referred to as the 'working bourgeoisie'. It presents a theoretical discussion of the bases for labour aristocratic advantage. In particular, this part of the work argues that the labour aristocracy is formed on the basis of 'settler-colonial', metropolitan and 'native' ascendancy attendant to the formation of imperialist economies. It focuses especially on the metropolitan and native labour aristocracies as two sides of the political economy of imperialist *embourgeoisement*. It concludes that the material benefits associated with living in an imperialist country accrue to all but the poorest and most oppressed sections of global North society. As such, it is not simply capitalists of the North whose incomes derive in large measure from imperialism but, to varying degrees, all citizens of the developed countries. Chapter 9 presents a brief history of that strand of Marxist and socialist thought which emphasises the ways in which imperialism and national oppression create the conditions for a material and ideological split within the international workforce. Chapter 10 defines the metropolitan labour aristocracy as that section of the international working class whose relative affluence is sustained by the unrequited transfer of value from the exploited countries to the exploiting countries in the capitalist world system. Chapter 11 describes how native labour aristocracy status in the imperialist countries is conferred by localised discrimination against non-nationals from the exploited countries.

Part IV presents an overview of social-imperialist (or imperialist socialist) political practice over the last century, demonstrating that anti-imperialism has neither been properly prioritised by the metropolitan left in its political practice nor has it been organically integrated into left understandings of class struggle. The part concludes with final comments on the importance of the foregoing analysis for anti-imperialism, socialism and international labour solidarity in today's world. Chapter 12 details the tradition of social imperialism in the half century before the First World War, a watershed moment in labour history when the socialist parties in each of the major belligerent powers gave in to their pre-existing national chauvinist and racist tendencies in a catastrophic way. Chapter 13 examines the history of social imperialism following the Great Class War of 1914–18. It finds that virtually every major strand of socialist praxis in the imperialist countries has for the past century tended to negate the international solidarity of workers in favour of capitulation, collusion and compromise with a ruling class sated with imperialist transfer value. Chapter 14 looks at the *embourgeoisement* of Marxism itself suggesting that Western Marxism has been tailored over the last century according to the interests of the labour aristocracy in maintaining the imperialist world economy.

The Wealth of (Some) Nations concludes with a discussion of the prospects for socialist advance at the present conjuncture, stressing the necessity of anti-imperialism and the central significance of struggles against US hegemony in particular. There is a seemingly limitless capacity for Europeans and Euro-Americans to view their own societies as paragons of every virtue and those of Africa, Asia and South America as prone to every vice, whether the matter at hand is labour relations, gender relations, 'race' relations, art, music, culture, or what constitutes respectable political practice. This capacity is only matched by the even more evident ability of those in the global North to forget the source of the Third World's impoverishment and the First World's affluence, namely, over half a millennium of imperialist despoliation. As such, the book explains how opposition to capitalism must have an internationalist and anti-imperialist dimension and, conversely, how effective anti-imperialism must be rooted in the struggles of working people in the exploited countries. The book concludes that labour internationalism will only become relevant to the vast majority of workers in the developed countries when the so-called developing countries have succeeded in abandoning imperialism and establishing genuine national sovereignty on the basis of democracy and popular movement towards (and beyond) socialism.

Part I
The Mechanics of Imperialism

1
Value Transfer

The traditional Marxist view that capitalism thrives upon the imposition of repressive conditions on workers is correct, but historical capitalism (that is, 'actually existing capitalism') has largely displaced these conditions away from the core countries of the international capitalist economy and onto the subject peoples of its colonial and neo-colonial 'periphery'.[1] Capital accumulation under conditions of global monopoly has supplemented incomes in the global North, providing employees there with a share of 'imperialist rent' (that is, 'the above average or extra profits realised as a result of the inequality between North and South in the global capitalist system').[2] The benefits brought by imperialist rent are, to put it politely, an 'important factor' in curbing the internationalism of the populations of the global North.[3]

Labour organisations in the global North tend to follow the foreign orientation of their governments so that when the system of business internationalism is in the ascendant (from 'Pax Britannica' to the 'Washington Consensus') they support 'free trade', whereas the relative erosion of industrial and financial monopoly encourages protectionist business nationalism. In both cases, 'free trade' and protectionism are characterised by imperialist relations with oppressed populations appropriate to the shifting economic fortunes of the dominant capitalist concerns. Crucially, so-called developing countries have been systematically prevented – ultimately by means of aggressive war, *coups d'état* and internal subversion sponsored by the imperialist countries – from protecting their industries in the way that the developed countries have both in their transition to industrial capitalism and in their latest monopolistic phase.[4]

The global hegemony of imperialist institutions (financial, monetary, corporate, commercial, military and communications), especially those of the United States, is at least tacitly accepted and often enthusiastically championed by the working classes of the imperialist countries. The world's most militarist states, those of North America, the United Kingdom and (to a somewhat lesser extent) Western Europe, have citizens who are historically, culturally and sociologically conditioned to support imperialist war as a matter of duty, obedience, patriotism and citizenship.[5] This political quiescence of the metropolitan working class is facilitated by the imperialist transfer of value. The 'parasitism [of] the whole country that lives by exploiting the labour of several overseas countries and colonies' if enabled to continue eventually (re)produces the phenomenon of mass *embourgeoisement* therein.[6] This explains why there has neither been a revolutionary mass movement nor widespread working class opposition to colonialism or imperialism within an advanced capitalist country. Insofar as the imperialist project proves itself successful, populations in the centres of the capitalist world economy have consistently voted for parties and governments engaged in war, intimidation and ramped up exploitation on an ever expanding planetary scale. As the recipient of value transferred from the underdeveloped countries, the dual class position of the metropolitan working class is reflected in its fundamental acceptance of the imperialist system and its ruling ideologies.

> With a relatively low level of legal non-military struggle they [metropolitan workers] can build big trade unions and negotiate welfare concessions. In return they offer to seek nothing else. That is, they guarantee the security of the state and the domestic stability needed to pursue military policies overseas. The imperialist state is a dialectical unity of colonial militarism and domestic collaboration which determines these specific necessary class alliances, characteristic of contemporary world capitalism.[7]

In this chapter, we argue that to analyse the production and distribution of value and surplus value within each nation without looking beyond its borders is to adopt a kind of 'methodological nationalism' that is both scientifically and politically indefensible.[8] As US theorists of monopoly capitalism Paul Baran and Paul Sweezy have written:

> [Even] today there are many Marxists who seem to think of capitalism as merely a collection of national capitalisms instead of seeing that the international character of imperialism has always had a decisive effect on the nature and functioning of the national units which compose it.[9]

In a subsequent part of the present work we will attempt to gauge metropolitan *embourgeoisement*, that is, the extent to which workers' incomes in the major imperialist countries reflect a petty-bourgeois or middle class social position when understood at the appropriate international level. In this part we describe three interrelated means by which the most affluent countries exploit 'peripheral' countries within the imperialist world system, namely, (1) colonial tribute; (2) monopoly rent; and (3) unequal exchange. Each of these mechanisms of *value transfer* shapes the global class structure and the social role of its various agents. In sum, by contrast with the views of Austrian political economist Joseph Schumpeter who wrote that 'capitalism is by nature anti-imperialist', and for whom imperialism is a fundamentally irrational expression of a pre-modern will to power, we argue that imperialism is theoretically and empirically inseparable from capitalism both historically and currently.[10]

CAPITALISM, CRISIS AND
THE NECESSITY OF IMPERIALISM

For Marx and Engels, capitalism is a system inherently prone to both cyclical and generalised crisis. *Cyclical* crises typically begin with falling demand in the sector producing means of production (what Marx referred to as Department I).[11] During the boom period of a business cycle, both the production of means of production (plant and machinery, expanded transportation, research and development and so forth) and the production of consumer goods grow in tandem. At a certain point, however, business expansion reaches the limits of the current market and investment in new production facilities drops off, leading inevitably to lower levels of employment, lower levels of income and, hence, insufficient effective demand for consumer goods. Restricted demand attendant to increased unemployment forces those capitalists in the sector producing consumer goods (Department II) to reduce costs of production and to renovate their plant and machinery, regardless of whether it is physically usable or not. Increased demand for the output of Department I must initially lag behind its capacity, however, and companies in Department II bid up the price of equipment and materials. In consequence, the profit rate in Department I rises above that in Department II and new capital flows into the former, prompting its capitalists to invest as heavily as possible. Yet by the time this new productive capacity has become fully operational, demand from Department II must necessarily have declined since the attendant approach of full employment drives wages up and poses a threat to the rate of profit, hence stymieing further investment. Still the expansion of production does not typically stop at this point. Rather, there ensues a period of speculation, 'fuelled by the expansion of credit due to the slowing of productive investment and the accumulation of idle money capital. Purchasing commodities in the hope of further price increases, speculators would accumulate stocks. As speculative began to prevail over real investment, the final turning point of the cycle would draw near.'[12]

Capitalism passes through these cycles repeatedly, with their duration and intensity increasing according to a more general tendency for capitalism to break down entirely. This *generalised* crisis is endemic to the logic of capital accumulation. As capital accumulation demands ever higher investments in machinery and fixed assets (c, constant capital) – necessary both to undercut competitors and to block the tendency of rising wages – the share of new value-creating, 'living' labour-power (v, variable capital) in production diminishes. Over time, the surplus value (s, the difference between the value of the workers' wages and the value generated during the course of their employment) needed to maintain a constantly expanding capital outlay declines and so, in tandem, does the rate of profit (r, defined by Marx as $s/c + v$). With every new advance in the technological foundations of capital accumulation, that is, investment in machinery and plant as a proportion of total production investment, there is a decrease in capitalists' inclination to invest in productive, surplus value-creating labour. The resultant underemployment of labour ensures not only that less surplus value is being produced, but also that capitalists are increasingly unable to realise surplus value through the sale of commodities. As a result, there is not only less demand in the consumer goods sector but, consequently, also reduced demand for the means of production.

To ensure the optimal rate of profit, capitalists are forced to increase production, to introduce new technology and to throw an ever increasing quantity of articles onto the market. Exploitation, however, limits the popular consumption of these commodities. Whereas capitalists struggle to keep wages as low as possible to reap higher profits, wages represent a considerable part of the effective demand required to yield profit from sales. As such, if capitalists increase wages, they limit their potential profits, but if wages are lowered the market will be concomitantly constrained. In both cases (restricted profits and restricted markets, respectively), capitalists will cease making new investments. The imperialist solution to capitalism's problems, then, has two sides: profitable investment opportunities in the dependent countries and the expansion of an affluent market in the imperialist countries, created by a transfer of value in the form of superprofits and cheap goods to sustain superwages.

Marx had specified the principal means by which the tendency for the rate of profit to fall (TRPF) is countered as follows: (1) cheapening of the elements of constant capital (machinery and materials); (2) raising of the intensity of exploitation (longer working days, more efficient labour organisation, lower unit labour costs); (3) depression of wages below their value (superexploitation, the payment of below-subsistence wages) and below their current value; (4) relative overpopulation (or increased unemployment); and (5) foreign trade.[13] All five means of countering the TRPF together ensure that capitalism becomes a mode of production in which value is increasingly produced and realised at the level of an imperialist global economy. As a means of combating economic stagnation, an imperialist solution has been pursued vigorously by the world's leading monopolies and their representative states from the late nineteenth century until today. From that time, capitalism has sought trade and investment opportunities in the low-wage countries at the same time as it has created a mass consumer market in the imperialist countries, sustaining itself by a transfer of value reflected in both superprofits and superwages.

IMPERIALISM, DEPENDENCY AND THE GEOGRAPHICAL TRANSFER OF VALUE

The word 'imperialism' derives from the Latin word *Imperium*, meaning several countries ruled by a single overarching authority. In abstract economic terms, imperialism is the systematic unrequited transfer of resources from foreign territories. Imperialism in this sense predates capitalism by several thousand years at least, the Roman, Mongol, Chinese, African, Arab, Amerindian, Indian, Spanish, Ottoman and Russian empires being exemplary in this regard. Wood has distinguished between the 'Empire of Property' typified by the Roman Empire and the Spanish Empire, the 'Empire of Commerce' typified by the Arab Muslim Empires, and the Venetian and Dutch Empires, and the 'Empire of Capital' typified by the British Empire. Only in the transition from the Empire of Commerce to the Empire of Capital did capitalist imperatives first come to constitute the driving force behind imperialism.[14]

Specifically capitalist imperialism functions to bolster the accumulation of capital, that is, the advance of money for the express purpose of purchasing inputs to produce outputs which are then sold for more money, and so on. The plunder of gold from the Americas, forced labour, slavery, colonial levies, and mercantilist profits (based on the promotion of manufactured exports from and the restriction of manufactured imports to the core markets of the world economy), were ways in which capital at the centre of the world economy was augmented very early on at the expense of the economies of the 'periphery'. As such, Austrian Marxist economist Rudolf Hilferding's notion that imperialism emerges only during the final, monopoly phase of capitalism is liable to mislead. Rather than being, as Lenin wrote, the highest stage of capitalism, it is much more the case that imperialism is 'the permanent stage of capitalism'.[15]

The geographical transfer of value (GTV) is the process through which the value produced by workers in one locale is realised (a) by the capitalists who have employed these workers, with profits being reinvested elsewhere; and/or (b) by the capitalists who have employed these workers but is also added as excess profits to capitalists in other locales.[16] Although in both cases the realisation of surplus value occurs both within and outside the area wherein it has been produced, the first case (a) may be referred to as *direct* GTV and the second (b) as *indirect* GTV. Direct GTV arises where straightforward intervention by capitalists and their agents ensures that surplus value produced locally is transferred elsewhere. The forms this intervention takes include war, plunder, taxation, profit repatriation and transfer pricing, typically mediated through the state in combination with industrial and financial capital.[17]

Indirect GTV, meanwhile, operates through the capitalist market and, specifically, according to the transformation of values into prices of production and into actual market prices.[18] This transformation results in the altered division of the total sum of surplus value among individual capitalists having their firms in diverse regions, so that each region's money-profits are not proportional to the surplus value inherent in the commodities they sell. Ultimately, since the price of an individual commodity is not necessarily equal to its value, although the total sum of values remains constant, the transformation of values into prices at the level of the international market ensures that surplus value is redistributed from one locale to another.[19]

Influential British Marxist Bill Warren argued that imperialism was a force tending to spread capitalism and, hence, socialism worldwide. He wrote:

> If ... world capitalism is characterized not only by uneven development, but by changing hierarchies of uneven development ... then, new power centres are arising throughout the Third World. [The] empirically observable trends: of rapidly advancing industrialization; of burgeoning economic nationalism (involving increasing indigenous control and ownership of previously foreign-owned domestically located assets); of growing sectoral diversification (especially the growth of capital and intermediate goods industries); and of the development of capitalist social relations in the more primitive sectors, are sufficiently widespread to enable us to say that throughout the underdeveloped world the post-war period has witnessed a major upsurge of national capitalisms. The result is that the balance of power has shifted away from the dominance of a few major imperialist countries towards a more even distribution of power. Imperialism declines as capitalism grows.[20]

Contrary to these views, we argue that imperialist value transfer acts to thwart the evolving development prospects of the exploited countries and regions relative to those of the exploiting countries and regions of the capitalist world system. Relatedly, it is a mistake to suggest that the incorporation of the countries of the global South into globalised imperialist structures operating principally in the interests of the United States and its major imperialist allies has created straightforwardly and omnipresent capitalist production relations therein. Such views may be fairly character-ised as 'Warrenite fantasies'.[21] The exploited countries of the global economy remain internally disarticulated at the sectoral level, with dependent bour-geoisies following extraverted patterns of accumulation. In consequence, there is an admixture of feudal, semi-feudal and capitalist relations of production throughout the dependent South.

The Dependency theory of the 1960s and 1970s made explicit the enduring relationship between the terrible poverty in the Third World and the incredible opulence of the First World.[22] As one of the founders of Dependency theory, Brazilian economist Theotonio Dos Santos, has written, dependence is

> a situation in which the economy of certain countries is conditioned by the development and expansion of another economy to which the former is subjected. The relation of interdependence between two or more economies, and between these and world trade assumes the form of dependence when some countries (the dominant ones) can expand and be self-starting, while other countries (the dependent ones) can do this only as a reflection of that expansion, which can have either a positive or negative effect on their immediate development.[23]

The Dependency theory-inspired import substitution industrialisation (ISI) programmes adopted by many Third World nations in the 1960s and 1970s, in which state support for the economy played a central role, stimulated growth in Latin America and Africa (where gross domestic product (GDP) rose by 5 per cent and 4 per cent per annum, respec-tively, between 1960 and 1982) and the Asia-Pacific region registering an average increase of 7 per cent a year.[24] Neoliberalism evolved as an anti-protectionist, anti-labour strategy to re-subordinate the Third World to global imperialist interests; roll back the economic challenge posed by the newly industrialising countries and Japan; and dismantle the social contract between monopoly capital and the labour aristocracy.[25] Its implementa-tion relied on the electoral 'conservatism' of a defiantly middle class base in the imperialist nations (including the better-off sections of the traditional labour aristocracy), comprador autocracy in the least developed nations and export-oriented oligarchy in the semi-peripheral nations of the capitalist world system.

Undoubtedly, profound changes in the global economy associated with neoliberalism have refuted Dependency theory's assumption that the possibility of industrialisation in the dependent countries is permanently blocked by imperialism. Indeed, the partial industrialisation of certain large countries in the global South following the adoption of export-oriented industrialisation (EOI) growth strategies in the late 1970s coincided with the (temporary) waning of Dependency theory as a school of thought. Nonetheless, the growth of manufacturing in many countries of the global South has not meant an end to their exploitation. As we wish to demonstrate, value transfer based on low-wage production in countries denied their independence has taken on new and historically unprecedented dimensions as a result of the continued operation of international relations of imperialist exploitation. As British economist John Smith writes:

> Dependency theory's [continued relevance] hinges upon its perception that the wide and growing differences in wages and living standards between workers in imperialist nations and neo-colonial southern nations is reflected in a higher rate of exploitation of workers in the oppressed nations and a mitigation of the rate of exploitation in the imperialist countries; the 'dependent' nations losing and imperialist nations gaining because the former 'exchange more labour for less labour.'[26]

The present work develops this key insight of Dependency theory, emphasising the fact that imperialism is the indispensable condition for the reproduction of imperialist societies as a whole, and not simply the financial wherewithal of particular groups of capitalists therein. As the Dependency theorists recognised, the economies of the 'peripheral' countries in the world economy are constituted as such by their formation according to the requirements of the metropolitan centres. Thus the countries of Africa, Asia and Central and South America have provided slaves, gold, spices, fuel, primary products and/or manufactures according to metropolitan capitalist requirements at particular times. Dependency brings about an international division of labour wherein the development of some countries ('the centre') is facilitated by the exploitation of others (thus constituted as 'the periphery') for which autochthonous development is effectively forestalled.[27]

Though in recent decades many poor countries have benefited from trade and have experienced high growth rates, globalisation has also been characterised by the economic stagnation of backward areas, rising income inequality between countries and unequal power relations at the international level.[28] Relatively high growth rates for the newly industrialising countries (NICs) of the 'periphery' in recent decades have not led to a convergence of per capita GDP globally. Though export-oriented industrialisation has paid dividends for the (distinctly non-neoliberal) *dirigisme* of a select group of East Asian countries granted free access to Western markets, it has not even begun to close the enormous gap in living standards between the world's rich and poor countries. As imperialist capital shifted production to low-wage countries, the developmentalist states of East Asia (variously, the Republic of Korea, Hong Kong, Singapore, Taiwan and China) registered significant growth in productivity and technological capacity, and a concomitant spread of business elites involved in production for Western markets. Neoliberal global labour arbitrage – that is, 'the pursuit of higher profits through the substitution of higher-paid labor with low-paid labor' – has led to a drop in wages worldwide and, hence, rising inequality within countries.[29]

The economic growth of large NICs during the 1980s and up until the Great Recession of 2007–08 was and is entirely conditional upon the growth of global markets in which the imperialist countries are the final, dominant link in the global value chains thereby established. Thus, for example, even after more than two decades of rapid growth, there is still a wide development gap between China and the high-income countries, with China's national income being only one-fifth, and national income per person only 16 per cent, of that of the high-income countries. China's exports, meanwhile, are only 13 per cent of those of the high-income countries, and it has just nine firms in the G1,400 list of companies and none in the top 100. Its household wealth is only 4 per cent of that of the high-income countries.[30]

Economic downturn and crisis in the countries of the global North leaves the countries of the global South in an especially vulnerable position. As such, neoliberalism has left intact the basic structures of dependency as outlined by Dos Santos and Smith above. These structures, typified by a clear division between what may be called producer and consumer states, ensure a continued trend towards North-South divergence.[31]

DEPENDENCY AND THE INTERNATIONAL CIRCULATION OF VALUE

What Amin calls 'autocentric accumulation', that is, the tendency for capital at the centres of the capitalist world economy to shape its own development by balancing increases in productivity with increases in wages, results in an expansion of the internal market and the stable development of both Department I and Department II industries. As suggested above, where wages do not increase at a rate sufficient to balance demand in both Departments, an external growth of the market is necessary, typically conferring subordinate or 'extraverted' economic functions upon the periphery as consumer in the last resort of the excess output of core capital. Since the final quarter of the nineteenth century, however, the increase of real wages at the centre occurred at a faster than optimal rate, necessitating the expansion of the imperialist system in the form of the export of capital as opposed simply to the export of commodities. Thus began in earnest the process of transforming the 'periphery' of the capitalist world economy into a direct supplier of surplus value.

The imperialist transfer of value under capitalism takes many forms, both historically and currently. Historical penetration of the economies of Africa, Asia and South and Central America by those of Europe and North America, and their subsequent under- and even de-development, has occurred according to stages in the growth of the capitalist mode of production, from the predominance of commercial capital in the sixteenth and seventeenth centuries, to industrial commodities export in the eighteenth and nineteenth centuries, to the era of financial capital export in the twentieth century, and up until neoliberal globalisation today. 'Primitive accumulation' of capital and of 'free (wage) labour' is both a historical fact and a contemporary reality, as witnessed in today's imperialist wars of encroachment upon national and common property in the Middle East, as well as the ongoing land grabbing and resource colonialism practised in Africa, South America and elsewhere.[32] At the same time, currency imperialism (today largely based on the aforementioned primitive accumulation, especially of Middle East resources by core companies and their subsequent sale in dollars) ensures that countries are able to amass huge deficits on the basis of debts that become less valuable over time. In addition, the new forms of unequal exchange and global labour arbitrage encapsulated in the global commodity chain and the new international division of labour (NIDL) allow for developed, high-wage countries to capture value from less developed, low-wage countries.

THE MECHANICS OF GLOBAL VALUE TRANSFER

We may briefly present here seven mechanisms of value transfer. We will describe each of these succinctly, before proceeding in Chapters 6 to 8 to provide further substantial proof of imperialist transfer of value.

1. 'Brain drain'. Richer countries gain one-sidedly from highly educated professionals migrating from the global South, many trained through aid-funded bursary programmes. The effects of this 'brain drain' and human capital export from the global South are the curtailment of long-term development there:

> The world periphery lost between 1960 and 1980 human capital to the tune of $16 billion to the centre. Critical, skilled and opposition elements leave the periphery, with the benefits of such a human capital import reaped by the centre in the long run.[33]

Leaving aside the question of the extent to which worker remittances tend to be spent on luxury consumption and on imports, claims that migration benefits both the source and the destination country are dubious. If such arguments were correct we might expect Jordan, Mexico, Jamaica, the former Yugoslavia, Greece, Portugal and other highly dependent capitalist countries to have become 'economic miracles'. Conversely, major imperialist countries such as Japan and the United States send their managers abroad, but never their workforce. Indeed, it is a sign of economic weakness globally for a country to be a net exporter of its labour.[34]

2. Illicit capital flows. Well-connected firms and persons are able to circumvent regulation and taxation through misinvoicing imports and exports and withholding money in tax havens.[35] Corporations report false prices on their trade invoices so that they can transfer money out of developing countries and into tax havens and secrecy jurisdictions ensuring that developing countries lose US$875 billion through trade misinvoicing each year.[36]

3. Northern trade barriers. Northern business interests gain from restricting the import of goods from the global South while demanding 'free trade' for their own heavily subsidised output. As a senior policy adviser for Oxfam noted at the turn of the century, each year developing countries lose about US$700 billion as a result of trade barriers in rich countries: for every US$1 provided by the rich world in aid and debt relief, poor countries lose US$14 because of trade barriers.[37]

4. Northern dumping. Particularly during times of crisis, the leading capitalist powers turn to protectionism, with protected home markets ensuring that monopolies can sell their goods at higher than foreign prices. With the resultant embellished income, they can increase their output and dump some of it abroad, reaping profits even where foreign prices received are lower than the average unit cost of production.[38] While the North restricts imports from the global South it insists on its own ability to dump goods on Southern markets regardless of the effects on local industry. Haiti is a paradigmatic example of the consequences of this. In 1986 Haiti was largely self-sufficient in rice, a staple food for its people. Forced by foreign donors and lenders, however, and after the country was flooded with (subsidised) rice from the United States, ten years later the country was importing 196,000 tons of foreign rice at the cost of US$100 million. National rice production became negligible and Haiti's poor became dependent on the rise and fall of world grain prices.[39]

5. Repayment of debt. Debt repayment constitutes a drain of value from global South to North. In 2000, low-income countries paid a net sum to their creditors of US$101.6 billion, or more than three times what they had received in aid grants that year, whereas in 1999 they paid almost five

times more than they received in aid grants.[40] From 1992 to 2000, debt repayments as a share of poor country earnings from exports and services changed as follows: repayment of loan principal rose from 14 to 19 per cent; repayment of interest on loans rose from 8 to 10 per cent, and in 1999 total debt repayments (interest plus principal) consumed 28 per cent of the earnings of lower-income countries.[41] Developing countries pay over US$200 billion in interest each year to foreign creditors, much of it on old loans that have already been paid off many times over. Since 1980, developing countries have paid out over US$4.2 trillion in interest payments to global North-based creditors.[42]

6. Unfavourable terms of trade. The purchasing power of global South exports tends to decline relative to that of global North imports.[43] As Heintz notes:

> [During] periods of productivity-led growth, prices of manufactured goods will rise relative to prices of primary products. Since primary commodities also tend to be price inelastic [the quantity of them demanded or supplied being unaffected when their price changes], the income terms of trade – that is, receipts from exports relative to imports – will also fall, leading to a widening income gap between industrialized and developing countries.[44]

For non-primary products, too, the commodity or net barter terms of trade of the global South's manufactured goods relative to the machinery, transport equipment and services exports of the global North declined from 1975 to 1995.[45] Over the course of the 1980s the developing countries suffered a cumulative loss in total export earnings in real terms of US$290 billion, an annual average loss of US$25 billion. For the non-oil African countries, excluding South Africa, that figure represents almost minus 120 per cent of GDP, a massive and persistent loss of purchasing power.[46]

7. Trade-Related Intellectual Property Rights (TRIPS). The vast majority of patents on intellectual property are held by Northern institutions. Three-quarters of patent filings received by the World Intellectual Property Organization (WIPO) in 1999 were from five countries, namely, the United States, Germany, Japan, the United Kingdom and France. Fully 97 per cent of all patents are held by nationals of Organisation for Economic Co-operation and Development (OECD) countries, with 90 per cent of all patents in the world being held by global corporations. Around 70 per cent of all patent royalty payments are made between subsidiaries of parent enterprises, proving that they are not, as apologists claim, designed to share knowledge or encourage innovation.[47] As a result of TRIPS, developing

countries had obligations to pay US$60 billion extra annually, according to World Bank-related estimates.[48]

Our approach highlights the transfer of labour time and accumulated capital from the poorest to the richest countries in the global economy. While accepting the theoretical and empirical validity of the seven distinct types of international exploitation described above, we argue that (1) colonial tribute; (2) the direct provision of additional surplus value to foreign creditors, investors and monopolies; and (3) trade involving the unequal exchange of commodities embodying different quantities of value represent overarching mechanisms of imperialist value transfer. Each varies in importance according to the level and type of monopoly advantage exercised within the world system, and is typical of a specific constellation of forces and relations of production internationally. Hence phases of imperialism reflect the historical development of capitalism and its military and political bulwarks worldwide. A historical taxonomy of international economies of exploitation would account for dynamic changes in the characteristic methods of transferring economic surplus from and to exploited and imperialist countries, respectively. Following Braun, we may broadly distinguish four eras of international relations underpinning the transfer of value from the global South to the global North:

1. Colonialism. This period played a crucial role in the primitive accumulation of capital and allowed for the beginning of the industrial revolution in Western Europe. It lasted roughly three hundred years, from the sixteenth to the beginning of the nineteenth centuries.
2. Commercial Expansion. This period cemented the 'periphery' of the capitalist world system as a supplier of raw materials and an outlet for the purchase of the manufactures of the global North. It lasted for much of the nineteenth century.
3. Capital Export. This period involved the export of capital to the global South where capital was scarce and wages low. It lasted from the end of the nineteenth century to the economic crisis of the 1930s.
4. Unequal Exchange. This period, gaining special prominence from the 1980s onwards, has constituted the global South as a supplier of both raw materials and industrial products at low prices predicated upon huge differences in real wages North and South.[49]

In the following chapters we will consider the historical and contemporary features of both direct and indirect GTV in the form of (1) colonial tribute; (2) monopoly rent; and (3) unequal exchange.

2
Colonial Tribute

Between the sixteenth and nineteenth centuries, the major international motors for European capital accumulation were silver and gold exports from South America to Spain and Portugal; profits from the Dutch spice trade; the trade in African slaves carried in British and French ships; profits from slave labour in the British West Indies; profits from the opium trade; and colonial land revenue. In each case, colonialism as the expansion and acquisition of control of overseas territories by rival European powers, many featuring unmitigated slavery, provided the impetus for nascent capitalist accumulation.[1] In the seventeenth and eighteenth centuries, Blaut has estimated that the number of labourers and slaves in plantations, haciendas, factories and mines in the colonies was at least as large as the proletariat of Europe itself.[2] As economic historians Acemoğlu et al write:

> [The] rise of Western Europe after 1500 is due largely to growth in countries with access to the Atlantic Ocean and with substantial trade with the New World, Africa, and Asia via the Atlantic. This trade and the associated colonialism affected Europe not only directly, but also indirectly by inducing institutional change. Where 'initial' political institutions (those established before 1500) placed significant checks on the monarchy, the growth of Atlantic trade strengthened merchant groups by constraining the power of the monarchy, and helped merchants obtain changes in institutions to protect property rights. These changes were central to subsequent economic growth.[3]

Accordingly, much of the differential growth of Western Europe between the sixteenth and early nineteenth centuries may be accounted for by the expansion of Atlantic trading nations directly involved in trade and colonialism with the New World and Asia, namely, Britain, France, the Netherlands, Portugal and Spain, a pattern in large measure reflecting the direct effects of Atlantic trade between Europe and America, Africa and Asia. Originally the product of the degeneration of landed property relations characteristic of late feudalism (that is, the marketisation of land to exploit expanding urban trade networks and overcome the increasing limits to serfage set by the deconcentration of land ownership) capitalism was catalysed by this expanding system of continental value transfer.

THE RATIONALE BEHIND CAPITALIST COLONIALISM

During the 1850s committed proponents of free trade considered that the costs of administering and enforcing British colonial diktat would outweigh any potential or actual economic benefits derived from it. For authors then and since, including those ostensibly opposed to it, the nations of Europe and North America did not substantially benefit from colonialism; rather, it was only a thin stratum of private investors, officials and migrant workers who benefited.[4]

Adam Smith, for example, is well known for having insisted that colonies were a never-ending source of war and expense for the colonising country. It is less well known that his opposition to colonialism was fundamentally based on opposition to colonial *monopolies* in trade and investment as opposed to colonialism *tout court*. For Smith, colonialism was permissible if the colony contributed net revenue to the metropolis within a system of free trade for all members of an Imperial Federation.[5] In the early nineteenth century, there were precious few consistent free trade anti-imperialists, except perhaps the most famous, manufacturer and Radical free trade supporter Richard Cobden. As Marx recognised in 1853,

> when India had been in the process of annexation, everyone had kept quiet; once the 'natural limits' had been reached, they had 'become loudest with their hypocritical peace cant.' But, then, 'firstly, they had to get it [India] in order to subject it to their sharp philanthropy.' ... In 1859 Marx was writing that 'the "glorious" reconquest of India after the Mutiny' had been essentially carried out for securing the monopoly of the Indian market to the Manchester free traders.[6]

Nonetheless, some authors have argued that the Empire was an overall burden on the British economy. Not only did Imperial preferential duties ensure that British consumers paid over the world market price for West Indian commodities like cotton, ginger, indigo, molasses, rum, pimento and sugar, but the costs of occupying and administering the colonies, not to mention defending them from rival colonial powers was a severe drain on the British state budget.[7] Yet this view of the negligible role of Empire in Britain's economy is scarcely tenable.

Australian economic historian G. S. L. Tucker has shown how Victorian proponents of colonialism argued that the investment of British savings in countries where wheat and other primary goods could be produced more cheaply than at home would tend to raise and maintain profit rates, and thereby enlarge Britain's sphere of investment.[8] A declining rate of profit, by contrast, could be averted neither by investing in one form of manufacture instead of another, nor by transferring capital to agriculture rather than industry. Instead, profits could only be maintained and extended by exporting capital and labour to the colonies, 'where they would produce the food and raw materials that England required, and at the same time create new and growing markets for her export industries'. In so doing, Britain would no longer be so dependent on foreign markets and the exigencies of foreign tariff policies. Rather, by setting up a 'colonial *Zollverein*' (or customs union) it would be able to control its own economic destiny.[9]

Despite being a staunch opponent of slavery in the United States and the West Indies, English liberal economist and political theorist John Stuart Mill was nonetheless firmly convinced of the benefits of colonialism to human progress, so much so that he vouchsafed the option of the *enslavement* of colonised peoples. For Mill, whose advocacy of a liberal pluralist voting system based on citizens' educational standards was explicitly formulated so as to exclude the representation of the broad working class (fearing that its numerical preponderance would lead to political domination), freedom applied 'only to human beings in the maturity of their faculties' and could not be demanded by minors or 'those backward states of society in which the race itself may be considered as in its nonage'.[10] In Mill's view, 'a ruler full of the spirit of improvement is warranted in the use of any expedients that will attain an end, perhaps otherwise unattainable'.[11] He demanded the 'barbarians" (*sic*) 'obedience' for purposes of their education for 'continuous labour', the supposed foundation of civilisation. In this context, writes the late Italian historian Domenico Losurdo, Mill did not hesitate to theorise a transitional phase of 'slavery' for 'uncivilized races',[12] since there were 'savage tribes so averse from regular industry, that industrial life is scarcely able to introduce itself among them until they are ... conquered and made slaves of'.[13] Mill was characteristically sanguine as to the benefits of colonialism to the British economy:

> It is to the emigration of English capital, that we have chiefly to look for keeping up a supply of cheap food and cheap materials of clothing, proportional to the increase of our population; thus enabling an increasing capital to find employment in the country, without reduction of profit, in producing manufactured articles with which to pay for this supply of raw produce. Thus, the exportation of capital is an agent of great efficacy in extending the field of employment for that which remains: and it may be

said truly that, up to a certain point, the more capital we send away, the more we shall possess and be able to retain at home.[14]

For British historian Bernard Porter, the centrality of the developing world to British capital accumulation was threefold:

Firstly: in so far as it was developing, and not merely stagnant it followed that it required more capital than it could provide itself: and this Britain could supply. In the 1890s, ninety-two per cent of the new capital Britain invested abroad went outside Europe, and half of it to the developing countries of Africa, Asia and Australasia. Secondly: from the commercial point of view it was a market which overall bought more from Britain than it sold – just; and such markets were becoming very rare. Thirdly: it was a market which, in so far as it had not been cornered by European rivals and surrounded by their tariffs or saturated with their capital, was still 'open'. 'Open' markets were getting hard to find in the protectionist nineties; but if Britain's products were to be sold abroad at all, those that were still open had to be kept open.[15]

Economic historian Phyllis Deane has listed six major ways that foreign trade contributed to catalysing what she refers to as the first industrial revolution. First, foreign trade generated demand for the products of British industry. Second, it provided access to raw materials which widened the range and cheapened the products of British industry.[16] Third, international trade provided underdeveloped countries with the purchasing power to buy British goods. Fourth, it provided an economic surplus which helped finance industrial expansion and agricultural improvement, with the profits of trade having 'overflowed into agriculture, mining and manufacture'. Fifth, international trade helped to create an institutional structure and business ethic which was almost as effective in promoting home trade as foreign trade. Finally, the expansion of international trade in the eighteenth century was the principal vehicle for the growth of large towns and industrial centres such as Liverpool and Glasgow.[17]

COLONIALISM, SLAVERY AND CAPITALIST INDUSTRIALISATION

The plundering of the Americas functioned as a means of primitive capital accumulation on a Europe-wide scale, overwhelmingly profiting two (mercantilist) latecomers, the Netherlands and England, at the expense of the more advanced colonial (but largely feudal) powers of Spain and Portugal.[18]

The enormous flows of precious metals plundered from Mexico and Peru financed Europe's lucrative trade with East India, enabling the relatively less prosperous European merchants of Holland, England, Portugal and France to monopolise Asian markets and to 'displace, subordinate and subsequently dominate' Asia in its own locale. At the same time, the re-export of Asian colonial goods contributed to burgeoning markets in Europe, the Americas and Africa and, crucially, allowed fledgling capitalists in Western Europe to transfer labour-power from agriculture to industry.[19] By the turn of the nineteenth century, an estimated 100 million kilograms of silver had been drained from South America and imported into Europe, first into Spain and then to the rest of the continent as payment on Spain's debts. If this quantity of silver had been invested in 1800 at a 5 per cent rate of interest it would be valued at around US$165 trillion today, more than double the world's GDP in 2015.[20] Ultimately, the creation of a Eurocentric world market was funded by the precious metals of the 'New World'.[21]

Meanwhile, the international division of labour established through the Atlantic triangular (more accurately, quadrilateral) trade generated profits through buying cheap and selling dear at each of its nodes. Especially in the eighteenth and nineteenth centuries, the capitalist slave trade provided outlets for Western European manufactures, that is, ironware, textiles, arms and ammunition especially from Liverpool, Plymouth, Bristol and London. These were sold to African notables in return for slaves (of whom around 15 million were transported from Africa to the colonies between 1700 and 1850), who were then shipped to the Caribbean islands to produce tobacco, sugar, indigo, molasses and, later, raw cotton. These goods were shipped to New England (New York and Boston), from where they were exported to England to enter into its manufactures as raw materials.

The profits from transatlantic slavery and plantation colonialism (obtained to the detriment of the indigenous peoples of the Americas and the people of Africa and those of African descent enslaved according to its requirements) were reinvested in the metropolitan countries, financing such crucial technological innovations as the world's first steam engine by James Watt, and providing much of the capital required to finance early capital accumulation in shipping, insurance, agriculture and technology.[22] Blackburn has provided in-depth analysis of the contribution of slavery to overseas demand in the early decades of the industrial revolution and has compared mercantile and plantation profits with the investment needs of the iron and textile industries and the wider British economy.

[The] colonial and African trades around 1770 accounted for 96.3 per cent of British export of nails, and 70.5 per cent of the export of wrought iron.[23] Around the same time British exports of iron manufactures were equivalent to 15–19 per cent of the country's iron consumption. Textile exports accounted for between a third and a half of total production, with colonial and African markets looming large ... Stanley Engerman calculated that annual British slave trade profits running at around £115,000 a year in 1770 could have amounted to 7.8 per cent of total British domestic investment and to 38.9 per cent of total commercial and industrial development.[24] Once plantation production and trade are taken into account, the possible contribution grows very considerably ... The gains of the planters and merchants were so large that, despite themselves, they made a contribution to accumulation. The Atlantic trades and plantations were generating a surplus equivalent to 50 per cent or more of British investment in every branch of the economy – agriculture and infrastructure as well as manufacturing – on the eve of the industrial revolution.[25]

Hickel estimates that the United States alone benefited from a total of 222,505,049 hours of forced labour between 1619 when slaves were first brought to the North American colony of Jamestown, Virginia, to aid in the production of lucrative crops such as tobacco, and the abolition of slavery in 1865. Valued at the US minimum wage, with a modest rate of interest, that uncompensated labour would be worth US$97 trillion today.[26]

The centrality of colonialism to European advance was recognised by many European intellectuals of the nineteenth century, not least renowned German sociologist Max Weber, who portrayed it in the following unambiguous terms:

> The acquisition of colonies by the European states led to a gigantic acquisition of wealth in Europe for all of them. The means of this accumulation was the monopolizing of colonial products, and also of the markets of the colonies, that is the right to take goods into them, and, finally, the profits of transportation between mother land and colony.[27]

Whereas Marx had correctly observed that 'the veiled slavery of the wage labourers in Europe needed the unqualified slavery of the New World as its pedestal',[28] in an 1865 book entitled *The Coal Question*, English economist William Stanley Jevons had frankly described the benefits brought to Britain by its colonial and industrial monopolisation of the world's resources:

> The plains of North America and Russia are our corn fields; Chicago and Odessa our granaries; Canada and the Baltic our timber forests, Australia contains our sheep farms and in Argentina and on the Western prairies of North America are our herds of oxen; Peru sends her silver, and the

gold of South Africa and Australia flows to London; the Hindus and the Chinese grow our tea for us, and our coffee, sugar and spice plantations are all in the Indies. Spain and France are our vineyards and the Mediterranean our fruit garden; and our cotton grounds, which for long have occupied the Southern United States are being extended everywhere in the warm regions of the earth.[29]

Occupying a structurally analogous position to today's multinational firms, historian Paul Kennedy has noted that in order to transfer this wealth to the metropolitan countries, exclusive trading companies like the East India Company (English, Dutch and French), the Africa Company, the Hudson Bay Company and others were established.[30]

Overseas colonialism transformed the industrial division of labour in Britain in at least two fundamental ways. First, a large part of the proletariat was employed in forms of work that presupposed colonies, namely, shipbuilding, harbour building and, later, sugar refining and textile production, with each of these industries providing a stimulus for other derivative ones. For example, large quantities of labour were required to clear forests and transport the timber used to manufacture the ships that formed the backbone of British colonial expansion. Likewise, towns such as Liverpool, Glasgow and Derry originated as nodes in the growing network of international shipping based on the Atlantic trade. The construction of ports and harbours required the labour-intensive reclamation of marshy coastal lands, the felling and transportation of timber and rubble, and the building of seawalls, breakwaters, piers, quays and jetties.[31] Second, what Marx referred to as the 'reserve army of labour', the dispossessed population unable to find gainful employment, was exported to the colonies as settlers, garrison and otherwise, or enrolled as indentured servants.[32] By and large, this section of the metropolitan population was indebted or considered criminal, vagrant or rebellious and was regarded by the 'great and the good' as the 'rank multitude' who 'cannot live at home'.[33]

In Britain, the absorption of the 'surplus population' in market activities and the expanded reproduction of capital depended upon 'the exploitation of a widened sphere of activity beyond the boundaries of the domestic market'.[34] Specifically, the combination of 'English' capital, African slave labour and American land used for commercialist plantation slavery acted as a spur to British domestic development. Adding timber imports to sugar and cotton, the 'New World' (*sic*) contributed some 25 to 30 million 'ghost acres' to Britain alone, that is, roughly double the size of Britain's own total arable land.[35]

The plantation economy was central to the expansion of foreign trade, with the import of luxury items from the 'New World' (tobacco, sugar, coffee and so forth) providing goods in global demand and enabling the colonial powers to re-export trade to the rest of Europe. Meanwhile, access to cheap sources of cotton lowered the cost of production in the economically crucial textile industry, boosting the competitiveness of British exports.[36]

VALUE TRANSFER AND HISTORICAL UNDERDEVELOPMENT

During the colonial era (from the sixteenth to the mid-twentieth century), colonial administrators and businessmen justified extreme exploitation by the insistence that 'inferior' indigenous workers need only be paid a subsistence wage.[37] (Shades of this argument may be found in Eurocentric left arguments today.) Meanwhile, colonial employers could afford to pay indigenous workers a miserable wage less than was required to maintain their families because the workers were earning a wretched subsistence in the home village or tribal reservation in conditions of tributary peonage requiring high levels of both remittance and actual labour.[38]

Though providing abundant enormous benefits to Europe and its settler offshoots, colonialism practically ruined the economies of the oppressed countries. India, for instance, had more than 20 per cent of the world's GDP in 1820, but less than 4 per cent when the country became formally independent from Britain 130 years later.[39] In uprooting the native ruling class, hitherto the primary consumer of quality artisanal products, and also by introducing machine-made goods imports, traditional crafts were effectively decimated by colonialism. Tribal peoples and peasants were deprived of their customary usage of land through its being made a vendible asset with exclusive ownership restricted to a small group of wealthy individuals. The destruction of traditional industry, the concentration of land ownership and the extraction of surplus ensured an open or disguised excess supply of colonial labour that served to rationalise low wages.[40]

Though initially some opportunistic alliances were formed between the prospective capitalists of the colonies, that is, its native merchants and financiers, and the conquering Europeans, the relationship between the two groups rapidly became an extremely unequal one in which domination was exercised by the latter. In consequence, and just as intended, most of the surplus extracted by colonial capital was transferred to the metropolitan countries or, as from the nineteenth century onwards, to captured territories of white settlement in North America and Australasia. This ensured that the indigenous or national bourgeoisie of the colonial world that managed to stay afloat had little left with which to expand their own capital. Given the military and political disparity, the institutional changes required for a fully capitalist society were not made due to the retardation or elimination of this class by colonial competitors. Only when intra-imperialist conflicts became sufficiently acute did the local bourgeois and petty-bourgeois strata of the colonial countries (many with roots in commercial trade with the colonial metropoles) find space to effectively struggle for a larger retention of the national surplus.[41]

The 'head start' of European countries in capital accumulation and their political hegemony ensured a virtual monopoly of industrial production in relation to the countries that would become known as the Third World. Even after decolonisation, the continued outward flow of surplus and the consequent failure to reinvest in the production of capital goods remains a major economic handicap, and helps keep the so-called developing countries perennially underdeveloped relative to the advanced capitalist countries.[42] World Bank data on global inequality reveals that per capita income has a persistent effect on wealth redistribution, with the former colonial and dependent countries still having relatively low levels thereof. Moreover, global inequalities in redistribution over the last generation or so reflect both the influence of colonialism and the history of exposure to socialism. Income equality is markedly higher in former colonising countries and lower in formerly colonised societies. Meanwhile, a history of socialism increases the presence of redistributive institutions, in part compensating for the effects of lower national incomes.[43]

THE IMPERIALIST MODE OF PRODUCTION

The articulation of modes of production depends on the course of class struggle and processes of accumulation, dispossession and working class resistance at the international level. As a result of imperialism, the mode of production of less developed countries differs from that of developed capitalist countries, with the former characterised by economic relations based variously on (1) semi-feudalism, wherein economic surplus generated by small farmers and rural workers is appropriated by landowners and money-lenders as opposed to capitalists per se; (2) neo-colonialism, wherein economic surplus generated by the national workforce is appropriated by monopolistic foreign buyers and investors; (3) bureaucratic capitalism, wherein economic surplus is appropriated by state officials or by persons with close connections to the bureaucratic apparatus, or by some combination of the above. The relative prevalence of semi-feudal, comprador and/ or bureaucratic capitalism in the economies of the global South tends to prohibit therein the growth of hegemonic 'national' bourgeoisies rooted in industrial production for domestic markets.

Crucially, imperialism depends upon the maintenance of 'income deflation' in the peripheral countries so that petty producers there have restricted effective demand for their own products and so do not push up the prices of primary commodities, in the process threatening the value of metropolitan industry, currency and investment.[44] So-called 'fiscal responsibility' as well as the shift in agricultural earnings to favour multinational distributors over direct producers are two means by which such income deflation has been achieved under neoliberal globalisation; onerous taxation was another such means in the colonial era.

From the 1950s to the 1970s, incomes were rising and poverty rates declining in the recently liberated former colonies of the global South as redistributive and protectionist policies were pursued by their respective governments.[45] Meanwhile, the developmental successes of Japan and South Korea were facilitated by the relatively extensive land reform carried out under US tutelage after the Second World War as a safeguard against the ascendance of communist forces. Along with Taiwan, these countries were given the opportunity to protect their industries and were provided special access to US markets. As such, they were able to simultaneously raise the pay of their workers and repay the capital that the United States had exported to them.[46] Especially as the military contingencies of the Cold War developed, these East Asian economies, as well as those of Western Europe, were afforded massive aid in a successful effort by the US imperialist hegemon to prevent them pursuing independent courses of industrialisation, or policies that would otherwise subject their economies to the requirements of the US would-be hegemonic Soviet rival.

Those nations not needed as powerful allies in this battle to maintain global imperialism were to remain impoverished suppliers of cheap resources and labour for the global centres of capital.[47] As such, France, Britain and especially the United States set out to overturn the independence of nationalist states throughout the Third World, no matter how moderate and regardless of the extent of their electoral mandate. They did so through military intervention and armed subversion leaving millions dead across South America, Africa and Asia. Indeed, *force majeure* was and remains the ultimate guarantor for the continued siphoning of wealth from the weak to the powerful countries.

METROPOLITAN WORKERS UNDER NEOLIBERAL IMPERIALISM

Whereas capitalism was competitive in the Victorian age, metropolitan labour was supplemented but not compensated for by the labour of the exploited countries. In the subsequent age of monopoly capitalist trade and investment the average labour content of core countries' consumption has increasingly tended to exceed the labour (value) they supply to the global economy.[48] Under colonialism, the real wages, job opportunities, skill levels, productivity and living standards of metropolitan workers were dependent on the imperial division of labour, but its benefits were disproportionately enjoyed by relatively skilled upper strata of workers. That social base has broadened in the home countries of advanced monopoly capitalism in tandem with the development of the welfare state, global labour arbitrage, consumerism and the comprehensive tertiarisation of core nation employment structures. However, as we shall discuss further on, the development of imperialist globalisation within its home countries has had uneven impacts on different sections of society therein, tending to produce overlapping, widening, and in times of crisis polarising class, gender, ethnic/ racial and even national inequalities.

The class position of the wage-earner in the metropolitan countries vis-à-vis domestic capital is profoundly shaped by the international division of labour established by imperialism. In the 30 years before and after the First and Second World Wars, and for ten years in between, the systemic costs of wages rising in proportion to productivity were defrayed in the core countries by the additional value these obtained by accumulating the unpaid labour of dependent or colonial nations. This transfer had slowed down by the 1970s, however, with the rise of 'import substitution industrialisation' (ISI) in the global South, the limits of which set the terms for neoliberal 'export-oriented industrialisation' (EOI).

The period of neoliberalism under US hegemony has eroded the institutional advantages of global North labour relative to capital, even as it has augmented the purchasing power of its wages. Considered in relation to the share of their national workforces in global production, the net consumer countries of the late twentieth- and early twenty-first-century economy cannot balance their books without massive labour arbitrage involving exploitative trade and investment by their banks and monopolies. Globalisation on such terms has tended to deflate the value of labour-power relative to capital in every country, forcing precarious conditions upon all but the most skilled and in-demand sections of the workforce. As a result, rising underemployment, stagnating wage rates and deteriorating working conditions may be observed in the richest countries, though to a much lesser extent than in the poorest countries. Yet the basic class structure of the former colonial powers continues to rest on the appropriation of value from the poor countries in the form of underpriced commodities and servicing of loans and investments (accumulated labour). The relative decline in living standards has not yet led to widespread proletarianisation of the metropolitan workforce (as defined according to occupational and income trends globally), nor has it signalled the wholesale erosion of the global wage scaling that would entail.

3
Monopoly Rent

Competition between businesses results in ever higher degrees of capital concentration, and in production and distribution becoming controlled by one or a few giant conglomerates, that is, monopolies or oligopolies. A monopoly is a capitalist enterprise which is able to dominate national production, setting high prices for its products so as to maximise profits. The term 'monopoly' as used herein does not connote the occupation of a particular industry or branch of industry by a single firm but, rather, the transformation of capitalism from a mode of production wherein more or less free competition between firms obtained in its advanced centres to one in which giant firms, trusts and cartels control the market. In this chapter we will explore the various ways in which the development of monopoly capitalism as a global mode of production (what Amin has called 'generalised monopoly capitalism') facilitates value transfer from the exploited to the exploiting nations.[1] Monopoly engenders intense international competition in sales markets, in raw materials markets and in spheres of capital investment, with rival national capitals compelled to seek larger, captive markets abroad.[2] A further motivation for overseas expansion by monopoly capital is to exploit cheaper foreign labour-power. In the process, ever larger shares of the imperialist country's 'national' wealth is created abroad and transferred home by a variety of means (debt servicing, profit repatriation and unequal exchange being the three principal ones).

As noted above, if the growth in the organic composition of capital (c/v) is greater than the growth in the rate of surplus value (s/v), that is, if technological advance is occurring at a faster rate than is the exploitation of labour, the rate of profit will fall. The central problem of capital valorisation in the age of monopoly, then, is the production of extra surplus value, the appropriation of which is principally based on 'monopoly rent'. Monopoly rent is defined by Amin as the difference between the price of production (the cost of production plus the average rate of profit) and the actual market price where that is not set by the average rate of profit, but by the cartels and corporations dominating the production and sale of commodities.[3] Monopolies can conclude agreements among themselves to restrict output, allocate market share and impose price mark-ups on production costs (especially on raw materials and wages).[4]

Though competition normally forces down the prices of the output of relatively productive labour, monopoly ensures that this does not occur and that its products are overvalued when exchanged internationally. Conversely, the prices of global South goods are rendered far lower than they would be in the absence of price-fixing, transfer pricing, monopoly (whereby the rich countries are the only seller of certain key commodities, especially of advanced electronic and military technology) and monopsony (whereby the rich countries are the single major buyer of much of the Third World's output). Effectively, the technological and commercial monopolies of the major imperialist countries ensure that non-monopoly producers are only able to compete in labour-intensive, low 'value-added' sectors in which the countries of the global South compete with one another in a veritable 'race to the bottom'.

MONOPOLY RENT AND METROPOLITAN WAGES

The present domination of the world economy by Northern-based monopolies has dire consequences for the underdeveloped capitalist countries. Monopoly capitalism forces Third World producers to expend extra labour to pay 'imperialist rent', that is, superprofits obtained through trade and investment based on profound global differentials in the prices of labour-power of equal productivity.[5] Imperialist rents, according to Amin, remove about half of the potential profits of the global South.[6] Moreover, they exceed the capital that is annually invested in expanded reproduction of those societies, dramatically reducing their opportunities for investment in economic and social development.[7] In 2004, for instance, the US trade deficit alone consumed fully 80 per cent of all global savings in the form of foreign purchases of US municipal, state and government bonds.[8]

Monopolistic price fixing ensures that extra surplus value is imported to the imperialist economy at the expense of the country against which the monopoly is exercised. Although Europe and North America no longer have unrivalled ownership of the planet's major means of production, along with Japan they retain monopolistic control over the commanding heights of the global economy, in particular, commerce, finance, the extractive industries, military hardware and intellectual property. The major imperialist countries also have a monopoly on high-wage-labour and the mass markets this and this alone affords.

On the one hand, imperialism encourages the outflow of capital from the metropolitan areas of the world economy, thus decreasing the demand for labour and, *ceteris paribus*, the price of labour-power therein. At the same time, the purchase of low-priced commodities from the 'peripheral' areas of the world economy raises the standard of living of metropolitan labour, either directly through increasing the purchasing power of wages or indirectly by cheapening the costs of production of domestically produced wage goods.[9] The mass markets thus established tend to attract capital to the metropolitan centres of the world economy, raising the demand for labour and, hence, wages therein. By and large, insofar as a mass market based on working class consumption is precluded by the low wage levels prevailing in the countries of the global South, capital tends to accumulate at the centres of the world system. Meanwhile, as well as failing to establish the indispensable conditions for autochthonous market growth, cheap and abundant labour-power encourages low capital intensity and, hence, a smaller percentage of skilled and highly skilled labour in the workforce. As Emmanuel puts it, '[cheap] labour chases equipment and technicians from underdeveloped countries while equipment and technicians replace labour in the developed countries'.[10]

Capital accumulation requires consumer markets that it is only possible to grow if labour is adequately paid, and it follows that developing nations should primarily trade with one another insofar as the payment of equal wages internationally ensures that trading nations cannot thereby appropriate the wealth of others.[11] As Smith writes:

Whenever possible, countries in the underpaid developing world should be trading with each other. If trading countries pay roughly equal wages for production of the products traded, neither confiscates the wealth of the other and the efficiencies of the trade can function honestly.

By trading with each other while building industry, developing nations with low-paid labor can develop their economies much more rapidly than when trading with a nation with high-paid labor. If labor is idle and the treasury empty (it always is in the dependent trading nation – that is the essence of a monopolized world economy) raw material or semi-processed goods can be bartered for industries (technology) as opposed to trading those resources for trinkets.[12]

Conversely, under imperialism, the low-paid worker or nation must labour for a longer time to buy one unit of wealth from their high-paid counterpart, whereas the latter need only work a fraction of the time to buy one unit of wealth from the low-paid worker or nation.[13] As such, a 'capital accumulation advantage' results from a pay differential between equally productive workers globally. Smith provides the following example as an illustration:

The equally productive worker in the poorly paid Third World produces a unique widget, is paid $1 an hour, and is producing one widget an hour.

The equally productive worker in the developed world produces another unique widget, is paid $10 an hour, and produces one widget per hour. Each equally productive worker likes, and purchases, the other's widgets. All true costs are labor costs so we ignore monopoly capital costs, which go to the developed world and only increases the advantage anyway, and calculate the cost of those widgets at the labor cost of production, $1 an hour and $10 an hour. The $1 an hour worker must work 10 hours to buy one of the widgets of the $10 an hour worker but, with the money earned in the same 10 hours, the $10 an hour worker can buy 100 of the widgets of the $1 an hour worker. While in a homogenized market of many producers (a mixture of high-paid and low-paid labor) there is a 10 times differential in buying power, at this ten times wage differential, in direct trades between each other – or between countries – there is an exponential 100 times differential in retained wealth.[14]

Indeed, a capitalist employing a worker at $20 per hour can sell and still make a profit even when competing against capitalists employing workers at $1 per hour, as can be seen from the following useful example:

[A] capitalist takes $21 to pay for one hour of labor from worker A at $1/ hr and one hour of labor from worker B for $20/hr. The end result is a commodity which the capitalist sells for $36, yielding a profit of $15. In this case, labor in its abstract (or 'socially necessary') form creates $18/hr in value (the full value of the commodity ($36), divided by the two hours which produced it), and this represents the value of labor.

In this example, worker B is paid $20 for an hour of labor power: this price of labor power is higher than the value of labor. In this case, for one hour of work worker B is able to purchase 1.11 hours of abstract labor. Consequently, worker A must work 18 hours to purchase the one hour of abstract labor. To clarify further: in this example, $17 in surplus value is exploited from worker A (the abstract value of labor ($18) minus the price of labor power paid as wages ($1)). Of this $17, $15 is kept by the capitalist and $2 is handed to worker B on top of the full value of labor. Functionally, worker B is an exploiter.[15]

According to Smith, the exponential capital accumulation advantage of the higher-paid nation is equal to the high pay divided by the low pay squared, or $(Wr/Wp)^2 = A$, where Wr is the wages paid to equally productive labour in the rich country, Wp is the wages paid to equally productive labour in the poor country, and A is the capital accumulation advantage of the well-paid nation. In Smith's example above, if $10 is earned by the well-paid worker for every hour of her labour time, and $1 is earned by the low-paid worker for every hour of her labour time, the capital accumulation advantage is 100 to 1.[16] Whereas labour everywhere is equally capable of producing the same use values per hour given equal access to the technology, training and markets denied poor countries by the global North's monopolisation of land, resources, technology and high wages, even today the labour of workers in non-mechanised industries such as strawberry pickers, janitors, guards and so on, as well as a large part of the industrial labour of the global South is of equal productivity around the world.

The product that export platform countries in the developing World are selling is not merely cheap labour, but highly productive labour. In Singapore McGraw Hill produces in one year an encyclopedia that takes five years to produce in the U.S. ... Mexican metal workers are 40 per cent more productive than U.S. workers, electronics Workers 10 to 15 per cent more productive, and seamstresses produce 30 per cent more sewing per hour than their U.S. counterparts.[17]

Smith concludes that 'whenever the difference in pay is greater than the difference in productivity, a part of the production of the low-paid worker or nation is transferred to the high-paid country'.[18] In order to purchase a part of the manufactured output of the most industrialised countries, largely produced using Third World resources, dependent societies must sell a larger share of their own accumulated wealth. Alongside money wasted on the purchase of the West's military goods and the corruption of comprador elites, the indebtedness of the global South increases and, in turn, servicing that debt requires the sale of ever more resources.[19]

To maintain the resultant flow of uncompensated value transfer, the imperialist countries have denied other nations the use of technology and access to markets by means of monopolistic control of both. When any country threatens to make a decisive break in the imperialist chain of value creation and distribution, they are forcibly pushed back into line, as the history of foreign interventions over the past century and more amply attests.[20]

MONOPOLY CAPITAL AND THE IMPERIALIST TRANSFER OF VALUE

The relative absence of competition allows monopolies to capture a large share of the profits (and surplus value) generated in the entire commodity chain of which the monopolised segment is a part.[21] Large multinational corporations (MNCs) are able to increase their market share through purchasing smaller and more localised firms, dictating the prices, terms and conditions, and policy frameworks through which production is regulated. As Norfield writes:

> Imperialism involves the control of the global economy by groups of monopolistic companies. These can exert power over the operation of markets, whether by price fixing, by cutting prices to drive out competitors or by other means. For example, one clue to the nature of the world economy today is that the number of mobile phones sold worldwide in 2014 was 1.9 billion, but 41 per cent of these were made by just three companies: Samsung (South Korea), Apple and Microsoft (both US). Add just another eight companies and the total market share of this still small group rises to two-thirds. This despite the many changes in mobile phone technology over the last three decades, which might have been thought to work against such monopolistic developments.[22]

New firms entering the market face serious obstacles in competing with both the leading system integrator firms (those companies specialising in bringing together component subsystems and ensuring that those subsystems function cohesively) and those firms occupying the 'commanding heights' in virtually every segment of global supply chains (Table 3.1).

Firms from developing countries are joining the 'global level playing field' at a point at which the concentration of business power has never been greater. In developing countries that liberalized their business systems in line with the Washington Consensus policies, oligopolies were established not only by the world's leading systems integrators but also in the upper reaches of the supply chain. Few people can imagine that just two firms produce 75 per cent of the global supply of braking systems for large commercial aircraft, that three firms produce 75 per cent of the global supply of constant velocity joints for automobiles, or that three firms produce 80 per cent of the global supply of industrial gases.[23]

The commanding heights of global capitalism are dominated by firms from high-income countries. Despite the number of firms from low- and middle-income countries in the *Financial Times'* FT 500 index having increased from eight in 2000 to 79 in 2010, this is a very small number in relation to the combined population of these countries. Moreover, those developing country firms that do feature in the FT 500 are concentrated in a narrow range of sectors, including 23 banks, 16 oil and gas producers, 11 metals and mining companies, and 9 telecommunications service companies. Most of these firms operate in protected domestic markets and are often state-owned enterprises which cannot be acquired by multinational companies.

In the 2010 FT 500 there were no developing firms in aerospace, chemicals, electronic and electrical equipment, retail, gas, water and utilities, health care, pharmaceuticals, industrial engineering, media, oil equipment and services, personal goods, or information technology hardware, and there was just one in the automobile parts and components sector.[24]

In terms of research and development, developing country firms lag far behind those from high-income countries, with firms from the United States, Japan, Germany, France and the United Kingdom accounting for fully 80 per cent of the world's top 1,400 (G1,400). Five small European countries (Denmark, Finland, Sweden, Switzerland and the Netherlands), with a combined population of 42 million people, have 132 firms in the G1,400, while four 'BRIC' countries (Brazil, Russia, India and China), with a total population of 2.6 billion, have 34 firms in the G1,400. The low- and middle-income countries as a whole, which have 84 per cent of the world's population, have a total of just 37 firms in the G1,400.[25]

Table 3.1   Industrial concentration among systems integrator firms, 2006–09

Industrial Sector	Number of Firms	Global Market Share (per cent)
Large commercial aircraft	2	100
20–90 seat commercial aircraft	2	75
Automobiles	10	77
Heavy-duty trucks	4	89[a]
Heavy and medium-duty trucks	5	100[b]
Fixed-line telecoms infrastructure	5	83
Mobile telecoms infrastructure	3	77
PCs	4	55
Mobile handsets	3	65
Smartphones	3	75
Plasma TVs	5	80
LCD TVs	5	56
Digital cameras	6	80
Pharmaceuticals	10	69
Construction equipment	4	44
Agricultural equipment	3	69
Elevators	4	65
Soft drinks	5	>50
Carbonated soft drinks	2	70
Beer	4	59
Cigarettes	4	75[c]
Athletic footwear	2	55

Notes: All estimates of global market share are rough approximations only.
a. NAFTA only.
b. Europe only.
c. Excluding China.

Source: Nolan 2012, p. 18; *Financial Times*, various issues; company annual reports.

Much of the global North's agricultural consumption, meanwhile, originates in the global South where it is produced cheaply (often by small farmers), with as much as 60–70 per cent of Northern food items having tropical or sub-tropical import content.[26] Alongside around 450 million farm labourers, there are an estimated 1 billion farmers on around 450 million farms worldwide, of which 85 per cent are small-scale. These small-scale farms produce around half the world's food, but are paid extremely low prices for their output while being charged high prices for seeds, fertilisers, pesticides, energy and animal seeds.[27] Profits are largely captured by a handful of the world's largest companies based predominantly in the global North. Recent figures show that the concentration of agricultural production by the global North's agricultural monopolies ('agropolies') has reached unprecedented heights:

- The market share of the top four livestock breeding companies in the world is 99 per cent.
- The market share of the top ten seeds corporations is 75 per cent.
- The market share of the top ten fertiliser corporations is 55 per cent.
- The market share of the top eleven pesticide corporations is 97.8 per cent.
- The market share of the top four grain and soya corporations is 75 per cent.
- The market share of the top ten processing corporations is 28 per cent.
- The market share of the top ten retail corporations is 10.5 per cent (the hundred largest supermarket corporations had a 35 per cent share of global food retail sales in 2007).
- Three companies roast 40 per cent of the global coffee harvest and five companies trade in 55 per cent of the coffee.[28]

While primary products such as the above are vital to Third World economies, the prices assigned to them by the MNCs who dominate their production and marketing are 'highly discriminative'.[29] In consequence, only a fraction of the final sales price of these commodities is retained by the exporting countries.

Growers' prices ... typically represent a small fraction of the retail price for finished products, ranging from as low as 4 percent for raw cotton to 28 per cent for cocoa. Even with bananas, which require almost no processing, international trading companies, distributors and retailers claim 88 per cent of the retail price; less than 12 per cent goes to the producing countries and barely 2 percent to the plantation workers.[30]

Value added at the level of the MNC (as at the level of imperialist countries and regions) is expanded by externalising costs of production, especially of intermediate inputs and consumer goods, to low-wage nations. Commodities produced by low-wage workers in the labour-intensive export industries, and not just those of the primary goods sector, obtain correspondingly low prices internationally. As soon as these goods enter into imperialist country markets, their prices are multiplied several fold, sometimes by as much as 1,000 per cent. As Chossudovsky comments, 'value added' is thus 'artificially created within the services economy of the rich countries without any material production taking place'.[31] Rather, the rich, imperialist countries import Third World goods reflecting cheap labour prices, below their real value as measured in socially necessary labour time. This underpayment – which Jaffe refers to as 'hidden surplus value' – is not justified by any lower productivity obtaining in Third World mining, agriculture or industry; where entirely different products are produced (and many of the global South's agricultural exports, in particular, simply cannot physically be produced in the global North), productivity data is not comparable. Where similar or identical commodities are produced in the global South and the global North, respectively, as in gold, copper, uranium, and coal mining, oil and iron extraction, as well as in the manufacture of textiles, automobiles, and even certain heavy and/or high-tech industries, there is little or no difference in productivity as measured in physical terms, and the global South is, in fact, more productive in many sectors. Instead, the process of undervaluation of Third World produce on the world market may be explained as follows, with reference to African exports:

The low selling price of African products has behind it 500 years of European undervaluing of African lives, African lands and African labour and wealth. Marx drew attention once to European undervaluing of American gold and silver. The undervaluing of African production in the pre-independence period was standard practice – used also for tax and customs evasion. But when the imported raw materials are sold as part of a European manufacture, they are sold at full world value. They are costed not at import but at world prices. The general rate of profit may be in the region of 100%, but the profit on the colonial products is 200%, even 1000%, as shown by recent research into British imports of electrical products from Hong Kong. The surplus value transferred in this manner I have called 'hidden' surplus value: colonial imports to the imperialist countries make up about 10% of total national incomes, and the hidden super-surplus value some 10% or more, so that it comprises the entire declared surplus value in the gross national products of those countries. To this major element we must add the surplus value made either through direct investments or through the German-developed loan-contract system; and the Lomé Convention guarantees to Europe a regular supply of cheap, undervalued raw materials and at the same time preserves the character of the independent African countries as primary producers and the colonialist world social division of labour. The combination of the two methods of super-exploitation, through loans and through undervalued imports, has frustrated every ambition of independence.[32]

Transfer pricing is another prominent mechanism of imperialist value transfer, and occurs when a multinational firm charges its foreign subsidiary or affiliate above cost for parts, goods and services as a means of reducing its tax burden. In 1977 the United Nations Conference on Trade and Development (UNCTAD) estimated that half of all exports from Africa, 45 per cent of those from Asia and 35 per cent of those from Latin America to the United States were intra-firm exports. More recently, in 2009 Folfas estimated that at least 35 per cent of world trade is intra-firm trade between subsidiaries and their parent companies, the number of these having increased threefold from 37,530 in 1995 to 78,817 in 2007.[33] The World Trade Organization (WTO), meanwhile, estimates that fully half of all international trade is within MNCs.[34] The MNCs' share in global technology transfer is around 80 per cent and 65–70 per cent of this total takes place in intra-firm exchange.[35] Intra-firm trade and the associated transfer pricing has become a principal mechanism for overcharging on imports and undercharging on exports in order to hide profits and remit them. Transfer pricing is used by MNCs to shift declared profits between jurisdictions with differential tax rates, thus minimising their legal corporate taxation. A parent company in a high tax country may purchase goods from its subsidiary in a low tax country at a price substantially above the market price paid therein. The subsidiary can then report high profits which will be taxed at a lower rate.[36]

Alongside price-setting and transfer pricing, a third way that value is transferred from underdeveloped countries by way of their economic domination by global North-based monopolies is the repatriation of profits from foreign investment, almost all of which is under the control of MNCs.[37] Capital exports by the leading monopolies raise profit rates in their countries of origin by (1) tying unequal exchange to loans; (2) ensuring exclusive orders for exported commodities at high prices; (3) controlling raw materials sources; and (4) exacting tribute from indebted nations. Leaving aside the enormity of portfolio investment whereby the investor is not involved in the management of a company she or he invests in, between 1970 and 1978, direct investments in underdeveloped countries totalled $US42 billion, while profits from these investments repatriated to investing countries amounted to US$100 billion.[38] Thus for every new dollar invested in the underdeveloped countries as a whole during this period, MNCs repatriated US$2.4 to their country of origin.[39] More recently, it has been estimated that foreign investors take around US$500 billion in repatriated profits out of developing countries each year.[40]

CAPITAL EXPORT IMPERIALISM

The export of capital to dependent and oppressed nations wherein labour may be more intensely exploited does not occur only when crises arise in the imperialist countries, but is the essence of capital accumulation in the age of monopoly. Export of capital is principally due to monopoly capital's relative inability to realise high enough rates of profit domestically in comparison to returns from exporting capital to a country with higher rates of exploitation. Over time, the increasing organic composition of capital in the home countries of monopoly capital ensures a correspondingly diminished rate of profit. This is principally compensated for by investment in colonial and neo-colonial countries where capital is relatively scarce, where the masses are subjected by violent means to the rule of foreign capital and where cheap labour is made abundant by the persistence of pre-capitalist, extraverted relations of production.[41] Since the rate of exploitation is higher in such countries, rates of profit in the centres of world capital can be sustained by those monopoly firms with sufficient global reach.[42]

The export of capital from the developed to the less developed countries is disproportionately one-way as can be seen by comparing the foreign direct investment (FDI) originating from developing countries with that from developed countries. This generates a net outflow of capital in the form of repatriated profits, royalties, services, and repayment of debt and interest.[43] Crucially, a greater quantity of surplus value creating labour is commanded by financially equivalent trade with and investment in the industries of developing countries than it is in the developed countries.[44] Were global South workers involved in the production of commodities for metropolitan markets suddenly to be remunerated at the same rate as workers therein, the profit margins of the world's leading capitalist powers would be wiped out.[45]

Critics of capital export as a means of value transfer question why capital does not simply migrate en masse to the low-wage countries of the world. Such reasoning does not properly consider that the tendency for the rate of profit to equalise internationally means that the industry with the lowest wages is not necessarily the most profitable. Nonetheless, since profit rates do, in fact, tend to be somewhat higher in low-wage countries (in both the extractive industries and in manufacturing) a further reason for why Northern capital does not migrate in its entirety to the South must be forthcoming. One may be readily discerned insofar as a total emigration of capital to the global South would destroy capitalism's driving engine, namely, effective demand for products produced in the global North. In low-wage countries the major consumer base consists of capitalists as opposed to workers. Since global export outlets are correspondingly limited, the result of too much capital migrating to the global South would be economic depression caused by a 'realisation' crisis of capital. Producing cheaply and selling at high prices, therefore, are contradictory goals that must be balanced by governmental policy.[46] In particular, protectionist state intervention in the economy is normally required to curb the potential destabilisation caused by international capital mobility.[47]

MONOPOLISTIC VALUE TRANSFER TODAY

Historic forms of plunder, slavery and colonial tribute have given the metropolitan areas of the capitalist world system a historic advantage over the rest of the world. Since that time, global value transfer has been based, inter alia, on production monopsonies (where buying power is monopolised), sales monopolies (whereby selling power is monopolised), exploitative trade, one-sided tariffs, extortionate loans and unequal exchange rates.[48] The value embodied in the commodities of the 'peripheral' country greatly exceeds the price paid for them by metropolitan countries and this difference constitutes a transfer of value to distant buyers.[49] Most of this transfer would not occur in a purely competitive economy, but depends upon the power of a few metropolitan firms to force down the prices, wages and profits of highly competitive 'peripheral' firms. In this relationship, the latter act as underpaid overseers of low-wage production for foreign monopoly capital and to that extent retain the central characteristics of the comprador elites of the colonial era.[50]

In the final decades of the nineteenth century the world economy was restructured by the metropolitan bourgeoisie in an attempt to reverse declining rates of profit. This shift in the development of capitalism largely revolved around the massive export of capital by giant banks and cartels aiming towards the generation of superprofits through monopolistic control over international markets. Likewise, from the 1970s onwards, a new imperialist structure emerged to combat declining rates of profit, this time characterised by a 'new international division of labour' (NIDL) entailing the relocation or outsourcing of metropolitan industry to 'peripheral' areas of the world where labour costs were significantly lower.[51] In recent decades, leading firms have off-shored a majority of production to the (semi-) periphery. Typically, 'the lead firm designs the product, establishes patent rights over its innovations, develops quality standards for component parts, organises and governs the supply chain, and controls the distribution and sales of the final product'.[52]

The expansion of manufacturing production has been linked theoretically and historically to the development of mass consumer markets, with production and consumption viewed as mutually reinforcing. Echoing Amin, Heintz suggests that mass production with wage increases tied to productivity improvements has supported a mass consumer market in the core countries which, in turn, sustains profits for further capital accumulation.[53] However, as we have noted, there is an inherent contradiction between production and consumption under capitalism, and the expansion of low-wage production overseas alongside the maintenance of mass purchasing power in the imperialist countries has proved an enduring process by which capitalism has managed to overcome its crisis tendencies. As Patnaik and Patnaik write:

[The] share of wages of the workers in the value added in the metropolis remains more or less constant, as many argue was the case between the late nineteenth century and the Second World War and even into the postwar period. The product wages of the workers in the metropolis, in other words, increase more or less in tandem with labour productivity. This acts to keep up the level of aggregate demand in the metropolis and to keep any tendency towards underconsumption at bay.[54]

Nonetheless, the globalisation of production processes relying on the enhanced exploitation of 'peripheral' wage-labour has definitively severed the link between production and consumption at the national level. Simply put, 'wages paid to workers in the export sectors of developing countries do not support purchasing power in affluent consumer markets'.[55] The growth in low-cost imports of particular goods that allow prices to fall and demand to rise does, however, sustain mass consumer purchasing power in the affluent imperialist countries despite deindustrialisation therein and dependent globalisation placing downward pressure on labour's share of income everywhere.[56]

The growth in manufacturing exports worldwide has contributed to the intensification of trade competition whereby the 'peripheral' countries compete not only with the exports of the established manufacturing sectors of the core countries, but also with each other to gain access to the markets of the affluent economies.[57] By virtue of their economies of scale and their brand name recognition, the largest global North-based retail conglomerates, multinationals and intermediate buyers are able to capture more value added along the global commodity chain than small, competitive producers and subcontractors.[58] As such, dependency increases with export-oriented industrialisation strategies predicated on supplying the consumer markets of the affluent imperialist countries.[59]

Overall, monopolistic economic position is established by a firm's securing low production costs as well as market domination through economies of scale, technological superiority, barriers to entry, patent rights, advertising, retail and international laws covering intellectual property rights. The ability to control the mark-up on the final price of commodities (the difference between total costs and revenue) enables potential rival corporations to set high prices so as to obtain high profits at the expense of both exploited workers and those smaller, far more numerous firms not in a position of monopoly.[60]

Monopsonistic position in the global economy, by contrast, is established when a few buyers dominate a market in which there are many sellers. Metropolitan buyers with monopoly positions in global markets ensure that fierce competition amongst smaller suppliers forces down costs and prices of production, as well as profits, the bulk of which accrue to the monopsonistic buyer.[61] In sum, in order to remain a competitive seller in a world market in which buying power is largely delimited to the metropolitan regions of the globe, subordinate capitalists must ensure that lower production costs are reflected in lower prices, and the monopsonistic final buyer thereby becomes a rentier obtaining imperialist rents. Often, as Clelland remarks, 'such firms are double rentiers since their high monopoly profit rates were already based on technology rents or design rent insured by legal barriers to imitation'.[62]

CONCLUSION

Expanded consumption in the metropolitan countries allows for the increased drain of value based on unequal production prices in the centre and the 'periphery' of the world economy. When unrequited value (or 'dark value') is exported to the metropolitan countries from the exploited countries, it can be distributed in three ways, namely (1) as profits; (2) as wage payments; or (3) as consumer surplus. Clelland estimates that whereas around 15 per cent of this unpaid surplus value transfer is transformed into profits, and 15 percent into wages, the vast majority of it is captured by metropolitan customers. Clelland calls the difference between the price of a commodity were it to be produced in the core countries and the actual price that benefits from the cheapness of 'peripheral' labour the *consumer surplus*.[63] He estimates that at the bare minimum, global value transfer is worth at least US$4,000 annually to average metropolitan households and concludes that collectively these gain more than the capitalist class itself.

4
Unequal Exchange

Unequal exchange occurs where there is a discrepancy between the value of a country's exports and that of its imports as measured in terms of labour, world market prices (actual or ideal) or ecological footprints. Non-equivalence arises when the current prices differ from the ratios of inequality inherent in one or all of these measures. As such, where prices do not accurately reflect the indirect and direct inputs of labour (or of biomass) in the imports and exports of two countries, one country may be said to use international trade to exploit another in terms of labour (or of biomass).[1] We will examine here two forms of unequal exchange of embodied labour hours whereby divergent sums of productive labour are bought and sold in international trade. We argue that rents accrue through unequal exchange to (1) capitalists afforded additional profits and profit-making opportunities by their possession of industrial, technological, financial and military monopoly and (2) metropolitan labour afforded high wages based on what Emmanuel refers to as 'institutionally different' rates of exploitation in the core and 'periphery' countries of the global economy, respectively.[2]

In terms of the rents accruing to capitalists we signify productivity and capital gains based on the different capital intensities of international firms engaged in trade with one another. An enduring historical system of political oppression underlies all processes of unequal exchange between the centre and the 'periphery' of the world economy. As such, these, too, are 'institutional' differences given international relations based on monopolies of force, industry and finance.[3] In the second category, we primarily intend unequal exchange per se, that is, imperialist trade gains based on the payment of divergent, institutionally inscribed wages in the core and 'periphery' countries of world capitalism, respectively. We suggest that monopoly capitalism can reinforce processes of unequal exchange based on metropolitan labour's high wages insofar as global patterns of retail monopoly militate against too severe reduction of metropolitan incomes. Conversely, compared with the labour aristocracy, transnational investors may be less interested in maintaining high metropolitan wages at the expense of immigrant labour, or at the cost of placing greater restrictions on international trade.

UNEQUAL EXCHANGE BASED ON DIFFERENT
ORGANIC COMPOSITIONS OF CAPITAL

Trade between firms and industries with a low and high 'organic composition of capital', respectively, ensures a transfer of value from the former to the
latter. Marx refers variously to the *technical composition of capital*, the *value*
(or price) *composition of capital*, and the *organic composition of capital*. He
writes: 'I call the value composition of capital, *in so far as* [emphasis added]
it is determined by its technical composition and mirrors the changes of
the latter, the *organic composition of capital* [emphasis in the original].'⁴ For
Marx, as capital (dead labour) accumulates and is increasingly employed
relative to wages (living labour), the organic composition of capital rises and
the rate of profit tends to fall. The qualifier emphasised in the above quote
is, however, highly significant since the value of labour-power (what Marx
called variable capital) 'can change without any change in the technical composition in circumstances in which workers themselves can receive more or
less, while producing with the same technology'.⁵

As capital is withdrawn from industries with low rates of profit and
invested in those with higher rates, output (supply) in the former declines
and its prices rise above the actual sums of value and surplus value the
particular industry produces, and conversely. Thus capitals with different
organic compositions (the ratio between constant and variable capital)
ultimately sell commodities at average prices and surplus value is distributed
more or less uniformly across the branches of production according to the
proportional share of capital – constant *and* variable – advanced.

Marxist economist Michael Roberts has noted how Marx discerned two
types of 'rent', that is, the capacity to appropriate (as opposed to generate)
additional profit in the global economy. He writes:

The first [type of rent is] 'absolute rent' where the monopoly ownership
of an asset (land) could mean the extraction of a share of surplus value
from the capitalist process without investment in labour and machinery
to produce commodities. The second form Marx called 'differential rent'.
This arose from the ability of some capitalist producers to sell at a cost
below that of more inefficient producers and so extract a surplus profit – as
long as the low cost producers could stop others adopting even lower cost
techniques by blocking entry to the market, employing large economies
of scale in funding, controlling patents and making cartel deals. This
differential rent could be achieved in agriculture by better yielding land
(nature) but in modern capitalism, it would be through a form of 'technological rent'; i.e. monopolising technical innovation.⁶

Monopoly firms can extract imperialist rent from producers with institutionally lower capital intensities. Polish socialist Henryk Grossman (1881–1950) was the first economist to develop a theory of value transfer based on Marx's ideas on non-equivalent exchange according to different organic compositions of capital (namely, the ratio between constant and variable capital outlay, that is, between the price of raw materials and fixed capital and the price of labour-power). In the following hypothetical situation, labour is exploited at a rate of 100 per cent in Europe and only 25 per cent in Asia, with different relative quantities of fixed capital used in each region. Here c = constant capital, v = variable capital, s = surplus value, the rate of exploitation (rate of surplus value) = s/v and the rate of profit = $s/(c + v)$.

In Asia, the value of the product is 16c + 84v + 21s = 121, and the rate of profit is 21/100 = 21 per cent. In Europe, the value of the product is 84c + 16v + 16s = 116, and the rate of profit is 16/100 = 16 per cent. For Grossman, in trade between the two countries the output of the more developed capitalist country with a higher average organic composition of capital is sold at prices above its value (the quantity of average socially necessary labour embodied), while the converse is the case with less developed capitalist countries. In this case, insofar as the rate of profit tends to equalise on the world market with higher rates attracting investment and thus creating a tendency towards an equal rate of profit globally, a uniform rate of 18.5 per cent is earned in both countries, with the European country selling at 118.5 instead of 116. As such, surplus value created in the Asian country is transferred to the technologically more developed country through trade because surplus is distributed according to capital invested, not value created.[7]

Contrary to Rosa Luxemburg, therefore, who theorised that imperialism was principally aimed at the realisation of surplus value through the export of a surfeit of unsaleable goods to non-capitalist markets, Grossman understood imperialism as facilitating the transfer of surplus value from one country to another by means of the form of non-equivalent exchange described above. Luxemburg may be further criticised insofar as it is clear that from the late nineteenth century it was not pre-capitalist territories that were imperialism's consumers of last resort, but the metropolitan proletariat itself.[8]

UNEQUAL EXCHANGE BASED ON WAGE DIFFERENTIALS

For Emmanuel, Grossman's theory of non-equivalent exchange is not specific to foreign trade but also occurs within national capitalist economies. He argues, moreover, that productivity differences between the global

North and the global South are not the cause of unequal exchange. Thus, for instance, Scotch or Cognac are still produced as they have been for hundreds of years, with similar levels of fixed capital, but they support wages at the European level while coffee or cocoa do not. Similarly, wood from Sweden and wood from Africa are produced using comparable methods, but Swedish and African wages are radically divergent.[9] As such, Emmanuel reserves the term 'unequal exchange' for international trade between countries with fundamentally dissimilar wage levels.

Both Adam Smith and Karl Marx had highlighted the possibility of the town exploiting the countryside through capitalist trade. In a manner highly reminiscent of Emmanuel's model of unequal exchange, Smith explains rural-urban value transfer as resulting from institutionalised wage differentials:

The wages of the workmen, and the profits of their different employers, make up the whole of what is gained upon both. Whatever regulations, therefore, tend to increase those wages and profits beyond what they otherwise would be, tend to enable the town to purchase, with a smaller quantity of its labour, the produce of a greater quantity of the labour of the country. They give the traders and artificers in the town an advantage over the landlords, farmers, and labourers in the country, and break down that natural equality which would otherwise take place in the commerce which is carried on between them.[10]

Likewise, commenting on Smith's views, Marx described the medieval European towns, and the incomes of both entrepreneurs and workers therein as growing at the expense of the countryside:

If the prices of the commodities which are exchanged between town and country are such that they represent equal quantities of labour, then they are equal to their values. Profit and wages on both sides of the exchange cannot, therefore, determine these values, but the division of these values determines profit and wages. That is why Adam Smith finds that the town, which exchanges a smaller quantity of labour against a greater quantity of labour from the countryside, draws excess profit and excess wages compared with the country. This would not be the case if it did not sell its commodities to the country for *more than* their value. (Emphasis in the original)[11]

As Raffer suggests, both of these statements are reminiscent of China's People's Liberation Army Commander Marshal Lin Biao's explanation of North-South divisions as revolving around conflict between the 'village' and the 'city', with the former understood as being the 'peripheral' countries and the latter the imperialist countries of world capitalism.[12] For Braun, the exploitation of the dependent countries that is effected through unequal exchange is the necessary correlate of the prosperity of the imperialist countries, and the relative wealth of both groups of countries reflects changes in their respective wage levels.[13] He provides the following realistic example of how international exploitation occurs through trade.

Table 4.1   Hypothetical distribution of net product before international wage equalisation

	Country A	*Country B*
Net Product	$2 trillion	$200 billion
Labour Force	200 million	200 million
Annual Wage	$5,000	$500
Annual Profits	$1 trillion	$100 billion

Balance of Trade (Imports = Exports) = $50 billion

Braun assumes that imports from the periphery may not be substituted, that is, that their price elasticities of demand are zero. In consequence, assuming profits remain unchanged, he finds that an equalisation of wage levels at $2,750 per capita in both countries shown in Table 4.1 would lead to a GDP of $650 billion in Country B and only $1.5 trillion in Country A. In short, equalisation of wages at this rate would imply a negative growth rate of 22.5 per cent in Country A, whereas a change of prices multiplying country B's exports by ten would boost these to $500 billion at current prices, multiplying the purchasing power of Country B tenfold. Like Emmanuel, Braun concludes that the level of trade at nominal prices and wage levels is a very poor indicator of the importance of North-South trade relations.[14]

If the metropolitan centre is thus dependent on cheap imports from the 'periphery', why then does it erect trade barriers to the same? According to Braun, trade restrictions (including subsidies for particular sectors of industry) are the 'condition of the expansion and reproduction of unequal exchange', that is, for consolidating the monopolistic position of metropolitan firms and safeguarding differences in North-South incomes.[15] Trade restrictions are therefore an indispensable precondition for the centre to establish periphery-export-prices at a low level and maintain trade based on unequal exchange. A monopoly of the centre in the reproduction of capital is thereby established.[16] As Braun writes:

[An] imperialist country is able to modify prices of production in its favour by a policy of trade restrictions (apart from other restrictions which as we have pointed out may exist) used by the State. This implies forcing a reduction of wages and/or profit rates upon the dependent country while they are increased locally. Analytically this has nothing to do with distortions of market prices in relation to prices of production that can be induced by monopoly action at the level of production or commercialisation.[17]

Amin has argued that where labour of the same productivity is rewarded at a lower rate in the periphery than in the core countries of capitalist world economy, international trade between the two involves a transfer of surplus value from the former to the latter.[18] Leaving aside these double factoral terms of trade, that is, the extent to which wage differences between North and South outstrip 'productivity' differences, it is possible to calculate imperialist value transfer through trade based on wage differentials alone. Thus in analysing imperialist value transfer through trade between the United States and the Philippines, Webber and Foot conclude:

For every dollar's worth of goods exported from the Philippines in 1961, approximately five times as many hours of labour had to be invested as in a dollars worth of goods exported from Canada. If an hour of labour in the Philippines had been sold abroad at the same price as an hour of labour in Canada, the revenue on Philippine exports would have amounted to 5.269 billion pesos instead of the actual 1.129 billion pesos (this refers to value-producing sectors only) – a difference of 4.14 billion pesos ($1,505 billion). This figure, though it includes the value flow from transfer pricing, compares with a total net direct profit expropriation by US companies (which were responsible for 91.62% of profits on foreign owned capital) between 1956 and 1965 of only $306.8 million.[19]

More recently, political economist Minqi Li has examined the labour terms of trade in the world economy, that is, the ratio between the labour time embodied in goods of a certain monetary value imported by a country and the labour time embodied in goods of a certain monetary value exported by the same country. For instance, in 2012 one million dollars of goods exported by China on average contained 60.7 'worker years' of direct and indirect labour input, while one million dollars' worth of goods imported by China contained an average 32.8 'worker years' of direct and indirect labour input. China's average labour terms of trade in 2012 was, then, 32.8 / 60.7 = 0.54, ensuring that each unit of China's exported labour exchanged for just over half a unit of its imported labour on the world market.[20] Li concludes:

In the early 1990s, China had unfavorable labor terms of trade (less than one) against every other region in the world. China in the early 1990s was clearly a peripheral economy within the capitalist world system. By 2012, China had become a net 'exploiter' in its trade with East Asian, South Asian, and African peripheral economies. However, China's labor terms of trade was only 0.14 against the United States and 0.20 against other 'high income economies' (which include all the core economies, high income oil exporters in the Middle East, and several semi-peripheral economies in Latin America and Eastern Europe). China's terms of trade against the Middle East, Eastern Europe and Latin America remained unfavourable. Overall, China continues to be a peripheral economy within the capitalist world system.[21]

Obviously, such a huge transfer of national wealth in the form of surplus labour has extremely negative consequences for the exploited countries' development opportunities, and equally positive ones for the exploiting country.

A MODEL OF UNEQUAL EXCHANGE
AND UNDERDEVELOPMENT

As the developed capitalist country having strict sovereignty over its trade and payments balances exports its commodities to the less developed country, deindustrialisation and the displacement of relatively uncompetitive producers increases unemployment in the latter while spurring market growth in the former. As a result of an oversupply of labour relative to demand, wages fall in the less developed country and the rate of profit rises. Meanwhile, the economy of the more developed country is characterised by a high rate of accumulation increasing demand for labour and, hence, by both rising wages and a falling rate of profit. Both due to its relative industrial weakness, as well as restricted access to global markets,[22] in order to pay for its imports the less developed country is compelled to export primary goods to fuel the industry of the more developed capitalist country. At the same time, conversely, the higher rate of profit consequent to the diminished wage levels of the less developed country attracts capital from the more developed country. This further induces capital movement from the more developed to the less developed country. As a result of the mobility of productive capital, an equilibrium rate of profit tends to emerge that is higher than that prevailing in both countries before trade occurred.[23]

As the rate of profit is equalised between more and less developed countries and regions, there is a concomitant transformation of values into prices internationally such that insofar as the organic composition of capital is higher in the more developed capitalist country, the prices of its commodities tend to be higher than their values as measured in terms of the average socially necessary labour required to produce them. Conversely, the prices of the commodities of the less developed country tend to be lower than their values, and trade between two such countries results in unequal exchange. Shaikh describes the process as follows:

[Since] wages tend to be much lower in the underdeveloped regions, in the absence of capital mobility between regions profit rates will tend to be higher in the underdeveloped regions than they will be in the developed regions. If profit rates are now equalized through the international mobility of capital, the profit rate in the underdeveloped regions will be lowered and that in the developed regions raised. It follows from this that profits (surplus value) are transferred from the former to the latter. Since profits are an important source of growth, the transfer of profits out of the underdeveloped regions is at the same time a reduction in their rate of growth relative to what it could have been in the absence of the intrusion of foreign capitals. This effect, which compares potential profits in the absence of capital mobility with actual profits resulting from the existing mobility of capital, is quite different from the question of whether or not the actual profits made by foreign capitals in the underdeveloped regions are then reinvested there or repatriated. To the extent that these profits are repatriated, this would of course add insult to injury. But the primary problem remains the transfer itself, which Emmanuel calls unequal exchange (in the narrow sense).[24]

Unequal exchange of commodities leads to an improvement in the rate of capital accumulation in the more developed country and, at the same time, in the productivity of labour therein. Ultimately, this means that for a given volume of employment the more developed country is able to produce more 'machines, wage goods, raw materials and luxury goods' than the less developed country.[25] As the rate of accumulation declines in the less developed country, wages there stagnate and profit rates rise. At the same time, since the organic composition of capital in the less developed country is lower than the average of the two countries, the reduction in wages forces down the price of its commodities. As such, the terms of trade (the secular ratio of a country's export prices to its import prices) move against the less developed capitalist country and underdevelopment is increased despite higher profit-seeking capital flowing there from the more developed country.[26]

In Tables 4.2 and 4.3, Sau provides a mathematical example illustrating the transformation of values into prices internationally and the positive correlation obtaining between global wage divergence and patterns of unequal exchange.

Table 4.2 Transformation of value and price

Economy	Constant Capital	Variable Capital	Surplus Value	Value	Profit Rate	Price
	c	v	s	$\pi = c + v + s$	$\Sigma s / \Sigma (c + v)$	$p = (c + v)(1 + r)$
A	200	100	50	350		300 x 1.25 = 375
B	100	200	100	400	150/600 = 25%	300 x 1.25 = 375
	300	300	150	750		750

Table 4.3 Value and price as wages rise in Country A and fall in Country B

Economy	Constant Capital	Variable Capital	Surplus Value	Value	Profit Rate	Price
	c	v	s	$\pi = c + v + s$	$\Sigma s / \Sigma (c + v)$	$p = (c + v)(1 + r)$
A	200	110	40	350		300 x 1.4706 = 455.88
B	100	100	200	400	240/510 =	200 x 1.4706 = 294.12
	300	210	240	750	47.06%	750.00

Note: In this example, the rate of surplus value is lower in A than in B; it is 0.3636 in the former, as against 2 in the latter.

In sum, for two countries to balance their trade with both bundles of traded goods fetching equal prices, the country with the higher wage rate must sell goods which have a proportionately smaller labour content.[27] The following example illustrates the dynamic in simple terms:[28]

Example:
Country A sells $1,000 of goods to Country B
Country B sells $1,000 of goods to Country A
Trade is balanced.

Suppose
Country A's $1,000 contains $500 of materials and profit and $500 of labour costs,
Country B's $1,000 contains $200 of materials and profit and $800 of labour costs

Assume further
Country A's wage is $1 per day
Country B's wage is $40 per day

Calculating labour content in terms of days of labour we find

For Country A, $500 of labour costs at wage $1 per day equals 500 days of labour

For Country B, $800 of labour costs at wage $40 per day equals 20 days of labour

Thus the country with the higher wage rate sold goods which have a proportionately smaller labour content, in this example, 20 days of labour performed by Country B were exchanged for 500 days of labour performed by Country A. Since average socially necessary labour time at the international level is the source of all value under capitalism, we can therefore say that there is an unequal exchange of values in trade between low-wage and high-wage countries in the world economy.

UNEQUAL EXCHANGE IN THE CAPITALIST WORLD SYSTEM

For Raffer, unequal exchange is based primarily on dependence and the underdevelopment it fosters. He describes the evolution of North-South relations in the following terms:

> Since the first contacts the South has been used by the North for its own economic development, reducing Southern 'development' to a mere reflex of IC [Industrialised Country] needs. No domestic base in the sense of [German economist and theorist of a national system of economic protectionism, Friedrich] List, no balance of productive forces, could be achieved. In the wording of Braun, these countries are now unable to effect their own economic reproduction. As long as this situation persists it matters little whether these countries specialise in agriculture, manufacturing industries or other fields. Their economies will always be dependent on the North; Unequal Exchange will persist.[29]

The development of a sustainable national and regional articulation between the production of mass consumption goods and the investment goods required to produce these is absolutely essential for the global South to attain a higher standing in the international market. Only those countries that are able to meet their own basic needs and can thus afford to stop trading where necessary are capable of withstanding the economic pressure exercised by the imperialist monopolies of the global North and thereby prevent unequal exchange from occurring.[30]

As Martinez-Alier writes: 'One peculiarity of human ecology is that, on the borders of rich countries, there are a sort of Maxwell's Demons ...,[31] which keep out most people from poor countries, thus being able to maintain extremely different per capita rates of energy and material consumption in adjoining territories.'[32] Whereas for Emmanuel the global North's monopoly on high wages is established mainly through the political and organising efforts of metropolitan labour, we suggest that the institutional bias favouring metropolitan wages is predicated upon colonial and neo-colonial relations.

Part II
The Econometrics of Imperialism

5
Imperialism and Its Denial

Before proceeding to provide an operational definition of economic imperialism, it is first necessary to examine some of the objections raised against theories of the same, particularly those which are hegemonic on the metropolitan left.

'PRODUCTIVITY' AND UNEQUAL EXCHANGE

It is often claimed by Marxists that workers in the 'periphery' countries earn such paltry wages as they do due to an alleged deficiency in 'productivity'. Critics of the theory of unequal exchange as a mechanism of imperialist value transfer suggest that since the productivity of developing country labour is much lower than that of developed country labour, the backward industries of the global South produce goods and services that are correspondingly less valuable than those of the far more advanced industry of the global North. As such, productivity differentials either reduce or completely negate the inequality inherent in exchange based on divergent wage levels. Indeed, this point has recently been made quite forcefully in the following terms: '[Global labour arbitrage] is a shift of work from the hands of those who create more value to those who create less.'[1] Although it is obvious that it would scarcely be profitable for corporations to shift production to areas where workers are only a fraction as productive as those in their home countries, we are compelled to take such logic seriously. There are several points to make against this view commonly held by socialists in the global North at least, where it functions as tacit justification for prioritising the demands of the world's richest ('most exploited') workers.

First, measuring productivity according to the market value generated by each unit of labour (whether in terms of labour time or of cost) is highly problematic. In denying the elementary truth that international wage differentials typically reflect divergent rates of exploitation Finger, for instance, declares that 'the value-enhancing ability of an hour of social labor is intrinsically linked to the quantity of social resources sacrificed to attain and preserve those skills'.[2] In other words, metropolitan workers are said to produce more (surplus) value because their costs of reproduction, that is, their wages, are higher. As John Smith has noted, were this true 'capitalists could increase the quantity of surplus value extracted from a workforce simply by paying them higher wages!'[3] Similarly, as Jedlicki argues, 'value-added' data already incorporates those wage and capital differentials which Western 'socialists' justify in the name of superior metropolitan 'productivity'. In doing so, 'a demonstration is carried out by using as proof what constitutes, precisely, the object of demonstration'.[4]

Second, one hour of average socially necessary labour time (what Marx called 'abstract labour') expended in a capital-intensive industry is the same as one hour expended in a labour-intensive industry. It is not the amount of capital at a worker's disposal that renders her more or less productive of value, but the amount of abstract labour that she contributes to the capitalist production process as a whole. As Marx writes:

Productive power has reference, of course, only to labour of some useful concrete form ... Useful labour becomes, therefore, a more or less abundant source of products, in proportion to the rise or fall of its productiveness. On the other hand, no change in this productiveness affects the labour represented by value ... *However then productive power may vary, the same labour [of equal skill and intensity], exercised during equal amounts of time, always yields equal amounts of value.* But it will yield, during equal periods of time, different quantities of value in use; more, if the productive power rise, fewer, if it fall. The same change in productive power, which increases the fruitfulness of labour, and, in consequence, the quantity of use-values produced by that labour, will diminish the total value of this increased quantity of use-values, provided such change shorten the total labour time necessary for their production; and vice versa.[5] (My emphasis)

Contrary to what some critics of unequal exchange imply, the higher physical productivity of labour, *ceteris paribus*, tends to reduce, not increase the per capita value of its output. Moreover, as Emmanuel argues, in the absence of political and/or trade union pressure being brought to bear on the labour market, technological progress tends to lower the value of labour-power (wages). As such, productivity increases are not necessarily correlated with wage increases, as can be observed by comparing the 'relatively small differences in productivity between centre and periphery [with wage differences between the two] and the fact that sometimes Third World workers are even more productive than workers from the centre ...'.[6] Historically, productivity increased rapidly in the earlier years of the industrial revolution in Britain, but wage levels tended not to rise in tandem. The growth of monopoly, however, has afforded increasing wages for a section of the working class having a modicum of social and/or economic capital at its disposal.

Relatedly, surplus value is not the difference between the price of labour-power and the final price of its product as is suggested by socialists who argue that metropolitan workers are the most exploited worldwide. Rather, it is the difference between the labour time required to produce the materials required for the worker's reproduction compared with the labour time he or she actually expends as a wage-earner. A *negative rate of surplus value* can and does apply in some regions of the world where workers are able to purchase with their wages more abstract labour than they themselves contribute with their labour-power.[7] We will examine the extent to which this is the case below. For now, it is necessary to understand that (1) a high proportion of the goods consumed by metropolitan workers are the product of highly exploited global South labour, and (2) a high proportion of the capital used in the production of consumer goods industries in the core countries is the accumulated or 'dead' labour of these same highly exploited workers. Addressing the first of these issues, Smith writes:

The Euro-Marxist argument that higher productivity in the North means that higher wages are consistent with higher rates of exploitation has been negated by a simple fact: as we know from the labels, the consumption goods consumed by workers in the North are no longer produced solely or mainly in the North; to an ever-greater extent, they are produced by low-wage labour in the Global South. Their productivity, their wages significantly substantially determine the value of the basket of consumption goods that reproduces labour-power in imperialist countries.[8]

In light of this, it is notable that even the small numbers of writers who are critical of value transfer view it largely or solely as enriching capitalists, but not most workers in the global North.[9] Broadly speaking, they see superprofits but not superwages. The mobility of productive capital, however, ensures that profit rates tend to be equalised internationally, with the consequent transfer of surplus value between countries. This tendency for the rate of profit to be equalised means that workers in the advanced countries benefit from unequal exchange. As Emmanuel writes, 'super-profits can only be temporary. Super wages, however, become automatically in the long run, the normal level of wages'.[10]

The third point against critics of alleged lower 'periphery' productivity is that the export industries of the Third World are not typically based on primitive production techniques, but on technological endowments similar to those of analogous sectors of metropolitan industry. More importantly, capital is mobile internationally and is therefore *capable* of levelling intra-industry technological differences across countries even if it does not in fact do so. International technology transfer is principally dictated by profitability criteria under circumstances wherein the extremely low price of labour-power has been used as a substitute for capital investment internationally. Thus a massive increase in the employment of cheap labour over the past four decades has coincided with decreasing investments in fixed capital. In sum, technological wherewithal is dependent not on what is necessary for the production of a given quantity of use values, but on what is optimal for the valorisation of capital. The introduction of labour-saving technology to the production process is foremost conditional, then, upon the prospective maximisation of profits.

It may be technically efficient to use a labour-intensive method of producing things, because although mechanisation saves on labour it involves using more of the other input, namely machines. Setting aside technically inefficient production methods, the real question is which of the possible technically efficient methods will give most profits: the more mechanised or the more labour-intensive one? A simple example shows how this question must be answered. Street cleaners can clean the streets more quickly if they are all equipped with vacuum cleaners. But this will not necessarily be profitable. If the vacuum cleaners are very expensive, it may cost less to use a more labour-intensive method. If the machines are cheap enough, then it pays to become more mechanised.[11]

Fourth, evidence for the alleged productivity gap which opponents of the theory of unequal exchange have traditionally posited as responsible for global wage divergence is highly suspect; in value terms, transfer pricing makes it extremely difficult to measure productivity in the different operations of one enterprise.

The enterprise's ability to set arbitrary prices for transfers of semi-finished goods within the same firm means that relative productivity between different branches of the firm will take on an arbitrary value. As in a single plant where, say, production line workers are paid different wages from cleaning workers, productivity (and hence the notion of exploitation) is indivisible.[12]

In Amin's understanding of the concept, unequal exchange is 'the exchange of products whose production involves wage differentials greater than those of productivity'.[13] However, where productivity differentials may realistically be said to apply, and bracketing the first two points raised above, these are not necessarily greater than wage differentials and, therefore, trade between low-wage and high-wage countries involves a transfer of additional surplus value from the former to the latter.

Fifth, the less developed countries have neither the government budgets, nor the industrial infrastructure in place to produce technological innovations which might compete with those of the developed countries.[14] Multinational corporations based in the developed countries have a monopoly of advanced technology for which the firms and countries of the less developed world must pay to use, and they thereby obtain a corresponding productivity gain.

Sixth, the final prices of goods produced in the 'periphery' using cheap labour and sold in the imperialist countries are inflated by the costs of advertising, marketing, retail, insurance and security. When added to the cost price, these enormous capital outlays make it appear that metropolitan workers employed in these sectors are producing huge quantities of additional value per unit of labour time, that is, that they are exceptionally productive compared to the 'peripheral' workers who actually manufacture a product or its vital inputs. In fact, no additional value is added to many products during these later phases of its circulation, but geographical and inter-sectoral price structures allow the redistribution of value created at the point of production. In sum, countries are exploited within the capitalist world economy by means of unequal exchange in the sphere of circulation, that is, in the difference between the selling prices of national producers and those of multinational corporations (monopolies).[15]

Seventh, some critics assume that labour cannot exploit labour. As Finger writes: 'Although from a formal standpoint, an unequal exchange of hours takes place in the exchange of commodities of equal physiological labour through unequal prices, skilled labour does not exploit unskilled labour.'[16] Superficially, this statement is correct; to exploit labour, one would first have to hire labour. Nonetheless, some strata of the working class clearly do benefit from the exploitation of other strata. Leaving aside the extent and spread of shareholding, home ownership, and savings in the form of deposit accounts and pension funds amongst the 'working class' – all of which constitute capital from which profits may be drawn – some sections of the same actively pursue political agendas that maintain and extend a parasitic relationship between themselves and oppressed workers. This agency may itself be described as exploitative. That is to say, where some workers seek to retain whatever bourgeois status their occupation, income and conditions of work afford them through alliance with imperialist, racist and/or patriarchal political forces responsible for the low-wage position of oppressed workers, they may justly be said to actively exploit said workers.

Marx and Engels themselves had admitted the possibility of one section of the working class 'exploiting' another. For Marx, the wages of workers in the unproductive sectors of employment must be paid for out of the exploitation of production sector workers, their numerical expansion being conditional upon the latter. Unproductive workers do not necessarily exploit productive workers even though, as a whole, they are 'parasites on the actual producers'.[17] Certainly, the wages of unproductive workers are determined according to the value of labour-power just as much as those of their productive counterparts, and they would not be hired if they did not deliver to the individual capitalist revenue in excess of the same. However, as Marx writes, the 'surplus labour' of the unproductive worker does not 'produce value any more than his [sic] ... necessary labour' does.

Marx noted another possibility, however, namely that a privileged section of the working class might be hired so as to directly exploit another, less privileged section. He wrote:

Since the quality and intensity of [piece-]work are ... controlled by the form of wage itself, superintendence of labour becomes in great part super-fluous. Piece-wages therefore lay the foundation of the modern 'domestic labour' ... as well as of a hierarchically organised system of exploitation and oppression. The latter has two fundamental forms. On the one hand piece-wages facilitate the interposition of parasites between the capitalist and the wage-labourer, the 'sub-letting of labour'. The gain of these middle-men comes entirely from the difference between the labour price which the capitalist pays, and the part of that price which they actually allow to reach the labourer. In England this system is characteristically called the 'Sweating system'. On the other hand, piece-wage allows the capitalist to make a contract for so much per piece with the head labourer – in manufactures with the chief of some group, in mines with the extractor of the coal, in the factory with the actual machine-worker – at a price for which the head labourer himself undertakes the enlisting and payment of his assistant workpeople. *The exploitation of the labourer by capital is here effected through the exploitation of the labourer by the labourer.*[18]

Finally, left apologists for global wage differentials contend that skilled workers generate more value than do unskilled workers since 'skilled labor power is itself the product of a greater expenditure of labor-time in its formation and maintenance ... than is the labor-power required for average and unskilled, brute [sic] work'.[19] As noted above, however, labour not engaged in the production of commodities does not generate any value at all, no matter how skilled it may be. Skilled labour employed in the production of commodities is indeed equal to a greater number of hours of unskilled labour. Yet that observation does not imply anything about the exploita-tion of one group of labourers by another. To determine whether anyone is 'exploiting' (or parasitic upon) anyone else, we would have to look at the distribution of the economic product, especially, but not exclusively, in the form of wages.[20]

As such, the issue at hand is whether within the world economy labour-power is (a) paid uniformly according to skill; and (b) similarly capable of obtaining skilled employment in any given national economy. In our view, a lack of employment opportunities in the underdeveloped and exploited countries, particularly in the health, education, military and science sectors (which in the major imperialist countries are heavily state subsidised), has led to a 'brain drain' of skilled mental labour migrating to the imperialist nations. This has embellished the overall skill level of the metropolitan workforce and depleted the general skill level in the 'periphery', Asia in particular, affording the imperialist countries higher levels of productivity and, *ceteris paribus*, higher levels of consumption.

Nonetheless, there is little evidence to suggest that increased employment of 'skilled' white-collar workers reduces levels of fixed capital investment by increasing labour efficiency. The late British Professor of Economics and quantitative macroeconomic historian Angus Maddison has shown that the proportional increase of white-collar employment exceeded the growth rate of gross non-residential fixed capital stock to GDP in the leading capitalist countries between 1950 and 1989.[21] That is to say, the great expansion in the unproductive sector of the imperialist countries did not lead to higher rates of profit during that period and its employees cannot be said to have therefore 'earned' their higher wages from a bourgeois point of view.

It is, moreover, false to claim that the major imperialist countries contribute more skilled labour to the global economy than other countries. Table 5.1 shows that low-income, lower middle-income, and upper middle-income countries provided 64.6 per cent of high-skilled employment, 86.1 per cent of medium-skilled employment, and fully 87.1 per cent of low-skilled employment to the global economy in 2015. It is clear, furthermore, that labour is not paid according to skill level, but according to the average value of labour-power multiplied by the level of demand for skilled labour within an economy. Not only is there a general oversupply of labour in the dependent economies that deflates wage rates, but lower levels of capital accumulation and civil infrastructure reduce the demand for skilled labour therein. As such, wildly different wages for the same work may be evidenced on a global scale.

Taking Ethiopia, Cambodia, Albania and the United Kingdom as representative of their respective per capita GDP income brackets, Table 5.2 suggests the following:

- Professionals in high-income countries earn over 44 times as much per month as those in low-income countries; 36 times as much as

Table 5.1 Employment by skill level, 2015

Reference Area	Employment – ILO modelled estimates (thousands)				Employment Distribution by Area – ILO modelled estimates (%)				World Employment Distribution – Author's estimates (%)		
	Total	Skill Levels 3 and 4 (High)	Skill Level 2 (Medium)	Skill Level 1 (Low)	Total	Skill Levels 3 and 4 (High)	Skill Level 2 (Medium)	Skill Level 1 (Low)	Skill Levels 3 and 4 (High)	Skill Level 2 (Medium)	Skill Level 1 (Low)
World	3 215 810	608 494	2 126 006	481 310	100.0	18.9	66.1	15.0	100.0	100.0	100.0
Low Income	253 930	11 357	205 745	36 829	100.0	4.5	81.0	14.5	1.9	9.7	7.8
Lower Middle Income	1 118 746	171 168	707 405	240 174	100.0	15.3	63.2	21.5	28.2	33.3	49.9
Upper Middle Income	1 268 287	210 171	914 952	143 164	100.0	16.6	72.1	11.3	34.5	43.1	29.7
High Income	570 466	215 573	294 030	60 862	100.0	37.8	51.5	10.7	35.4	13.9	12.6

Source: International Labour Organization (ILO) 2017. Employment by occupation – ILO modelled estimates, May. Online: www.ilo.org/ilostat/faces/oracle/webcenter/portalapp/pagehierarchy/Page3.jspx?MBI_ID=12 (accessed 13 November 2018).

Table 5.2   Mean monthly earnings by occupation and income type, various countries

Country	Occupation	Year	US Dollars	Country Type
Ethiopia	2. Professionals (ISCO-08)	2010	106	Low Income
Ethiopia	3. Technicians and associate professionals (ISCO-08)	2010	80	Low Income
Ethiopia	6. Skilled agricultural, forestry and fishery workers (ISCO-08)	2010	35	Low Income
Ethiopia	TOTAL. Total (ISCO-08)	2010	60	Low Income
Cambodia	2. Professionals (ISCO-08)	2011	129	Lower Middle Income
Cambodia	3. Technicians and associate professionals (ISCO-08)	2011	168	Lower Middle Income
Cambodia	6. Skilled agricultural, forestry and fishery workers (ISCO-08)	2011	155	Lower Middle Income
Cambodia	TOTAL. Total (ISCO-08)	2011	121	Lower Middle Income
Albania	2. Professionals (ISCO-08)	2016	499	Upper Middle Income
Albania	3. Technicians and associate professionals (ISCO-08)	2016	402	Upper Middle Income
Albania	6. Skilled agricultural, forestry and fishery workers (ISCO-08)	2016	219	Upper Middle Income
Albania	TOTAL. Total (ISCO-08)	2016	369	Upper Middle Income
United Kingdom	2. Professionals (ISCO-08)	2011	4709	High Income
United Kingdom	3. Technicians and associate professionals (ISCO-08)	2011	3404	High Income
United Kingdom	6. Skilled agricultural, forestry and fishery workers (ISCO-08)	2011	2403	High Income
United Kingdom	TOTAL. Total (ISCO-08)	2011	3365	High Income

Note: The earnings of employees relate to the gross remuneration in cash and in kind paid to employees, as a rule at regular intervals, for time worked or work done together with remuneration for time not worked, such as annual vacation, other type of paid leave or holidays. Earnings exclude employers' contributions in respect of their employees paid to social security and pension schemes and also the benefits received by employees under these schemes. Earnings also exclude severance and termination pay. Statistics of earnings relate to the gross remuneration of employees, that is, the total before any deductions are made by the employer. This is a harmonised series: (1) data reported as weekly and yearly are converted to monthly in the local currency series, using data on average weekly hours if available; and (2) data are converted to a common currency, using exchange rates for the series in US dollars and using 2011 purchasing power parity (PPP) rates for the series in constant 2011 PPP \$. The latter series allows for international comparisons by taking account of the differences in relative prices between countries.

Source: International Labour Organization (ILO) 2017. Mean nominal monthly earnings of employees by sex and occupation – harmonised series. Online: www.ilo.org/ilostat/faces/oracle/webcenter/portalapp/pagehierarchy/Page3.jspx?MBI_ID=435 (accessed 13 November 2018).

those in lower middle-income countries; and 9 times as much as professionals in upper middle-income countries.

- Technicians and associate professionals in high-income countries earn
over 55 times as much per month as those in low-income countries; 26
times as much as those in lower middle-income countries; and over 10
times as much as those in upper middle-income countries.
- Skilled agricultural, forestry and fishery workers in high-income
countries earn over 68 times as much per month as those in low-income
countries; 15 times as much as those in lower middle-income countries;
and over 10 times as much as those in upper middle-income countries.

WHAT IS IMPERIALISM?

From the foregoing account of the mechanics of global value transfer,
today's imperialist economies may be defined in both *nominal* and in *real*
terms. Nominally, imperialist economies are those which operate internationally on the basis of a net transfer of value from specified foreign
territories, while exploited countries are net exporters of value to said
foreign territories. This transfer is effected through monopolistic control
of global value chains in agriculture, industry and services, as well as rents
accruing to financial, mineral and physical force monopolies. In addition,
monopoly capital places an effective levy on trade and investment between
countries with highly divergent wage levels, with low-wage countries made
to supply substantially more of their socially necessary embodied labour in
trade with high-wage countries. In real terms, however, this one-sided relationship between countries or groups of countries has progressed to such an
extent that the major imperialist economies today, dominated by the largest
capitalist interests in the world, are able to secure a *net value transfer* to their
economies from abroad, that is, they import more value than they create
nationally, including from other *nominally* imperialist economies.

The consumer economy attendant to imperialism is most visible in those
countries that have achieved global hegemony. By contrast, even smaller
imperialist countries like China are massive net exporters of national
wealth to the major imperialist countries, both in terms of exchange value
(labour time) and in terms of price (net current transfers from abroad,
equal to the unrequited transfers of income from non-residents to residents
minus the unrequited transfers from residents to non-residents). Unequal
exchange in the strict sense is, of course, diminished in trade between
countries with comparable wage levels, though non-equivalent exchange
based on industrial or financial monopoly is not. While China's export of
monopoly capital to other countries in the global South allows it to capture

value added in places such as resource-rich Africa, in respect of global value chains a large proportion of the wealth that China imports from Africa and Asia goes into production for export, principally to the affluent, high-wage countries, including a United States without the capacity to pay. As such it is First World consumption disguised as Chinese consumption.

Nonetheless, the regional, semi-peripheral hegemons of the global South strive to take economic advantage of weaker neighbours. National capitals have a tendency to expand beyond their borders, and frequently resort to international war to secure their sovereignty. On a world scale, however, imperialism is primarily characterised by the economic preponderance of generalised monopoly and finance capital, which systematically denudes the semi-colonial countries of their national product. While some states are stronger and others weaker regionally, the newly industrialising semi-colonies have in common with the more agrarian ones their exploitation by the largest imperialist monopolies. In terms of capital export, imperialist China's foreign direct investment (FDI) inflows consistently exceed its outflows, with the excess of China's inward stock of FDI over its outward stock having increased from US$165 billion in 2000 to US$243 billion in 2009.[22]

Divisions between the imperialist countries and the underdeveloped countries have not disappeared in recent decades. Corporate and financial wealth is overwhelmingly concentrated in the major imperialist countries, and in terms of value transfer through non-equivalent and unequal exchange, even the imperialist countries of the 'periphery' are not net importers of value. In respect to capital export imperialism, the BRICS countries' outward FDI stock does not typically exceed their inward FDI stock, while their shares of global capital export are far smaller than those of the major value-importing countries. China's FDI in Africa and elsewhere is dwarfed by that of Europe, Japan and the United States. In addition, despite having greater shares of global trade than investment, according to the United Nations Conference on Trade and Development (UNCTAD), between 2005 and 2010 at least 40 per cent of the export earnings of the 'upper middle income countries' and 30 per cent of the export earnings of all 'low and middle income countries' was used to service debts owed to Western financial monopolies.[23] For critics of imperialism, it is imperative to tally the net balance of value production and distribution on a world scale, explain how this operates, and recognise the value accruing to monopolies of wealth and privilege globally (including those of the 'labour aristocracy').

There is a glaring imbalance in global consumption and production that has not been substantially lessened by the development of large monopolies and capitalist relations of production in the poorer nations, or by the extension of international regimes of trade and investment. The apparent political independence of the nation-states of Africa, Asia and Central and South America is heavily circumscribed by their economic integration with the capital, stock and commodities markets of the generalised monopolies of Europe, Japan and North America. This has rendered them net suppliers of value dependent on unstable economic growth in the principal investor economies. In most cases it is closely tied to political support for the US military institutions, installations and contracts, and fear of retribution should the dictates of 'free trade' and 'geo-strategy' demand.

The legal, political, financial and military structures of value transfer prevent independent, sustainable and balanced national development in the countries of the global South. This is particularly true with the neo-colonial extractivism hosted by resource-rich countries in the Middle East and Africa, but it is also true of those more independent countries of the Third World which have gained most from globalisation. Even as the export of commodities to the affluent West has assumed paramount economic signif-icance to these countries, their domestic growth has been restricted by the operation of Western agricultural, industrial, mineral and fiscal monopolies. The neoliberal growth strategies directed by the Bretton Woods Institutions from the 1970s onwards (principally the World Bank and the International Monetary Fund (IMF) have not proved conducive to balanced national or social development either in the 'producer' or 'consumer' countries. In particular, 'peripheral' economies have frequently been devastated as a result of debt, inflation and currency collapse precipitated by unfettered transna-tional capital flows.

THE 'LABOUR ARISTOCRACY' AS CAUSE AND CONSEQUENCE OF DEVELOPMENT

In the pre-neoliberal phase of imperialist capitalism, unequal exchange and unequal development had the same basis in the international variation in wage rates.[24] Essentially, if there is not sufficient purchasing power in society for the sale of commodities at a price yielding profit, then capital will not be attracted to invest in it. Prior to the neoliberal 'globalisation' of capitalist production (uneven and attenuated as that has been), the low wage levels of the global South did not represent a market with sufficient purchasing power to attract capital. Even in 2016, the city of Dublin, Ireland, with a population of 530,000 had a GDP of US$101 billion, while Morocco, having a population 66 times that of Dublin at 35.3 million had a GDP of US$100.6 billion. Prior to neoliberalism, the low wage levels of the exploited countries generated a market that was too small to attract sub-stantial quantities of capital and, therefore, only a relatively small number of factories based on the domestic market were set up therein. The production facilities that were established were geared towards production for export to the wealthy imperialist countries with high consumer purchasing power.

In explaining how investments in the imperialist countries lead to development while those in the exploited countries remain limited and marginal, Emmanuel has written:

> Why is it that European capital in the United States and Australia, and United States capital in Canada, have benefitted these countries by developing their economies, whereas in the Third World they have played a harmful role by forming enclaves? An enclave merely means a foreign investment that refuses to participate in the country's process of expanded reproduction. In less learned terms, it is an investment that restricts itself to the self-financing of the branch in which it is installed and then, once this expansion has been accomplished, repatriates the whole of its profits.
>
> The Société Générale de Belgique installed the Union Minière in the Congo and Canadian Petrofina in Canada. The former exploits copper miners, the latter oil wells. When the investment has reached its maximum potential, Canada Petrofina uses its profits to establish a refinery: for this purpose it even increases its capital, or it sets up a sister company, inviting its Belgian shareholders to subscribe to this by sending back to Canada the dividends previously paid to them. For several years Canadian Petrofina refrains from paying any money dividend and instead grants stock dividend. This is not displeasing to the Belgian shareholders since, unlike dividends paid in money, a stock dividend is not subject to income tax. Then the company interests itself in the distribution of oil products and buys a network of selling points. Next, it sets up a petrochemical industry, followed by a works to produce tank cars; and, after that, what? Perhaps a chain of department stores, or else a shoe factory. If the company does not do this, its shareholders will, by instructing their bankers to use the product of their dividends to purchase a wide variety of shares on the Montreal stock exchange. The Belgian shareholders receive pieces of paper and credit notes and that satisfies them, but their capital is Canadianized.
>
> In contrast to all this, the Union Minière du Katanga, once its program for equipping its copper mines is completed, ceases to expand and pays its dividends in money. It becomes an enclave. Why? Are we really to suppose that the heads of the Société Générale in Brussels are solely concerned to overdevelop Canada and 'block' development in the Belgian Congo? The reality is different. The simple fact is that in Canada the high standard of living of the people, resulting from the high wage level, constitutes a market for all sorts of products, whereas wages and standard

of living in the Congo are such that there is nothing there to interest any fairly large-scale capitalist – nothing except the extraction of minerals or the production of certain raw materials for export that have inevitably to be sought where they are to be found.

This situation is the effect, not the cause, of low wages, even though, once established, it becomes, through the capitalist logic of profit-seeking, a cause in its turn by blocking the development of the productive forces and, consequently, the process of creating conditions propitious to trade union struggle for the raising of wages.[25]

The low wage level and consequent underdevelopment of the exploited countries is a vicious circle; unequal exchange and the repatriation of savings to the imperialist countries ensure that insufficient capital remains for dynamic market development. The more limited investments are in these countries, the higher the rate of unemployment and the greater labour market pressure on wages. By contrast, high wages in the imperialist countries guarantee high rates of consumption and much larger markets catering to the same. These attract capital, and expanded development of the productive forces necessarily follows, thus strengthening the long-term industrial, political and economic prospects of the metropolitan workforce.

Following the advent of the neoliberal era, however, partial industrialisation of the global South within the capitalist world system was rendered practical both in technological terms (with the proliferation of containerisation, computers, the internet, flexible specialisation and so forth) and in political terms, with neoliberalism facilitating the free movement of capital and goods across borders, and the weakening of trade unions globally. This new system of globalised capitalist production made it possible to produce commodities in low-wage countries while maintaining the core imperialist countries as centres of administrative, consumer, military and financial power.

Without question, Southern industrialisation has brought profound changes to the imperialist world system; with much of the planet having freed itself from formal colonialism in the decades after the Second World War, the bourgeoisie of the newly industrialising countries has the potential to grow and develop outside the imperialist diktat of the countries of the global North, the United States in particular. Yet the durability of global wage divergence and the concentration of associated consumer markets in the former colonising regions, alongside Western financial, fiduciary and military hegemony are preventing the global South from delinking from the major imperialist countries at this time. A long struggle for South-South unity lies ahead, with those states of the global South having the support of their working populations in the vanguard.

6

Measuring Imperialist Value Transfer

We have argued that there is a net transfer of wealth from the so-called developing countries to the developed countries in the world economy. The imperialist transfer of value (ITV) causes the underdevelopment or maldevelopment[1] of the exploited countries and affords the core countries profits realised through the higher-than-average exploitation of 'peripheral' labour. There are numerous mechanisms by which this transfer occurs including dividends from Trade-Related Intellectual Property Rights (TRIPS, tax holidays, interest payments, repatriated profits, capital flight, trade misinvoicing, abusive transfer pricing and unequal exchange.[2] As described in Chapter 1 of the present study, economic imperialism produces visible and invisible, recorded and unrecorded transfers of value.

In order to estimate the magnitude of these outflows of value from the 'periphery' to the core of the world economy, we will first consult two recent studies undertaken by US-based group Global Financial Integrity, the first in collaboration with the Norwegian School of Economics, India's Jawaharlal Nehru University, Brazil's Instituto de Estudos Socioeconômicos and the Nigerian Institute of Social and Economic Research. We will subsequently refer to our own estimates of the value of unequal exchange, combining these respective totals to provide a conservative estimate of the annual imperialist transfer of value.

VISIBLE AND INVISIBLE VALUE TRANSFER

In estimating value transfer today, we will first consider those mechanisms relating to *net recorded transfers* (RecT), and in the second category, *illicit financial flows* (IFFs) or illicit outflows.[3] Recorded transfers (RecT) are comprised of a country's financial account balance, primary income, secondary income and capital transfers. A financial account is a component of a country's balance of payments that covers claims on or liabilities to non-residents, specifically with regard to financial assets (including direct investment, portfolio investment and reserve assets). Primary income in current accounts refers to receipts and payments of employee compensation paid to non-resident workers as well as investment income (that is, from migrant remittances as well as interest, profits and dividends generated from foreign investment). Secondary income refers to transfers recorded in the balance of payments whenever an economy provides or receives goods, services, income or financial items without receiving anything in return (for example, from military aid or overseas development aid). Finally, capital transfer involves the transfer of ownership of a fixed asset, the forgiveness of a liability, and the transfer of money that is linked to, or conditional on, the acquisition or disposal of a fixed asset.

Fundamentally, net RecT consist of negative balance of payments as well as outflows of capital (that is, the transfer by foreign companies of 'invisible' earnings from profits and dividends). Thus, for example, a net recorded outflow occurs when a country's servicing of its external debt exceeds its supply of new foreign capital. This means that the country must finance that excess with a trade surplus. As such, a net outward transfer of resources results, with said country having to increase domestic production of goods and services, lower domestic absorption of goods and services, or some combination of both sufficiently so as to cover service payments on its external debt.[4] Leakage in the balance of payments refers to the net loss of a country's domestic finance, that is, the transfer of savings, tax revenue and/or cash to another country. The importation of foreign goods, for example, means that the money of one country is transferred to another. Global Financial Integrity estimated that developing countries lost US$325.9 billion in recorded transfers to the developed countries in 2012.[5]

Whereas the above measures may be used to estimate recorded transfers, illicit financial flows mainly arise from fraudulent misinvoicing, 'same-invoice faking', or otherwise misstating the value or volume of exports or imports on a customs invoice. Manipulation of the price, quantity, or quality of a good or service on an invoice allows corrupt governmental officials, tax-evading corporations and criminals to move huge sums of money across international borders quickly, easily and surreptitiously.[6] The movement of money from criminal enterprises tends to affect outflows from developing nations more than inflows to those nations.[7] According to Global Financial Integrity, illicit financial flows out of developing countries are sizeable and growing, amounting to an average US$1 trillion annually over the last decade.[8] In 2014 between US$620 billion and US$970 billion in illicit financial flows left the 'developing countries' by way of deliberate developed country misinvoicing in merchandise trade.[9] This amounted to illicit financial outflows of between 14 and 24 per cent of total developing country merchandise trade.[10]

Transfer pricing, meanwhile, involves inflating prices as a means of shifting profits across territories to take advantage of differences in national tax laws.

In other words, corporations boost post-tax earnings by reporting higher taxable profits in countries where taxes are lower. Transfer pricing should be counted separately from trade misinvoicing, since in the case of the former there are not discrepancies between recorded exports and recorded imports because the same price is reported on both sides of the transaction.[11] As Baker notes, 'transfer pricing is used by virtually every multinational corporation to shift profits at will around the globe'.[12] In 2009, Christian Aid estimated that transfer pricing accounts for around US$365 billion a year in capital flight from the poorest 17 countries to the richest countries.[13] According to the same study, the amount of capital lost by the countries of the global South by means of transfer pricing in that year was around US$1.1 trillion.[14]

The foregoing measures of the imperialist transfer of value in terms of (1) Net RecT and (2) IFFs are based on market-based accounting that tacitly accepts the massive gap between the 'real' value of goods from the global South (as measured by the average socially necessary labour time required to produce them) and the low prices actually paid for them. In our view, the unrecorded transfers of value resulting from this discrepancy are the product of (3) Unequal Exchange, that is, the terms of trade between the exploited countries and the imperialist countries in the world economy.

UNEQUAL EXCHANGE

Unequal exchange is the idea that 'on the world market the poor nations are obliged to sell the product of a relatively large number of hours of labour in order to obtain in exchange from the rich nations the product of a small number of hours of labour'.[15] The underlying basis for commodities embodying different values exchanging for equivalent prices internationally is the profound divergence in wages between the imperialist countries and the dependent countries in the global economy. The miserably low wage rates within the 'peripheral' economies are predicated upon (1) the pressure imposed by their exports having to compete for limited shares of the largely metropolitan consumer market; (2) the drain of value, capital and natural resources that might otherwise be used to build up the productive forces of the national economy; (3) the unresolved land question creating an oversupply of labour; (4) repressive governments, benefiting from and accepting neoliberalism and, therefore, unable and unwilling to grant wage rises; and (5) militarised borders that prevent the movement of workers to the core countries and, hence, an international equalisation of returns to labour.[16]

To estimate imperialist transfer of value due to unequal exchange we must determine the value of exports from the 'peripheral' to the core regions of the world economy were labour-power in the former to be remunerated at the same level as it is in the latter. In algebraic terms,

$$T = d * X - X$$

where:

T = Magnitude of unrecorded value transfer due to unequal exchange;
X = Volume of exports; and
d = the distortion factor, that is, the deviation of the nominal price from the price according to quivalent wage rates globally.[17]

Table 6.1   Value of regional trade flows in each region's total merchandise exports (billions of US dollars)

	Exports to North America	Exports to South and Central America	Exports to Europe	Exports to CIS	Exports to Africa	Exports to Middle East	Exports to Asia	Total
World	2 508	587	5 844	399	453	561	4 216	14 851
North America	956	165	330	11	32	53	413	1 965
South and Central America	138	148	108	8	15	15	134	577
Europe	416	98	3 998	180	177	168	524	5 632
Commonwealth of Independent States (CIS)	33	6	308	109	9	19	88	588
Africa	85	14	184	2	62	19	123	508
Middle East	79	7	108	5	29	89	471	895
Asia	801	148	808	85	128	198	2 464	4 686

North American and European Exports to South and Central America, Commonwealth of Independent States (CIS), Africa, Middle East and Asia	1 821
South and Central American, Commonwealth of Independent States (CIS), African, Middle East and Asian Exports to Europe and North America	2 652

Source: WTO 2011, Table I.4. 'Intra- and Inter-Regional Merchandise Trade, 2010'.

To determine value added domestically we must determine what percentage of export sector prices is composed of capital and intermediate goods imports. Intermediate goods are goods such as raw materials, parts and fuel used in conjunction with capital goods (machinery and equipment) and labour in the production of final goods. The OECD's 'import content of exports' measure provides an estimate of the value of imported intermediate goods and services subsequently embodied in exports. Changes in the same can reveal the evolution of domestic value added due to exporting activities. In 2014, the average import content of OECD exports was 30 per cent and the average import content of non-OECD exports was 25 per cent.[18] By that measure, we may assume that the domestically generated value of South and Central American, Commonwealth of Independent States (CIS), African, Middle East and Asian exports to Europe and North America was around US$2 trillion (US$2,652 trillion * 0.75), and the domestically generated value of North American and European exports to South and Central America, Commonwealth of Independent States (CIS), Africa, Middle East and Asia was around US$1.3 trillion (US$1,821 trillion * 0.70).

Bracketing the difficulties involved in using value-added figures on productivity to measure rates of exploitation and the imperialist transfer of value (with low wages reflected in the low prices of global South exports), *ad arguendo*, we may placate defenders of global wage differentials and assume that productivity can be defined in purely price-based terms. A rough measure of labour 'productivity', GDP per person employed is gross domestic product (GDP) divided by total employment in the economy. Table 6.2 shows 'productivity' for low-, middle- and high-income countries from 2011 to 2017. It reveals a 'productivity' differential between labour in lower- and middle-income countries relative to labour in high-income countries of 0.21.[19]

Table 6.2   GDP per person employed (constant 2011 PPP $) by country type, 2011–17

Country Type	2011	2012	2013	2014	2015	2016	2017
Low Income	3 713.95	3 815.12	3 889.29	3 981.43	4 031.32	4 067.85	4 133.76
Lower Middle Income	13 829.96	14 259.64	14 746.54	15 249.94	15 756.06	16 248.74	16 848.70
Middle Income	20 519.10	21 276.72	22 038.00	22 730.36	23 330.26	24 042.13	24 891.00
Upper Middle Income	26 266.62	27 341.70	28 409.58	29 339.03	30 124.68	31 150.40	32 337.55
Average for Low and Middle Income	16 082.41	16 673.30	17 270.85	17 825.19	18 310.58	18 877.28	19 552.75
High Income	90 012.41	90 561.66	91 216.43	91 938.71	92 913.27	93 636.75	94 860.03

Source: World Bank 2017. Purchasing power parity (PPP) GDP is GDP converted to 2011 constant international dollars using PPP rates. An international dollar has the same purchasing power over GDP that a US dollar has in the United States.

Turning now to global wage differentials, data from the International Labour Organization shows that average monthly earnings in developing countries between 2013 and 2016 were worth around US$684 while average monthly earnings in developed countries during that period were worth approximately US$3,383. That is to say, wages in developed countries were five times higher than those in developing countries during this period.[20] Our estimated median monthly wage rate globally is US$1,350, which is twice as high as the average wage rate in developing countries and 60 per cent lower than the average wage rate in developed countries. Assuming capital outlay other than wage costs remained constant, and assuming international factor mobility of both capital and labour, price equalisation on the basis of equivalent wage rates globally would lead to a twofold increase in the price paid for developing countries' exports to developed countries, and a reduction in the price of developed country exports to developing countries of 60 per cent.

We may thus summarise the data necessary to estimate imperialist value transfer through unequal exchange as shown in Table 6.3.

Table 6.3 Data for unequal exchange calculation

1. Average Annual Wage for Developing Countries (w_1), 2012	US$8 208
2. Average Annual Wage for Developed Countries (w_2), 2012	US$40 596
3. Median Average Annual Wage Worldwide (W), 2012[a]	US$16 200
4. Price Distortion Factor for Non-OECD Exports to OECD (d_1), According to Equivalent Global Wage Rates (W/w_1)	−2
5. Price Distortion Factor for OECD Exports to Non-OECD (d_2), According to Equivalent Global Wage Rates (W/w_2)	0.4
6. Wage Differential between Developed and Developing Countries (W_Δ)	5
7. Productivity Differential between Labour in Lower- and Middle-Income Countries Compared with High-Income Countries (P_Δ)[b]	0.21
8. South and Central American, Commonwealth of Independent States (CIS), African, Middle East and Asian Exports to Europe and North America (X_1), weighted by Domestic Value Added, 2011	US$2 trillion
9. North American and European Exports to South and Central America, Commonwealth of Independent States (CIS), Africa, Middle East and Asia (X_2), eighted by Domestic Value Added, 2011	US$1.3 trillion

Notes:
a. ILO 2017.
b. World Bank 2017.

Our calculation for unequal exchange due to underpriced developing country exports is, then, as follows:

$$T_I = (d_I * X_I - X_I) * P_\Delta$$

$$T_I = (2 * 2 - 2) * 0.21 \qquad\qquad \text{US\$420 billion}$$

Our calculation for unequal exchange due to overpriced developed country exports, meanwhile, is as follows:

$$T_2 = X_2 - (d_2 * X_2)$$

$$T_2 = 1.3 - (0.4 * 1.3) \qquad\qquad \text{US\$780 billion}$$

The total value of unequal exchange to developed countries is

$$T = T_I + T_2 \qquad\qquad \text{US\$1.2 trillion}$$

The figure of US\$420 billion as an estimate of imperialist transfer value due to underpriced developing country goods must, however, be considered a gross underestimate. In a world where labour could travel between countries as freely as capital is able to, wage levels would converge and the alleged greater 'productivity' of European, North American and Japanese workers would be revealed for what it is, namely, a by-product of militarised borders and superwages. At the same time, were monopoly rents accruing to transnational corporate and finance capital attenuated by means of various measures undertaken to prevent leakages in the domestic production of the countries of the global South, the attendant and hitherto 'Westernised' capital gains would be more widely diffused at the global level. To that extent, we are justified in gauging unequal exchange solely on the basis of wage differentials alone, that is, in not thereby accounting for alleged 'productivity' differentials between core and 'periphery' countries, these being inexorably established by underlying wage and capital differentials. By that standard, our formula for calculating imperialist transfer (T) by means of underpriced developing country goods exports to developed countries is as follows:

$$T_I = d_I * X - X$$

$$T_I = 2 * 2 - 2 \qquad\qquad \text{US\$2 trillion}$$

Total value of unequal exchange to developed countries

$$(T = T_I + T_2): \qquad\qquad \text{US\$2.8 trillion}$$

Before proceeding to draw out the economic and social class implications of the sums of value transfer outlined above, we will briefly describe one more way in which the metropolitan workforce may justly be defined as a working bourgeoisie.

EMBOURGEOISEMENT AND THE PENSION SYSTEM

The metropolitan workforce has become structurally integrated into the global financial circuit by means of its savings, such that the pension funds to which it subscribes are objectively tied to world financial markets.[21] As Peter Gowan has written:

Yet another explanation [for the lack of regulation of highly speculative financial transactions in the US economy] might be that all the strategic social groups within American society have themselves been captured by the institutional dynamics of the financial markets. The income and wealth of the managements of the big corporations have become tied to future prices on the stock and bond markets, they have invested their savings in the investment banks, mutual and hedge funds and have been restructuring their own corporations to make the augmentation of 'share-holder value' their governing goal. And American workers also have come to rely upon the securities markets for their pensions, health care and even their wages, which have been increasingly combining cash with securities. Any regulatory drive would inevitably have a depressive effect on current activities and would therefore cut off the politicians involved in pushing for the regulation from important and broadly based political constituencies. This political barrier is then powerfully buttressed by the rentier ideology of laissez-faire and free markets. But the power of ideology should not be exaggerated. The lives of workers in modern capitalism are tied to capital not only through the wage relation, but also through the savings relation. If the savings relation is mediated through the state, as in Western Europe, workers' security is less tied to market developments and rentier interests. But if the savings relation is in the direct control of private financial markets, then workers themselves acquire a rentier interest.[22]

Pension schemes in the developed countries typically consist in the employee contributing a certain percentage of her salary into an account managed by a pension fund. This fund invests these savings in shares, bonds, securities, real estate and so forth, with a view to increasing the capital at the wage-earner's disposal. The World Bank has published information on pension coverage as a percentage of the working age population for 120 countries.[23] High-income OECD countries have the highest pension coverage (that is, the share of the labour force and working age population contributing during the last year), and highest pension expenditures in the world, with coverage estimated to be above 90 per cent. Yet less than 30 per cent of the global workforce is accruing pension benefits, while globally less than 20 per cent of the elderly is receiving benefits. Figure 6.1 shows average pension coverage rates by region.

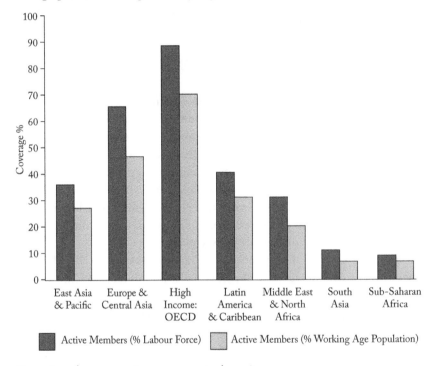

Figure 6.1   Average pension coverage rates by region

Source: Pallares-Miralles et al. 2012, p. 81.

Pension funds are especially important to the stock market where large institutional investors dominate. Globally, pension funds are the largest investment fund, ahead of mutual funds, insurance companies, currency reserves, sovereign wealth funds, hedge funds and private equity. The United States and Japan sit on half of the world's retirement wealth, with the United States having 38 per cent of the total and Japan having 12 per cent. Next is the Netherlands; with only 17 million citizens (0.23 per cent of the world population), it holds 7 per cent of pension assets. Norway and Canada are close behind with 6 per cent each.[24] In North America, pension funds' overseas investments stood at 16 per cent of the region's total portfolio in 2008, reaching 21 per cent in 2014. In Europe, the average percentage of pension fund portfolios allocated to foreign markets increased from 32 per cent in 2008 to 34 per cent in 2014.[25] We must conclude, therefore, that many workers in the North have invested heavily in stocks and bonds through their retirement account. These workers' economic and class interest is not as workers with nothing to sell but their labour-power. Rather, metropolitan workers' retirement years are directly linked to the wellbeing of imperialist capitalism. Large parts of the working population of the metropolitan countries live, or will live as rentiers on their pension capital.

CONCLUSION

The uneven development of the global economy ensures that some countries benefit from the accumulation of capital more than others insofar as 'profits expropriated from labour in one place are taken elsewhere to form the basis for consumption and further rounds of investment, which may be placed somewhere else again'.[26] Since industry along with agriculture is the source of all value circulated by the unproductive sectors of the economy, the globalisation of production and the associated chain of (surplus) value creation has huge implications as to the real economic basis of metropolitan wealth, including the affluence of metropolitan workers.

Presciently, English liberal economist and sociologist J. A. Hobson foresaw over a century ago that the imperialist exploitation of China must create states in Europe wherein elites of very rich financiers would live and employ a large part of the population in well-paid service jobs:

The greater part of Western Europe might then assume the appearance and character already exhibited by tracts of country in the South of England, in the Riviera, and in the tourist-ridden or residential parts of Italy and Switzerland, little clusters of wealthy aristocrats drawing dividends and pensions from the Far East, with a somewhat larger group of professional retainers and tradesmen and a large body of personal servants and workers in the transport trade and in the final stages of production of the more perishable goods: all the main arterial industries would have disappeared, the staple foods and manufactures flowing in as tribute from Asia and Africa.[27]

In the margins of the following illustrative passage from Hobson's book, V. I. Lenin had written 'N. B.' (*nota bene*, or note well): '[Economic parasitism will ensure that the] white races, discarding labor in its most arduous forms, live as a sort of world aristocracy by the exploitation of the "lower races", while they hand over the policing of the world more and more to members of these same races.'[28]

There is a hegemonic tradition in ostensibly Marxist thought which prides itself on making the labour of hundreds and thousands of millions of slaves, small producers and highly exploited workers in the export dependencies and colonies disappear from the ledger sheets and pay packets of the advanced capitalist countries. By contrast, we argue that a section of the international workforce had and continues to have a vested interest in maintaining the profitability of capitalist enterprise sustained by both colonialism and imperialism. The dimensions of this labour aristocracy, undergirded by an intercontinental imperialist economy of extreme exploitation (and even superexploitation whereby workers are not even paid the value of their labour-power, a subsistence wage), have expanded to encompass the overwhelming majority of metropolitan employees. The stratification of labour at the international level entails a relatively rigid caste-like social system for which white nationalism tends to become a basic organising principle.

Our perspective on the class structure of the imperialist economy today may be summarised as follows. First, the world economy is based on capital accumulation. Capitalist growth requires the exploitation of the working class and the dispossession of the working masses in the countryside. This proposition marks our perspective as being in opposition to mainstream bourgeois political economy but it is, of course, accepted by ostensibly leftist intellectuals. Second, in today's global economy most of the value (the average socially necessary labour required for the production of all commodities) and all of the surplus value (the difference between this value and the value of the labour-power of the productive workforce) is supplied by the nations of the global South. Third, value is transferred to the advanced capitalist countries by means of the imperialist exploitation of nations which, in the economic sense, principally involves the repatriation of surplus value by means of (1) capital export to low-wage countries and (2) the unequal exchange of commodities embodying differing quantities of value. It also entails the cheapening of the elements of constant capital through the plunder and undervalued production of raw materials and intermediate inputs for industry from Asia, Africa and South and Central America.

Fourth, we submit that the global class structure developed by imperialism is based on and perpetuates a hierarchical division of the international working class between those workers who are paid below the average value of labour-power and those paid above that value. Further, whereas it is still possible for workers paid above the value of labour-power to be exploited, the extent of imperialism today has ensured that the value of the wage in the major imperialist countries exceeds the per capita value of labour, that is, the 'average allowable wage with no surplus content', a measure of the average wage workers would receive in the absence of exploitation.[29] By this international(ist) standard, the metropolitan workforce is not exploited. Rather, the transfer of value from the Third World allows imperialist nations to pacify their working populations, constituting each as other than a proletariat (an exploited production workforce) in the strict sense. This view is opposed to the social-imperialist conceit that all workers everywhere have the same class interest in abolishing capitalism and the related notion that the same tactics and strategy may be applied to anti-capitalist struggle everywhere.

Finally, we argue that the movement towards (and beyond) socialism requires an end to imperialism and, following Amin, the de-linking of the oppressed nations from the imperialist political economy. Only as and when this occurs will the working class of the major imperialist countries come to have a material stake in an egalitarian and internationalist socialist system. The class interest of the working class of the major imperialist countries is at this time opposed to socialism and the metropolitan workforce can be expected to continue to either acquiesce in or vocally support the militaristic policy of their respective national governments. As Hosea Jaffe wrote more than a quarter of a century ago:

Today the majority of the 1,000 million people in socialist states were either colonial slaves themselves or else their parents were. Moreover, their present-day struggle with imperialism is a continuation of the struggle between the colonial toilers and capitalist colonialism. The fact that these workers did what the workers in the imperialist states did not do so is not, it goes without saying, almost, due to any inherent virtue in the colonial people or diablo [sic] or weakness in the 'advanced' workers (thus far, the most backward politically). It is due solely to their different objective social conditions (reflected, simply, in a 10 to 1 ratio of wages). For this reason, a change in these conditions (meaning: the weakening of colonialism) must tend to bring them together. This is no automatic process, however, for fascism in the 'home' country is an alternative possibility. For, if socialism is not imported from the confrontation of colonialism and anti-colonialism, fascism will be imported instead.[30]

The struggle against imperialism worldwide and the struggle against fascism in the imperialist countries (the ideological and political bulwark of imperialist capitalism, especially during times of crisis) are at the cutting edge of the socialist movement at the present conjuncture. As we shall see, however, the fundamentally bourgeois class structure of the major imperialist countries has ensured that the anti-imperialist and anti-fascist struggles therein are thoroughly marginalised.

With the exception of the first, the propositions above set our view apart from the mainstream 'left' in the major imperialist countries, determined as it is to secure the class privileges of its would-be constituency by any and all means, including by ignoring or by downplaying the global divide between oppressed and oppressor nations. The mainstream of the metropolitan left even insists that the most exploited workers in the world are the workers in the advanced capitalist countries, their allegedly greater productivity supposedly entitling them to much higher wages than their Third World/ global South counterparts. For such imperialist socialists, either value transfer does not exist at all, is negligible or has an insignificant impact on the global class structure since it benefits only (some) capitalists or a narrow upper stratum of workers in the First World. We insist that this is patently untrue, and we will attempt to prove this in the next chapter.

7
Measuring Colonial Value Transfer

We will examine here some of the ways in which colonialism transferred the wealth of America, Africa and Asia to Europe and to European-descended colonial elites. The metropolis thus constituted within a system of centre-periphery economic relations thereby gained increased real purchasing power and a major capital accumulation advantage. The 'Third World' countries, conversely, faced a concomitant loss in economic where-withal. To this day, the drain of cumulative historical value from the global South as a result of colonialism has in no way been compensated in the form of reparations or any allegedly palliative 'aid'.

THE METHODOLOGICAL NATIONALISM OF THE WHITE LEFT

For today's left the vast majority of workers in the metropolitan countries do not benefit in any way from the imperialist exploitation of working people in the oppressed countries. Some even hold the view that neither European nor North American workers derived any advantages from capitalism's earlier, specifically colonial exploitation. For these socialists colonialism must have brought benefits only to a handful of very rich capitalists, and these benefits can only have taken the form of profits. Colonial profits must not have been invested in either capital or consumer goods industries, and must not have led to any increase in labour productivity, or have stimu-lated economic growth that would have led in any way to greater demand for labour (the latter, presumably, entirely unrelated to wage levels). Rather, colonial profits must have been frittered away by these few capitalists on luxury items (though it could not have led to any increased demand for labour in industries producing said articles). Colonial consumer goods must only have been purchased by a handful of *haute* bourgeoisie, and must not have increased the real value of the average wage in any way. Likewise, colo-nial trade must have had no impact on the growth of Europe's urban centres and living conditions therein. Trade union growth was in no way related to the expansion of industries dependent on colonialism. Given a choice, neither European nor North American workers would have cared whether they lived in Bombay or Bristol, any stated or tacit preference for their own country being due mainly due to indoctrination by capitalist propaganda.

Leaving aside such absurd fantasies, we hope to show how colonialism enriched Europe at the expense of the colonies, and we provide empirical data demonstrating how burgeoning historical capitalism relied upon colonial value transfer. We will further provide details supporting the view, one that ought to be uncontroversial, that colonialism also enriched the working populations of Western Europe and North America, Empire facilitating a political shift from repression to inclusion therein. Colonial value transfers came in the form of (1) imported colonial mass consumption goods; (2) raw materials imports for expanding industry; (3) profits from colonial trade, taxation and investment; and (4) an area for the settlement of Europe's unemployed surplus population. We will examine several measures of colonial transfer herein, concentrating in particular on the British case. We encourage readers to research the impact of colonialism on other European economies and on the settler-colonial societies of northeast Ireland, North America, Australasia, Algeria, Israel and Southern Africa.

HIDDEN COLONIAL SURPLUS VALUE

Marxist author, teacher, activist and founding member of the Non-European Unity Movement in South Africa, his country of birth, Hosea Jaffe (1921–2014) coined the term 'hidden colonial surplus value' to describe the large amount of surplus value transferred to the imperialist countries by the oppressed countries of Africa, Asia and South America. This 'hidden surplus value' is the difference between the selling price of Third World exports and the selling price of these same exports in the imperialist markets.[1] The source of this cheapness is not purely 'economic', but intrinsically a matter of political economy, that is, the ensemble of power relations within which goods and services are produced, distributed and consumed. Specifically, the cheap prices of Third World goods are the result of the historical and contemporary matrix of imperialism, underdevelopment and value transfer.

For Jaffe, imperialist value transfers may be resolved into two components: repatriated profits and hidden surplus value. Repatriated profits represent only the *visible* portion of the value transfers generated by foreign investment and loan capital, while superprofits (derived from the extra or above average surplus value extracted from the labour of nationally oppressed workers) represent the *invisible* portions retrieved through capital export imperialism, unequal exchange and debt usury. As he has argued, the intra-imperialist rate of profit may be negative if hidden surplus value from invisible net transfers amounts to more than net profits. In such a case, value added $(s + v)$ is less than wages (v) and profits derive only from the exploited nations while wages are subsidised by superprofits. In short, were

Third World workers involved in the production of commodities for First World markets suddenly to be remunerated at the same rate as workers therein, the entirety of profits of the world's leading capitalist powers would be completely annulled.

Jaffe estimates that no less than 500 million people were killed by Europeans during the four centuries of its primary accumulation of capital in the Americas, Asia and Africa, an average of 100 million people per century at a time when total world population increased from 300 million to 1 billion. He writes: 'This 400-year long process left a permanent mark on the value of human labour power of the colonial workers and on the immediate "value" equivalent, in gold and its money representation, of the labour time of these workers.'[2] Jaffe argues that during the first half of the nineteenth century, the wages of British, French, Dutch and German workers differed little from the maintenance cost of slaves in the US, Brazil, Cape, and the Dutch and French colonies. The rate of exploitation for these two distinct groups of workers (those from oppressed nations and those from oppressor nations) was more or less equal. However, with the transition to imperialism in the second half of the nineteenth century, the ratio s/v rose for colonial and fell for metropolitan workers.[3]

THE DRAIN THEORY OF BRITISH COLONIALISM

Among the earliest writers to systematically analyse and oppose the parasitic relationship obtaining between a colonial and a colonising country was Parsi intellectual, teacher, cotton trader and early Indian nationalist Dadhabai Naoroji (1825–1917). Naoroji, India's 'grand old man', was the first Asian to become a member of the British Parliament (the House of Commons), which he was from 1892 to 1895. Naoroji formed the Indian National Congress together with A. O. Hume and Dinshaw Edulji Wacha, and his book *Poverty and Un-British Rule in India* drew attention to England's exploitation of the country. One of the few contemporary descriptions of England's colonial exploitation comes from Naoroji. In an appeal from 1882, 'On Justice for India', addressed to the British Parliament, and based on extensive statistical calculations of the transfer of wealth from India to Britain, Naoroji described how taxes, trading profits, the destruction of India's handicraft sector and monopoly prices on imports from England to India drained the country. In 1896, the Indian National Congress officially adopted Naoroji's 'drain theory' as their economic criticism of colonialism. Naoroji considered that by dint of its oppressed position, India was subject to British capitalist exploitation without being thereby enabled to reap any of the fruits of capitalist development.

For Naoroji, there were several underlying bases for this unrequited transfer of India's wealth to Britain. First, he argued, India is a vast country ruled by a handful of Europeans whose income is a 'moral drain', that is, a cost to British India. Second, India develops as a market for British manufactures and a supplier to Britain of its raw materials strictly because India's economic policies are dictated by Britain and in the interests of the British economy and the British capitalist class. Third, the Indian government under British rule is forced to pay an ever increasing list of official overseas expenses which Naoroji calls Home Charges (Table 7.1). Fourth, rather than creating domestic employment and income, India's public expenditure out of the proceeds of taxation is instead used to pay for the infrastructure required by Britain to more effectively plunder the country. Finally, India's transformation into a 'mere agrarian appendage and a subordinate trading partner' of Britain ensures that it has become a typical colony dominated from afar.[4]

Table 7.1   India's annual balance of payments of current account, 1869–70 to 1894–98 (£ millions, quinquennial average)

	Balance Merchandise Trade	Net Treasure Imports	Balance Visible Trade (1+2)	Home Charges	Other Invisible	All Invisibles (4+5)	Balance of Payments Current Account (3+6)
	1	2	3	4	5	6	7
1869–73	+22.6	−8.4	+14.2	−8.8	−15.6	−24.4	−10.2
1874–78	+21.0	−6.4	+14.6	−9.3	−18.0	−27.3	−12.7
1879–83	+23.8	−7.1	+16.7	−10.7	−17.7	−28.4	−11.7
1884–88	+23.8	−9.2	+14.6	−12.3	−18.0	−30.3	−15.7
1889–93	+25.2	−9.7	+15.5	−13.5	−19.4	−32.9	−17.4
1894–98	+20.7	−5.6	+15.1	−13.9	−18.9	−32.8	−17.7

Note: A plus sign (+) indicates net exports of goods: a minus sign (−) indicates net imports of goods and net exports of remittances, service charges and other invisibles.

Source: Banerji 1982, Tables 34A and 40A; cf. Karmakar 2001, p. 70.

For Naoroji, the introduction of commercial relations in agriculture, capital investment in crop production, the imposition of a rural tax in kind and the consequent monetisation of the Indian economy was not conducted on the basis of a thorough extirpation of the system of landlordism and a redistribution of landholdings amongst the peasantry, as in autochthonous capitalism, but on the incorporation of the landed class into a system of cash crop export dependency dominated by foreign capital. As such, Naoroji's 'drain theory' was a precursor to Marxist theories of semi-feudalism and the 'development of underdevelopment'.[5]

Naoroji argued that the transfer of capital from India to Britain effected by colonial subordination precluded India from implementing development opportunities in the form of infrastructural investment, education and so forth. This view was later echoed by US Marxist economist Paul Baran who, having estimated that around 10 per cent of India's national product was transferred to Britain each year in the early decades of the twentieth century, wrote that '[far] from serving as an engine of economic expansion, of technological progress, and of social change, the capitalist order in these [underdeveloped] countries has represented a framework for economic stagnation, for archaic technology, and for social backwardness'.[6]

Naoroji estimated that Britain exacted an annual 'tribute' from India of huge proportions. Following the Mutiny of 1857, India's First War of Independence, he estimated that the annual transfer from India to Great Britain amounted to a total of £30 million.[7] Consulting Bank of England data (Table 7.2), we can say that between one-third and one-half of Britain's gross fixed capital formation (GFCF), with the attendant *productivity gains of British labour*, was financed exclusively through the drain of India's wealth from colonial tribute.

Table 7.2   Selected data on the British economy, 1830–1920

	Household Consumption, £ million	Gross Fixed Capital Formation (GFCF), £ million	Government Consumption, £ million	Net Trade, £ million	GDP at Market Prices, Expenditure Side Measure, £ million	GFCF as % of GDP
1830	448	25	31	−3	501	4.99
1840	490	55	33	−9	566	9.72
1850	508	47	38	2	593	7.93
1860	715	59	51	4	828	7.13
1870	954	87	55	17	1153	7.55
1880	1146	107	70	−29	1379	7.76
1890	1253	106	85	9	1468	7.22
1900	1637	205	182	−78	1922	10.67
1910	1877	158	182	1	2216	7.13
1920	5246	578	520	112	6356	9.09

Note: Gross fixed capital formation is the value of acquisitions of new or existing fixed assets by the business sector, governments and households – excluding their unincorporated enterprises – less disposals of fixed assets and typically including land improvements; plant, machinery and equipment purchases; and the construction of roads, railways and the like, including schools, offices, hospitals, private residential dwellings, and commercial and industrial buildings.

Source: Mitchell, Chapter XVI, Table 5, pp. 831–5; cf. Bank of England 2014.

BRITISH INCOME IN THE ABSENCE OF EMPIRE

US economist Michael Edelstein specialising, inter alia, in the economics of the British Empire in the nineteenth century has attempted to measure what Britain gained from the underdeveloped parts of its Empire. He has done so through positing a counterfactual condition, namely, that the afore-mentioned countries had remained independent.

Edelstein argues that if the Empire territories had remained free from British rule they would not have participated in the international economy to the same extent that they in fact did. Thus, he writes, the British Raj brought a more peaceful, unified and commercially oriented political economy to India than would have been the case if the country had remained inde-pendent. While India was by no stretch of the imagination a peaceful place under British rule, and it may have been more commercially engaged abroad than Edelstein supposes, his working assumption that Britain's trade with India and the other non-Dominion regions would have been a quarter of its existing level in 1870 and 1913 in the absence of British rule is plausible.[8]

Edelstein estimates the gains made by Britain from trade with its colonies in the following terms:

Summing the 75 per cent reduction to British exports to the non-Dominion colonies and the 30 per cent reduction to British exports in the Dominion regions (weighted by their respective shares in British colonial exports), British colonial exports in 1870 and 1913 would have been 45 per cent of their actual levels under this 'strong non-imperialist' standard of the gains from empire. (The shares of white-settler and non-white-settler colonies in British exports to the colonies were approximately 45 per cent and 55 per cent, respectively. With their 'strong' non-empire levels hypothetically reduced to 0.7 and 0.25, respectively, of their actual levels, British exports to both types of colonies would have been = 45 per cent (0.7) + 55 per cent (0.25) = 45.25 per cent of actual levels.)

The 'strong' gain is the difference between the actual British empire exports and this hypothetical 45 per cent level in the absence of empire. British exports of goods and services to the empire were approximately 7.9 per cent and 11 .9 per cent of GNP in 1870 and 1913 therefore the 'strong' gain from empire was 4.3 per cent (i.e. 55 per cent of 7.9 per cent) of GNP in 1870 and 6.5 per cent of GNP in 1913.[9]

According to the Bank of England figures listed in Table 7.2, GFCF was 7.55 per cent of Britain's GDP in 1870 and 7.13 per cent of its GDP in 1910. Using Edelstein's 'strong non-imperialist' standard, we may therefore suppose that around 57 per cent of Britain's fixed capital investment in 1870 and 91 per cent of its fixed capital investment in 1910 was funded by its colonial trade.

BRITISH-INDIAN MERCHANDISE TRADE
AND CAPITAL ACCUMULATION

Specifically colonial trade differs from domestic and other foreign trade. Crucially, the colonial market is kept compulsorily open while the metropolitan market is strictly protected, in the case of Britain against Asian textiles, for example, draconian tariffs duties were applied for 150 years. Moreover, as Indian economist Utsa Patnaik notes, 'colonial goods for export were purchased out of local tax revenues raised from the colonized population as in India, or by the export-goods equivalent of slave rent as in the West Indies'.[10] In effect, either the money paid to the colonial goods exporter by the colonial power came out of high taxes that the latter had itself paid to the colonial state, as in the case of India, or the export goods were the commodity form of economic surplus directly taken in the form of rent (slave rent as in the West Indies and land rent as in Ireland). Finally, India's foreign exchange earnings were appropriated by Britain so as to settle its trade deficits with continental Europe and the United States.

As shown in Table 7.1, the nominal balance of trade includes more than direct merchandise trade, making it appear that Britain ran a trade surplus, not deficit, with its colonies. For no matter how great the trade surplus became (in 1913 India had the second largest trade surplus earnings in the world at £71 million), much larger fictitious, invisible political charges were imposed to nullify the increased export earnings and, in fact, produce a small deficit on current account. Thus, as Patnaik highlights, countries with large and growing merchandise export surpluses such as India and Malaysia had more than their export earnings siphoned off by Britain through politically imposed invisible burdens and had to borrow, while the country with a large and growing trade deficit, Britain, was able to siphon off the exchange earnings of its colonies and more than offset its current account deficit with sovereign regions, so that it actually exported capital to these regions on an increasing scale.[11]

Describing a similar economic relation between Britain and its Jamaican colony, historian Fernand Braudel writes:

In fact the balance of trade for Jamaica, even calculated in colonial pounds works out at a slight advantage for the island (1,1336000 to 1,3335000 pounds sterling) but at least half of the total for imports and exports made its way invisibly back to England, in freight charges, insurance, commissions, interest on debts and transfers of money to absentee landlords. All in all the net benefits for England in the year 1773 was 1,500,000 pounds sterling. In London as in Bordeaux the proceeds of colonial trade were transformed into trading houses, banks and state bonds. They made the fortunes of certain powerful families whose most active representatives were to be found in the House of Lords.[12]

India's foreign exchange earnings were appropriated by Britain so as to settle its trade deficits with continental Europe and the United States. As such, it was not only Britain's industrialisation that relied upon the underdevelopment of the colonised world. During the period immediately following the Napoleonic wars most of Britain's capital exports were directed across the Channel, helping to create new textile industries in France, Holland, Prussia and Russia.[13] The capital derived from overseas sources thus financed not only Britain's industrial revolution, but also continental Northwest Europe's, with that extracted from India alone comprising over 50 per cent of annual British capital exports in the 1820s and the 1860s. This plunder of India was 'not carried on under the competitive rules of the game, which we have consciously or unconsciously come to associate with the heyday of capitalism in Europe and North America', but rather through monopoly privileges, racial discrimination and outright violence.[14]

The unpaid trade surpluses provided by the most oppressed colonies of the British Empire allowed British capital accumulation to advance rapidly. By calculating the direct merchandise import surplus from India and the West Indies into Britain and using this as the measure of surplus transfer from these colonised regions, Patnaik estimates the level of Britain's rates of capital formation that were thereby made possible. She finds that the combined colonial transfer expressed as a percentage of Britain's savings is at least 62.2 in 1770, 86.4 in 1801, 85.9 in 1811 and 65.9 in 1821.[15] Britain's early capital accumulation was intimately connected to its plunder of the colonies. More broadly, value transfer raises the profitability of metropolitan business not only by cheapening the costs of constant and variable capital, allowing for much higher rates of consumption of both, but also, as in the colonial era and in the United States and the United Kingdom today, by affording increased rates of capital formation (and, to the extent that includes investment in consumer goods industries, also higher labour productivity) through unpaid trade surpluses.

Colonialism was crucial to British and European capital accumulation; imperialist trade and investment in the Third World is the very foundation of the capitalist world economy, and not only historically. As historian and first Prime Minister of Trinidad and Tobago Eric Williams wrote, '[t]he colonial system was the spinal cord of the commercial capitalism of the mercantile epoch'.[16] In the nineteenth century, the most important sectors in the world economy were the processing industries of Europe and the United States. Colonial goods were bought and sold in staple markets or trade centres (sugar, coffee, cotton exchanges), and then processed in factories into consumer products. These were then transported to retail markets and ended up at the consumer.[17] Thousands of companies and individuals benefited from the entire fabric of colonial relations. The social (industrial, commercial, civil, cultural and political) infrastructure built upon wider economies of colonial and neo-colonial trade and investment have tended to benefit not only business owners but also wage-earners in the metropolitan countries.[18]

COLONIALISM, POPULAR CONSUMPTION AND LABOUR REFORMISM

It is clear from the above that European capitalists derived enormous wealth from colonialism. The British economy was in large measure the product of commercial hegemony achieved through imperialism, allowing Britain to become industrialised with a large proletarian population. The question remains, however: to what extent did the European proletariat itself benefit from colonialism? We argue here that despite creating much of the surplus value produced by their respective nations in the earlier part of the industrial capitalist era, the European proletariat between 1875 and 1950 (the era of high imperialist colonialism) received real incomes dependent on colonialism, and its employment was a function of the maintenance of colonialism. The divide between the workers of the colonial nations and those in the colonised nations widened as imperialism advanced so that both the living conditions and the political horizons of each group of workers became increasingly polarised. We will examine here how colonialism raised the living standards of all European workers, particularly those organised workers poised to exploit the scarcity of their skills, as well as their national and 'racial' privileges vis-à-vis the colonised.

The European working classes had, following the political reforms of the second half of the nineteenth century, organised into powerful trade unions. This allowed the upper layers of skilled workers to obtain better wages and working conditions as well as the expansion of trade union rights. This wage increase – which occurred first in England and later in France, Germany and other Western European countries – contributed to the expansion of consumption power and to the reduction of the recurring overproduction crises that capitalism had hitherto suffered. Capital and revenues from the colonies made these wage increases for the metropolitan working class possible. Wages in England increased relative to prices by 26 per cent in the 1870s, 21 per cent in the 1880s and 11 per cent in the 1890s.[19] It was skilled workers who especially benefited, these earning approximately twice that of unskilled workers, then still living just above subsistence level.

Rising wage levels were only made possible without the profit rate falling below what was necessary for capital accumulation by the exploitation of an increasing number of people employed in the colonial regions as workers in plantations, mines and factories. Wages were set therein at subsistence level or less. This (super)exploitation of labour was the basis of the higher profits for capital invested in the colonies. The fall in the rate of profit that would have occurred as a result of rising wages in Europe was thereby compensated for by the increasing amounts of surplus labour performed in the colonies. On the one hand, capital benefited from rising wages at home by raising effective demand for commodities while, on the other, the low wages in the colonial areas maintained high profits. In this way colonialism solved the contradiction of capitalism in the North by dissolving the stagnating effect of higher wages within the system of enhanced exploitation of the proletariat in the South.

IMPERIAL CONSUMPTION

Economist Joan Robinson neatly summarised the link between colonialism, the development of capitalism in Europe and working class consumption patterns:

It was not only superior productivity that caused capitalist wealth to grow. The whole world was ransacked for resources. The dominions overseas that European nations had been acquiring and fighting over since the sixteenth century and others also, were now greatly developed to supply raw materials to industry … The industrial workers at home gained from imperialism in three ways. First of all, raw materials and foodstuffs were cheap relatively to manufactures which maintained the purchasing power of their wages. Tea, for instance, from being a middle-class luxury became an indispensable necessity for the English poor. Secondly the great fortunes made in industry, commerce and finance spilled over to the rest of the community in taxes and benefactions while continuing investment kept the demand for labour rising with the population … Finally, lording it around the world as members of the master nations, they could feel their self-esteem upon notions of racial superiority … Thus the industrial working class, while apparently struggling against the system, was in fact absorbed in it.[20]

The most important commercial crop at the beginning of the nineteenth century was sugar. Produced by slave labour, its sale generated enormous profits for sugar merchants, plantation owners and investors. Sugar consumption in Britain doubled between 1690 and 1740. By the 1830s and the advent of industrialised textile production, however, its market value had been exceeded by cotton. Britain was unable to produce cotton and imported all of it from America, where it was produced by slaves, and from Egypt and India, where it was produced by subsistence peasants. Raw cotton, sugar, rum and tobacco imports were shipped by the tonne into prosperous British ports like Bristol, London and Liverpool;[21] all originated in the expanding slave plantations of America and the Caribbean.

Many of Britain's primary products were producible exclusively in colonised tropical countries, though some were temperate food grains from colonies such as Ireland and India, as well as from the settler-colonial United States. The most important items of direct mass consumption for which there was substantial or complete import dependence were wheat (of which India was probably the third most significant source) and wheaten flour, rice, cane sugar (beet sugar production in continental Europe being fairly insignificant), tea, coffee and tobacco. Of these, only the first was produced in Britain but production was not growing as fast as population between 1700 and 1850.

At the height of the industrial revolution, during which time Britain was essentially self-sufficient in the 'temperate' foodstuffs (grain, meat and dairy products), by 1800 an estimated 18 per cent of beef and pork consumption, 11 per cent of butter and margarine consumption, and 12 per cent of wheat and wheaten flour consumption in Britain was met by Irish imports alone.[22] British importing of Irish grain, cattle, butter and so on contributed to the Hellish starvation in Ireland in the 1840s and 1850s, from which Ireland's population levels have not yet recovered almost two centuries later.

From the middle of the nineteenth century, a substantial general rise in incomes, particularly, as Davis notes, those of a large minority of the population (farmers, many kinds of skilled workers, the professional classes and rentiers), led to a sudden leap in demand for semi-luxury food and drinks and a sharp increase in the amount consumed per head. In this period Britain shifted to 'the kind of import dependence in which starvation, rather than inconvenience or even poverty, became the alternative to importing'.[23]

Whereas standard long-run real wage series simply divide the nominal wage by the price of an unchanging consumption basket, after Europe's 'discovery' of America, its consumption habits were profoundly transformed and dramatically improved.[24] Income gains from colonial goods imports such as tea, coffee and sugar added at least the equivalent of 16 per cent, and possibly as much as 20 per cent, of household income to British people's welfare by the middle of the nineteenth century. The intercontinental luxury trades of the early modern period transformed the European economy.[25] Crucially, it was not only the consumption habits of Europe's elites that drove this transformation, but those of its working and middle classes:

Who was drinking all of this tea and coffee? Surely not just wealthy elites, as the volumes are too high to even entertain the possibility of limited social access to hot caffeinated beverages. Some of the import volume was 'lost' to re-exports, but the ultimate consumers of these re-exports were, of course, just other Europeans (or their colonial counterparts). Eighteenth century commentators of all national stripes did not hesitate to ascribe consumption of these caffeinated luxuries, usually as a complaint, to the teeming masses of their social inferiors. Probate inventory evidence on the social diffusion of the artefacts associated with this consumption has been accumulating over the past several decades, and it suggests that it was indeed widespread across the social landscape.[26]

The mass consumption of colonial consumer imports proceeded apace with the liberalisation of trade, the incorporation of new producer countries in the international market and the decline of prices all predicated on the expansion of Empire. McCants summarises the main trends:

The consumption of tea, coffee, sugar, tobacco, porcelain, and silk and cotton textiles, increased dramatically in western Europe beginning as early as the closing decades of the seventeenth century, only to accelerate through much of the eighteenth century. The consumer setbacks associated with the period of the French Revolution and a continent at war, especially as triggered by the Napoleonic blockades, should properly be seen as a severe interruption to the trend which would otherwise have extended rather more seamlessly from the early modern trade system to the 'transport revolution' of the nineteenth century. Use of the new commodities brought by this trade spread rapidly, both in geographical and social space ... [The] presence of many of these so-called luxury goods is well documented down into the ranks of the working poor by the middle of the eighteenth century. There can be little doubt then, that European demand was fuelled not only by the rich with their growing 'surplus incomes' but by the much more numerous lower and middling classes of Europe's multitude of urban centres, followed by their rural counterparts.[27]

Between the sixteenth and nineteenth centuries around 15 million slaves were exported by European merchants from Africa to the slave colonies on the opposite side of the Atlantic to produce many of these luxury items or their raw materials. As many as one in five slaves died during the journey, after enduring cramped, filthy and dangerous conditions. Many more would die later on the plantations as a result of disease, overwork and horrifying maltreatment. The expansion of the transatlantic slave trade can be located in the growth of profiteering fuelled by popular consumer demand, behind which lay the sale into bondage of many millions of Africans.

SOCIALIST INTERNATIONALISM AND ANTI-IMPERIALISM TODAY

Since decolonisation, there has been a shift from value transfer based on colonial tribute to that based on imperialist rent, that is, 'the above average or extra profits realised as a result of the inequality between North and South in the global capitalist system' dominated by Western monopolies.[28] The mass *embourgeoisement* of the metropolitan working classes via receipt of value transferred from the exploited nations and the attendant political pacification is not admitted by socialists in the imperialist countries. Yet the point to be grasped by the genuine left – those struggling to see an end to capitalism and imperialism alike – is that so long as imperialism functions, internationalist labour movements in the core imperialist countries will be strictly delimited. Fighting for higher wages and better living conditions for First World workers is reactionary outside of the struggle against impe-rialism. Government deficit spending, expanded welfare measures and protected industry in the affluent countries are not necessarily socialist measures. Those groups, whether ostensibly left wing or right wing, which act to preserve the inequality of imperialist relations invariably promote national chauvinist solutions to problems of unemployment and declining living standards. As Baran has written:

[Under imperialism] there evolves a far-reaching harmony between the interests of monopolistic business on one side and those of the underlying [metropolitan] population on the other. The unifying formula of this 'people's imperialism' ... is 'full employment.' With this formula on its banner, monopolistic business has little trouble in securing mass support for its undivided rule, in controlling the government openly and compre-hensively, in determining undisputedly its external and internal policies. This formula appeals to the labour movement, satisfies the requirements of the farmers, gives contentment to the 'general public,' and nips in the bud all opposition to the regime of monopoly capital.[29]

The increasingly respectable fascist movement promises the highest levels of parasitism for white workers, national business interests unhappy with international competition, and the petty-bourgeoisie opposed to the fiscal requirements of globalised finance capital. The left's denial of gigantic imperialist value transfer thus adds fuel to the fire of right-wing populism.

8
Comparing Value Transfer to Profits, Wages and Capital

In this chapter, we will compare the foregoing estimates of transfer value to the value of profits, fixed capital and wages in the global North and to the costs of various social and economic goods in the global South (including the cost of the elimination of hunger worldwide, as well as the value of profits, savings and fixed capital investment). Before doing so, we will focus on the role of capital export in the imperialist transfer of value.

CAPITAL EXPORT TODAY

Though the theory of unequal exchange is one which most mainstream (imperialist) socialists are unwilling to countenance, it is important to recognise that classical Leninist theories of value transfer centred on the mechanics of capital export are by no means irrelevant to understanding the *embourgeoisement* of imperialist country workers. Over a century ago, Lenin had stated unambiguously that the 'export of capital, one of the most essential economic bases of imperialism, still more completely isolates the rentiers from production and *sets the seal of parasitism on the whole country* that lives by exploiting the labour of several overseas countries and colonies'.[1] Needless to say, the phrase 'whole country' implies that metropolitan workers, too, are parasitic on those countries exploited by capitalist monopolies.

Due to his concentration on monopoly as a new stage of capitalism, and capital export as its necessary outcome, however, Lenin only discussed foreign investment imperialism, and not unequal exchange. As such, we will for the moment concentrate our attention on foreign direct investment (FDI) as a means of imperialist value transfer. Despite the central importance of outsourcing to imperialist political economy, capital export (in the form of FDI, portfolio investments and debt) remains a significant means of value transfer, and has become increasingly so over the last two decades:

> For developing countries as a whole, profits repatriated from FDI investments grew notably between 1995 and 2008. Repatriated income from

FDI in the developing world increased 747 percent, from $33 billion in 1995 to $276 billion in 2008. In other words, repatriated profits are growing faster than FDI inflows [for developing countries]. In 1995, repatriated profits represented 29 percent of FDI inflows, but, by 2008, repatriated profits represented 36 percent of FDI inflows.[2]

In Table 8.3, we have estimated the number of developing country workers in industry that are employed by developed country capital (If). We find that 55.5 million industrial workers in developing countries are directly employed by capital from developed countries. We arrive at that estimate via the following procedure:

1. We start with the size of the entire industrial workforce of all developing countries (Id); that size is Id = 556.7 million (Table 8.1). Next, we estimate how many industrial workers in developing countries might be dependent on FDI (F). Here we use a rate of F = 15.1 per cent, and we estimate that 84.1 million of the industrial workers of developing countries are FDI-dependent (15.1 per cent of 556.7 million = 84.1 million). The rate of 15.1 per cent is the rate of FDI as a percentage of gross fixed capital formation (GFCF), which we have used as a proxy for that in industry as a whole and applied it here to the labour force (Table 8.2).

2. We refine our first estimate of 84.1 million because FDI that flows into developing countries does not only originate in developed countries; one part of that FDI inflow originates in other developing countries. In fact, FDI inflow into developing countries breaks down into 1/3 from other developing countries and 2/3 from developed countries. For our purposes, we apply the rate of F' = 66 per cent and arrive at our final estimate as follows:

$$Idf^* \ F' = If'$$
or
84.1 million * 0.66 = 55.5 million

The calculation is similar to the World Bank's method of calculating a country's export-weighted workforce, but instead of the total number of *all* workers being weighed against the figure for exports as a proportion of a country or region's GDP (as in the World Bank calculation), the total number of developing country industrial workers is here weighed against the figure for FDI inflows originating in developed countries as a proportion of industrial investment in the developing countries.[3]

Table 8.1   Total male and female employment by sector, world and regions (millions)

	Agriculture				Industry				Services			
	1999	2007	2008	2009	1999	2007	2008	2009	1999	2007	2008	2009
World	1038.9	1056.8	1061.2	1068.1	533.2	659.5	668.5	666.4	1010.8	1267.3	1299.2	1316.7
Developed Economies and European Union	24.8	18.7	17.8	17.5	122	119.3	117.9	109.8	296.1	338.4	343.3	341.1
Total for Developing and Transition Economies	1014.3	1038.1	1043.4	1050.6	411.1	540.2	550.5	556.7	714.6	929	956	975.6
Share of Developing and Transition Economies in World Total (%)	97.6	98.2	98.3	98.4	77.1	81.9	82.3	83.5	70.7	73.3	73.6	74.1

Source: ILO 2011a, Table A11. 'Employment by Sector and Sex, World and Regions (millions)', p. 68.

Table 8.2   Gross fixed capital formation, 2012 (current US dollars)

World	18 139 575 107 337.50
OECD Countries	9 954 339 957 755.81
Non-OECD Countries	8 185 235 149 581.69

Source: World Bank 2017. Gross Fixed Capital Formation (current US dollars). Online: https://data.worldbank.org/indicator/NE.GDI.FTOT.CD (accessed 17 November 2018).

Of course, Table 8.3 does not depict the extent of global value transfer through capital export imperialism, unequal exchange or any other means of global labour arbitrage. It is essential to understand, however, that industrial workers in the global South are much more exploited and work more intensively than their counterparts in the North. This is true whether exploitation is understood narrowly, in terms of lower unit labour costs, or in terms of the infinitely higher rate of surplus value (the ratio between the 'necessary labour', that is, the wages, and the 'surplus labour') pertaining in the South. Socially necessary labour (that is, value) is the average labour time required to produce a commodity under normal production conditions with labour of average skill and intensity. For present purposes, a greater quantity of (surplus) value-creating labour is commanded by financially equivalent trade with and investment in the industries of developing countries than it is in the developed countries.[4] Leaving aside this matter, however, the above calculation attempts to estimate the size of the developing country industrial workforce employed in developed country-owned or developed country-controlled enterprises. Accordingly, we find that the total number of developing country workers in industry effectively employed by developed country capital (55.5 million) is about 10 per cent of the developing countries' industrial workforce (556.7 million), but over 50 per cent of the developed countries' industrial workforce (109.8 million). This demonstrates that before even accounting for differences in the rate of surplus value and, hence, in the quantity of value transfer effected by means of international trade and investment dominated by the monopolies of the developed countries, FDI by developed country capital in developing country industry ensures that the equivalent of over one-third of its total industrial workforce (55.5 million/165.3 million x 100 = 34 per cent) is employed by developed country capitalists in developing country industry. As such, *ipso facto*, no more than two-thirds of the value added in developed countries (the agricultural workforce therein being negligible) is contributed by developed country workers.

The above calculation demonstrates the inadequacy of ostensibly Marxist treatments of national economy that do not account for the quantity of labour performed in foreign operations. Multinational firms make invest-

Table 8.3 Developing and transition countries' industrial workforce in foreign enterprises compared with industrial workforce of developed countries, 2009

Industrial Employment of Developing and Transition Economies, million (Id), 2009	FDI as Percentage of GFCF of Developing and Transition Economies (F)	FDI-Weighted Industrial Employment in the Developing Countries, million (Id*F), (Idf), 2009	Percentage Share of Developed Country FDI in Total Developing Country FDI (F')	Developing Country Industrial Employment Weighted by FDI Inflows from Developed Countries, million (Idf*F'), (If'), 2009	Developed Country Industrial Employment, million (D), 2009
556.7 million	15.1%	84.1 million	66.6 %	55.5 million	109.8 million

Note: Transition economies are those moving from an ostensibly centrally planned economy to a fully market-oriented economy. In the data provided, the United Nations Conference on Trade and Development (UNCTAD) has designated transition economies as those of Southeast Europe (Bosnia and Herzegovina, Montenegro, Serbia, the Former Yugoslav Republic of Macedonia and Albania) and the Commonwealth of Independent States (CIS), that is, the former Soviet Republics of Armenia, Azerbaijan, Belarus, Kazakhstan, Kyrgyzstan, Moldova, Tajikistan, Turkmenistan, Ukraine, and Uzbekistan and the Russian Federation. Cambodia, China, Laos and Vietnam, which the International Monetary Fund lists as Transitional Economies, are classed by UNCTAD (2014) above as developing economies. GFCF (formerly gross domestic fixed investment) includes land improvements (fences, ditches, drains and so on); plant, machinery and equipment purchases; and the construction of roads, railways and the like, including schools, offices, hospitals, private residential dwellings, and commercial and industrial buildings. According to the 1993 System of National Accounts (SNA), net acquisitions of valuables are also considered capital formation. FDI is a controlling ownership in a business enterprise in one country by an entity based in another country. It is typically made by setting up a foreign subsidiary, by acquiring a share in an overseas company, or through a merger or joint venture. The figure for FDI as percentage of GFCF is for 2010. The World Bank states that 'more than one third of FDI inflows to developing countries now originate in other developing countries', thus around two-thirds of FDI inflows to the developing countries originate in the developed countries (World Bank 2011, p. 5).

Source: UNCTAD 2014, Annex Table 05; 'FDI Inflows as a Percentage of Gross Fixed Capital Formation, 1990–2013'; ILO 2011a, Table A11. 'Employment by Sector and Sex, World and Regions (millions)', p. 68; World Bank 2011, p. 5.

ments globally that contribute to their rate of profit domestically. Regardless of the effects of wage differentials on the prices of production in different countries, and of whether investors choose to invest in expensive capital domestically or in cheap labour abroad, each worker within a firm contributes the same per capita value as every other working with comparable vigour.

GAUGING THE IMPACT OF VALUE TRANSFER IN TODAY'S GLOBAL ECONOMY

Before we can begin to assess the impact that imperialist value transfer must have on today's economies, we must first define and estimate various relevant measures of a country's income.

Profits

According to Eurostat's definition – Eurostat being a Directorate-General of the European Commission whose main responsibilities are to provide statistical information to the institutions of the European Union – gross operating rate is an indicator of profitability that corresponds to the share of *gross operating surplus* in turnover. Gross operating surplus is the surplus generated by operating activities after the labour factor input has been recompensed. It can be calculated from the value added at factor cost less the personnel costs. Turnover is the total of all sales (excluding VAT) of goods and services carried out by an enterprise in a given sector during the reference period. In 2015, the average gross operating rate for all economic sectors in the 28 countries of the European Union was 17.2 per cent.[5] According to the World Bank, world GDP in 2015 was around 75.8 trillion, and OECD GDP was US$46.7 trillion.[6] As such, we may estimate that profits in the core imperialist countries were worth approximately US$8 trillion in the same year.

Meanwhile, gross savings represent the difference between disposable income and consumption and replace gross domestic savings, a concept used by the World Bank and included in World Development Indicators editions before 2006. Gross domestic saving is equivalent to GDP minus final consumption expenditure, and it is expressed as a percentage of GDP. Gross domestic saving consists of the savings of the household sector, the private corporate sector and the public sector. Gross capital formation is a function of gross domestic savings. Table 8.4 shows gross savings as a percentage of GDP for low-, middle- and high-income countries.

For high-income countries, in 2015 gross savings were 22.6 per cent of GDP, whereas for low- and middle-income countries gross savings were 31.3 per cent of GDP, or US$10.1 trillion and US$8 trillion, respectively.

Table 8.4   Gross savings as a percentage of GDP, 2008–15

	2008	2009	2010	2011	2012	2013	2014	2015
High Income	21.8	19.8	20.7	21.3	21.7	21.9	22.4	22.6
Low Income	15.7		14.6	17.1	17.0	16.0	16.4	13.9
Lower Middle Income	28.8	28.7	31.7	30.4	29.4	27.8	28.5	27.4
Low & Middle Income	34.4	32.1	33.9	33.3	32.7	31.6	31.6	31.3
Middle Income	34.6	32.3	34.1	33.5	32.9	31.8	31.8	31.5

Source: World Bank 2017. Gross savings (% of GDP). Online: https://data.worldbank.org/
indicator/NY.GNS.ICTR.ZS (accessed 17 November 2018).

Gross fixed capital formation

GFCF (formerly gross domestic fixed investment) includes land improvements (fences, ditches, drains and so on); plant, machinery and equipment purchases; and the construction of roads, railways and the like, including schools, offices, hospitals, private residential dwellings, and commercial and industrial buildings.

Wages

The annual share of labour in total national income is normally calculated as total labour costs in a country divided by nominal output. According to UNCTAD, labour's share of national income in Latin America was approximately 60 per cent that of OECD labour's share of national income in 2008. In the same year, labour's share of the national income in Asian countries, the transition economies and African countries were an average 67 percent, 63 per cent and 53 per cent, respectively, of OECD labour's share (Figure 8.1). The International Labour Organization (ILO) notes:

Since 1994 the wage share in Asia has declined by roughly 20 percentage points ... The pace of the decline accelerated in the past decade, with the wage share falling more than 11 percentage points between 2002 and 2006. In China, the wage share declined by close to 10 percentage points since 2000 ... In African countries, the wage share has declined by 15 percentage points since 1990, with most of this decline – 10 percentage points – taking place since 2000 ... The decline is even more spectacular in North Africa, where the wage share fell by more than 30 percentage points since 2000.[7]

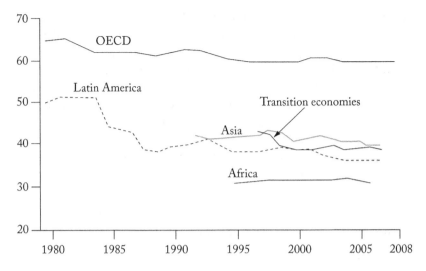

Figure 8.1 Share of compensation of employees in national income, selected country groups, 1980–2008 (per cent)

Note: UNCTAD (2010) notes: 'Unweighted averages. Data refer to net national income for OECD countries and to gross national income for other country groups. Latin America comprises: Argentina, Brazil, Chile, Colombia, Mexico and Peru; Asia comprises: Bahrain, China, Hong Kong (China), the Philippines and the Republic of Korea; Africa comprises: Egypt, Kenya, Mozambique, Namibia, Niger, Senegal, South Africa and Tunisia; Transition economies comprises: Armenia, Azerbaijan, Belarus, Kazakhstan, Kyrgyzstan, the former Yugoslav Republic of Macedonia, the Republic of Moldova, the Russian Federation, Serbia and Ukraine; OECD comprises: Australia, Austria, Belgium, Canada, Denmark, Finland, France, Germany, Iceland, Ireland, Italy, Japan, Luxembourg, the Netherlands, New Zealand, Norway, Portugal, Spain, Sweden, Switzerland, the United Kingdom and the United States.'

Source: UNCTAD 2010, Chart 5.1. 'Share of Compensation of Employees in National Income, Selected Country Groups, 1980–2008', p. 142.

Reports on the falling wage share in national economies do not, of course, account for the growth of the working class therein so that, adjusting the level of wage share decline thereby, we are forced to conclude that the rate of exploitation has increased more in the global South in recent decades than it has in the global North. More importantly, however, the wage share measure of exploitation does not account for the massive divergence in wages between countries such that one hour of labour in a rich country earns a worker enough money to purchase the product of ten hours of labour in another. On the basis of GDP figures that incorporate wage and capital differentials, most Marxists consider that workers in the export processing zones and outsourced factories and plantations of the global South are so hopelessly unproductive that their labour only entitles them to a fraction of the commodities produced by metropolitan labour. It is very clear, however, that this measure of exploitation, namely, that calculated according to the share of wages in national income, demonstrates clearly that global South workers are more exploited than those in the global North. Indeed, if this were not so, and the share of wages in prices were raised accordingly, we might expect global South goods imports to the OECD to be worth considerably more than what they are at present. Needless to say, this would put a heavy dent in global North profit margins and pay packets alike.

OTHER RELEVANT MEASURES TO CONSIDER WITH REGARD TO VALUE TRANSFER

According to the United Nations, solving world hunger would have cost around US$30 billion in 2008.[8] Adjusted for inflation, that figures rises to around US$34.2 billion in 2017. Meanwhile, according to the OECD, net official development assistance (ODA) flows from member countries of the Development Assistance Committee (DAC) of the OECD totalled US$131.6 billion in 2015. Adjusting for inflation and the appreciation of the US dollar, this represented an increase of 6.9 per cent in real terms, the highest level ever achieved for net ODA. Net ODA as a share of gross national income (GNI) was 0.30 per cent, on a par with 2014.[9] The United Nations estimates that it would cost US$54 billion to provide basic education to all children in low- and middle-income countries (at present, they note a gap in this cost of US$26 billion).[10]

COMPARING VALUE TRANSFER TO OTHER ECONOMIC RESOURCES

The 'imperial endowment' enjoyed by the Western European world has provided it with inconceivably large subsidies for its industry and industrial productivity in the form of:

- The addition of nearly 10 million square miles to Western Europe's 2 million square miles of territory by 1900, and the ongoing occupation of a quarter of the earth's most productive land.
- The theft of up to 20 million Africans and their subsequent enslavement.
- The indentured servitude of millions of Asian workers.
- The onerous taxation of millions of colonial peasants.
- The plunder of hundreds of tons of gold and thousands of tons of silver from Latin America alone, without which Western capital markets would have been impossible.

- The import of underpriced colonial foods, industrial materials and medicines including cotton, maize, wheat, rice, potatoes, rubber, tea, tomatoes, turkeys and countless other products.
- The deliberate destruction of colonial industries and the capture of guaranteed markets for Western manufactures.
- The wholesale restructuring of underdeveloped markets to serve Western interests.
- The unrestrained use of land and natural resources as dumps for toxic waste and other noxious by-products of industry.
- The unequal trade and tariff regulations that negatively impact the profit margins of Third World exporters.[11]

Table 8.5 compares our previous estimates of value transfer from the global South to the global North with various measures of economic wherewithal. It demonstrates that imperialism provides an indispensable cumulative boon to those countries receiving transferred value and, at the same time, a major impediment to economic growth and social wellbeing for those countries subject to imperialist value transfer.

The data depicted in Table 8.5 demonstrates that, by a conservative estimate, at least three-quarters of the profits of the capitalist class in the developed countries (that is, the 'top 1%' fixated upon by social democrats) is derived from the exploitation of workers in the underdeveloped countries. The rest of the developed country profits are likely to be accounted for by discrimination against non-white workers therein.[12] More revealingly, in terms of socially necessary labour time accruing to the metropolitan economies, for every worker employed therein, there is 0.56 'peripheral' country employees working unseen and for free alongside them. Meanwhile, there is approximately 2.4 times more transferred labour time in the metropolitan countries than there is industrial labour time expended therein. In sum, the intensive exploitation of the workers of the exploited countries enables the capitalist class of the global North to afford high wages for its employees, a gigantic tertiary sector, unending military build-up, enormous capital outlays and gigantic profits, without the capitalist system going into freefall.

IMPERIALISM AND THE EXPLOITATION OF LABOUR

The law of value as understood by Marx states that goods produced for sale on the market (that is, commodities) possess value according to the quantity of socially necessary labour required to produce them, and that this quantity is the sum of all of the quantities of labour, direct and indirect, that are used in the process of production.[13] Today, the sum value of all commodities and, hence, the prices of production are determined on a global scale insofar as

Table 8.5 Comparing value transfer to economic resources in developed and developing countries

Transfer (T)	Monetary Value of Transfer (US$)	Share of Transfer in Developed Country Profits, P (US$8 trillion), 2015 (P/T)[a] (%)	Share of Transfer in High-Income Countries' Gross Savings (US$10.1 trillion), 2015 (Sa/T)[b] (%)	Proportion of Low- and Middle-Income Countries' Gross Savings (US$8 trillion), 2015 (Sb/T)[b] (%)	Proportion of OECD Countries' GFCF (US$10 trillion), 2012 (T/Fa)[c] (%)	Proportion of Non-OECD Countries' GFCF (US$8 trillion), 2012 (T/Fb)[c] (%)	Proportion of Cost to Solve World Hunger (US$34 billion), H, 2017 (T/H)[d] (%)	Transferred Annual Labour Time, L, from Non-OECD Countries (T/Average GDP per Non-OECD GDP per Employee, P, US$19,553) (millions of workers)[e]	Share of Transferred Labour Time, L, in Total OECD Labour, La (468.4 million), 2009 (La/L)[f] (%)	Share of Transferred Labour Time, L', in Total OECD Industrial Labour, ILa (109.8 million), 2009, (ILa/L')[f] (%)
Visible Value Transfer[g]	$326 billion, 2012	4	3	4	3	4	959	16.7	3.6	15.2
Illicit Value Transfer[h]	$970 billion, 2014	12	10	12	10	12	2853	49.6	10.6	45.2
Transfer Pricing[i]	$1.1 trillion, 2009	14	11	14	11	14	3235	56.3	12.0	51.3
Disguised Value Transfer (Unequal Exchange)[j]	$2.8 trillion, 2012	35	28	35	28	35	8235	143.2	30.6	130.4
Total	$5.2 trillion	75	52	75	52	75	15282	265.8	56.8	242.1

Sources:

a. Eurostat 2017. Gross Operating Rate by NACE Rev. 2. %. Online: http://ec.europa.eu/eurostat/tgm/table.do?tab=table&init=1&plugin=1&language=en&pcode=tin00155 (accessed 17 November 2018); World Bank 2017. GDP (current US$). Online: https://data.worldbank.org/indicator/NY.GDP.MKTP.CD (accessed 17 November 2018).

b. World Bank 2017. Gross savings (% of GDP). Online: https://data.worldbank.org/indicator/NY.GNS.ICTR.ZS (accessed 17 November 2018).

c. World Bank 2017. Gross Fixed Capital Formation (current US dollars). Online: https://data.worldbank.org/indicator/NE.GDI.FTOT.CD (accessed 17 November 2018).

d. Rosenthal and Martin 2008.

e. World Bank 2017.

f. ILO 2011a, Table A11. 'Employment by Sector and Sex, World and Regions (millions)', p. 68.

g. Global Financial Integrity 2016, Table 3. 'Recorded Transfers (RecT) to and from All Developing Countries, 1980–2012 (billions of U.S. dollars)', p. 11.

h. Global Financial Integrity 2017, p. viii.

i. Christian Aid 2009, p. 8.

j. Author's calculation (present work).

capital has the ability to circulate across every country to secure the highest rate of return on its investment. The law of worldwide value implies that there is an upper limit to the exploitation of (a group of) workers established by the per capita value of labour, that is, by the extent to which workers earn more value through the sale of their labour-power than they themselves produce. By formulating a global rate of exploitation we can estimate the level beyond which workers in and outside the high-income countries are exploited. In the following calculation we shall make two untenable assumptions that favour the notion that metropolitan workers are exploited, namely, (1) that only waged or salaried employees produce value and (2) that all workers are equally productive of value.[14] Moreover, we shall leave aside the fact that not all of GDP is available for personal consumption. In 2007, for example, 22 per cent of global GDP was consumed in gross domestic investment (GDI), that is, investment in physical plant, machinery, stock and so forth. A further 17 per cent was used for public consumption (state construction of roads, schools, hospitals, weapons of war and so on). That allows, then, for 61 per cent for personal consumption.[15] Bracketing these matters, Table 8.6 illustrates the rate of exploitation at the level of the world market.

Table 8.6   Data for global rate of exploitation calculation

Average Wage (v_1) in High-Income Countries, 2012	US$40 596
Average Wage (v_2) in Low- and Middle-Income Countries, 2012	US$8 208
Total Full-Time Equivalent Workforce (P_1) in High-Income Countries	458 million
Total Full-Time Equivalent Workforce (P_2) in Low- and Middle-Income Countries	1.29 billion[a]
Total Wage Costs for High-Income Countries ($V_1 = P_1 * v_1$)	US$18.6 trillion
Total Wage Costs for Low- and Middle-Income Countries ($V_2 = P_2 * v_2$)	US$10.6 trillion
Total Wage Costs for World (V)	US$29.2 trillion[b]
World GDP (W), 2016	US$75.8 trillion
GDP of High-Income Countries (W_1)	US$48.6 trillion
GDP of Low- and Middle-Income Countries (W_2)	US$27.2 trillion
Total Surplus Value ($S = W - V$)	US$46.6 trillion
Global Rate of Exploitation ($E = S/V$)	1.6
Average Annual Wage (V_x)	US$16 200
Maximum Wage Beyond Which No Surplus Value is created ($M = V_x E$)	US$25 920
Average Annual Wage for Developed Countries (V_1)	US$40 596
Average Annual Wage for Developing Countries (V_2)	US$8 208
Factor by Which Average Developed Country Workers are Exploited ($E_1 = M/V_1$)	−1.6
Factor by Which Average Developing Country Workers are Exploited ($E_2 = M/V_2$)	3.2

Sources:
a. ILO LABORSTA Database; Köhler 2005, p. 9.
b. ILO 2017; ILO LABORSTA Database; Köhler 2005, p. 9.

PRODUCTION AND CONSUMPTION ON A WORLD SCALE

Divergent global rates of exploitation have profound consequences in terms of the amount of wealth that workers in different countries consume. Figure 8.2 compares total contribution to global production to share of total working class and middle class household consumption for the world's population, ranked in order of income. In the Lorenz curve used to depict global income equality, where the x-axis is cumulative population and the y-axis is cumulative income, perfect income equality is expressed in a diagonal straight line. The reality of income distribution, however, shows a curve that is more or less flat for the first two-thirds of its trajectory, but rises ever more steeply towards the end. The definition of the 'Gini Inequality Index' is the ratio between the area bounded by the curve and the straight diagonal, and the total area under the straight line. Plotted according to international income distribution, we refer to this as the 'world consumption curve'. Smith has suggested that generating a 'world production curve' by plotting each country's production of social wealth and superimposing this on said consumption curve can reveal much in regard to global exploitation.[16] In a world without exploitation, the two curves would be identical, that is, each person/household would produce what they consume. In fact, however, the global production curve diverges greatly from the consumption curve. In Figure 8.2, the area bounded by the two curves to the left of their intersection ought to be the same as the bounded area to their right were the world's workers to consume what they themselves produce. The ratio between this area and the area under either of the two curves (by definition identical, since total production = total consumption) might be called the 'global exploitation index'. The countries closest to the point of intersection are those whose total contribution to global wealth is closest to their total consumption of it. All countries to the right are net exploiters, that is, imperialists, and all countries to the left are net exploited.

According to mainstream economic doctrine, since markets equalise the income of workers, capitalists and nations with the value of their product, the production curve must be identical to the consumption curve; any deviation of one from the other being the result of the interruption of market forces. As the neo-classical marginalist economist John Bates Clark put it:

[Where] natural laws have their way, the share of income that attaches to any productive function is gauged by the actual product of it. In other words, free competition tends to give labor what labor creates, to capitalists what capitalists creates, and to entrepreneurs what the coordinating function creates. To each agent a distinguishable share in production, and to each a corresponding reward – such is the natural law of distribution.[17]

Marx pointed out the fundamental error in this view: workers are paid not for what they produce, but for what they consume. As such, the two curves described and depicted below directly juxtapose neo-classical and Marxist value theory. Moreover, by graphically illustrating the great disjuncture between contribution to global production and share of global consumption, Figure 8.2 refutes the views of those on the left who persist in denying the effects of global labour segmentation and stratification on the transformation of the global class structure.

For the non-Marxist, marginalist view of income distribution, global wage differentials are the result of productivity differentials conditioned by differences in the level of the productive forces at different societies' disposal. However, as Marx argued, it is only living labour and not machinery or constant capital which adds value. According to Marx, an hour of average socially necessary labour always yields an equal amount of value independently of variations in physical productivity, hence the tendency for labour-saving technological change to depress the rate of profit.[18] Although increased productivity results in the creation of more use values per unit of time, only the intensified consumption of labour-power can generate added (exchange) value. Since wages are not the price for the result of labour but the price for labour-power, higher wages are not the consequence of (short-term) productivity gains accruing to capital. Rather, in a capitalist society, the product of machinery belongs to the capitalist, not the worker, just as in a feudal or tributary society part of the product of the soil belongs to the landlord, not the peasant. As Engels writes:

Marx demonstrates that machinery merely helps to lower the price of the products, and that it is competition which accentuates that effect; in other words, the gain consists in manufacturing a greater number of products in the same length of time, so that the amount of work involved in each is correspondingly less and the value of each proportionately lower. Mr. Beaulieu forgets to tell us in what respect the wage earner benefits from seeing his productivity increase when the product of that increased productivity does not belong to him, and when his wage is not determined by the productivity of the instrument.[19]

In Figure 8.2, the economically active population (EAP) is defined as all persons who furnish the supply of labour for the production of goods and services. As such, the EAP includes hundreds of millions of persons

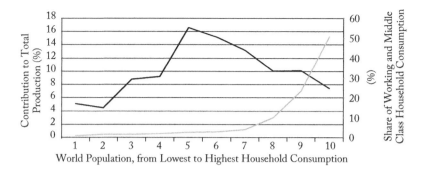

Figure 8.2   Global production versus global consumption

Note: Author's calculation.

Source: Cope 2013, p. 118; CIA World Factbook 2018; ILO LABORSTA Database; Köhler 2005, p. 9; Piketty and Saez 2004, Figure 1. 'The Top Decile Income Share, 1917–2002', p. 48; United Nations 2018; World Bank 2018.

engaged in private, so-called subsistence farming in the Third World. We have favoured Eurocentric assumptions that subsistence farmers contribute nothing to global production (even though the majority contribute money to capitalist landlords and/or supply goods for sale on domestic and international markets), and have (erroneously, *ad arguendo*) assumed that capitalistically employed workers are the sole source of value. Total global production is defined as the working hours of full-time equivalent production sector wage-employment in all countries.[20] The total production workforce was obtained by multiplying the EAP in each country by the rate of full employment for its corresponding global income quintile,[21] and then by multiplying this total by the percentage of each country's workforce in industry and agriculture. Hypothetically defining 'underemployment' as a worker's being employed for only one-third of the hours of a full-time worker, the figure thus obtained was then multiplied by 133 per cent.

To calculate capitalists' share of household income expenditure, Piketty and Saez' measure of the income share of the top echelons of the US income distribution has been used as a global benchmark.[22] Capitalists typically earn more than they can possibly consume, and much of their household consumption is reinvested. Since accumulated wealth is almost entirely in the hands of capitalists, the share of wealth of the top 10 per cent of the population has been subtracted from total household consumption expenditure figures for each country. Doing so allows a more focused comparison of relations between the world's working and middle classes, the major bone of contention between exponents and opponents of the labour aristocracy thesis outlined in the present work. Rather than adjusting each country's figure by the ratio of its Gini index to that of the United States (so that for countries with more unequal income distributions like Brazil or Pakistan, a larger portion of its national income would be subtracted), we have assumed a flat rate of 42 per cent for capitalist household income expenditure in all countries.

To suppose that the stark inequalities illustrated here are purely the result of superior economic efficiency and skill levels on the part of the core capitalist nations, or that they are the reward of a section of the global working class for its exceptional militancy, is to stretch reality to breaking point.

Part III
Foundations of the
Labour Aristocracy

9
Anti-Imperialist Marxism and the Wages of Imperialism

In this part of the work, we will explore the concept of the 'labour aristocracy', or what may be referred to as the 'working bourgeoisie', and we shall develop a theory of the bases for labour aristocratic advantage.[1] We identify three distinct types of labour aristocracy in the capitalist world system, each corresponding to specific social relations of production; (1) the settler-colonial labour aristocracy whose ascendancy is established through the denial of self-determination to those nations residing on indigenous land seized by the settler population;[2] (2) the metropolitan labour aristocracy whose ascendancy is maintained by value transfer from the dependent countries; and (3) the native labour aristocracy whose ascendancy is based on localised discrimination against ostensible non-nationals from the dependent countries. The labour aristocracy in each case involves itself in colonial and imperialist political structures insofar as it attempts to enforce its advantages. For reasons of space, we will focus here on the metropolitan and native labour aristocracies as two sides of the political economy of imperialist *embourgeoisement*.[3] This part of the present work aims to explain how the material benefits attendant to living in an imperialist country accrue to all but the poorest and most oppressed sections of global North society. As such, it is not simply capitalists of the North whose incomes derive in large measure from imperialism but, to varying degrees, all citizens of the developed countries.

There is a red thread running through Marxist and anti-imperialist thought which emphasises the extent to which the working classes in the world's wealthiest countries are the beneficiaries of imperialism, and argues that the attenuation of these workers' opposition to capitalism as a system of international value transfer is predicated upon their receipt of these benefits. As US novelist and socialist Upton Sinclair said, however: 'It is difficult to get a man to understand something, when his salary depends on his not understanding it.'[4] Unsurprisingly, the idea that Western workers owe their high living standards to imperialism is something that the Western left in almost all of its ideological permutations cannot permit itself to understand or accept. Thus leftists holding widely divergent views on historically existing socialism and its leaders, on the character of various governments in the global South (particularly those targeted for regime change by US imperialism), and on the prospects for socialism around the world, share virtually identical views on class and on imperialism's class structure.[5]

In spite of the hegemonic social-imperialist views of the mainstream metropolitan left there is, nonetheless, a tradition of anti-imperialist and internationalist Marxism that does not shy away from the causes and consequences of what Lenin referred to as the 'split in socialism', namely, between those socialists struggling for the betterment of a narrow upper stratum of the working class within capitalism and those seeking the rule of the whole working class outside it.[6]

MARXISM AND THE 'BOURGEOIS PROLETARIAT'

Marx identified early on the relation between working class conservatism and labour stratification, writing in 1862 that: 'England has largely discredited itself more than any other country – the workers by their Christian, slavish nature, the bourgeois and aristocrats by their enthusiasm for slavery in its most direct form. But the two manifestations supplement each other.'[7] Marx had explicitly referred to a working class 'aristocracy' in a section of the first volume of *Capital* entitled 'The Effect of Crises on the Best Paid Section of the Working Class'. In it he argues that economic crisis in the 1860s was tending to push the labour elite in Britain into the ranks of the wider British working class materially and, by implication, politically.

Marx's lifelong friend and collaborator, Friedrich Engels, had also made a number of statements concerning the extent to which colonialism and imperialism had afforded workers in the metropolitan countries a standard of living that was not entirely afforded by their own labour, but by the highly exploited labour of millions of workers and peasants in the dependent countries. Whereas Engels had famously written to Marx in 1858 that '[the] English proletariat is actually becoming more and more bourgeois', and that 'for a nation that exploits the whole world this is of course to a certain extent justifiable', he had anticipated the end of this *embourgeoisement* with the breakdown of Britain's industrial monopoly.[8] Unfortunately, Britain's hitherto unique position as the 'workshop of the world', having indeed broken down with the rise of German and US industry in the late nineteenth century, was revitalised on the basis of imperialist domination of the underdeveloped countries.

Lenin, too, was clear that there was a close correlation between imperialism and what he called opportunism (or the growth of reformist economism within a labour movement dominated by the most affluent sections of the workforce). In 1916 he asked: 'Is there any connection between imperialism and the monstrous and disgusting victory opportunism (in the form of social chauvinism) has gained over the labour movement in Europe? This is the fundamental question of modern socialism.'[9] Lenin lambasted the reactionary influence within the labour movement of a 'stratum of workers-turned-bourgeois'(as he termed it in his 1920 Preface to the French and German editions of *Imperialism: The Highest Stage of Capitalism*), yet he tended to vacillate in his assessment of the precise diameters of this 'labour aristocracy' nurtured by imperialism.

As we have noted, in 1916, Lenin stated clearly that whole nations were parasitic on the labour of the exploited countries.[10] In the turbulent decade before the First World War, however, Lenin went between approving Engels' view that 'colonial profits' provided the material basis for infecting the whole metropolitan proletariat with national chauvinism,[11] to espousing the view that a virtually unbridgeable chasm separated the complacent chauvinism of a narrow, bourgeois elite of workers from the revolutionary potential of the impoverished mass of workers in capitalism's heartlands.

Undoubtedly, this apparent fluctuation in outlook reflected a real split within the European working class, and Lenin's desire to exploit the rising tensions between its two major components, the labour aristocracy and the metropolitan proletariat, for revolutionary ends. Indeed, his terminology referring to the 'bribery' of the labour aristocracy reflected the reality that in the two or three decades before the First World War, the foundations of labour aristocratic privilege had become *politically institutionalised*. That is, whereas in Britain at least for much of the second half of the nineteenth century, the skilled and unionised labour aristocracy had secured its position by means of market bargaining exclusively for its own sectional ends, this method of muting the anti-capitalist struggle was no longer tenable by the end of the nineteenth century. Instead, in a situation wherein far higher levels of union organisation prevailed and anti-capitalist ideology had a foothold in certain regions, the state itself had become a major battleground to secure working class ascendancy. This, indeed, 'was the logic behind Lloyd Georgeism – the growing together of reformism, Fabian state socialism and social imperialism – which reached its climax during the First World War'.[12]

In this context, it is not hard to see how Lenin might have assumed that 'buying' the leaders of the labour movement was the central aspect of ruling class strategy in his time, and that a concerted struggle against such practices would soon bring the broad mass of workers back into the revolutionary fold. What Lenin to some extent neglected, however, was that the foundation for mass-based social democratic politics was not merely the corruption of the labour leadership, but underlying it was the fact that the benefits of imperialist capitalism had come to be enjoyed by a much larger section of the metropolitan workforce. Social imperialism catered to their short-term material interests as much as it thwarted their longer-term interests as workers.

Lenin erred in implying that the differences between the metropolitan masses and the working elites were absolute differences in kind, rather than in degree.[13] Nonetheless, that virtually all European workers stood to gain from Empire became ever clearer as even the cataclysmic intra-proletarian bloodshed of the First World War could not shift the allegiance of most workers away from their own imperialist state. As author, MI5 informant and former colonial police officer in India, George Orwell correctly surmised:

For in the last resort, the only important question is, Do you want the British Empire to hold together or do you want it to disintegrate? And at the bottom of his heart no Englishman … does want it to disintegrate. For apart from any other consideration, the high standard of life we enjoy in England depends upon keeping a tight hold on the Empire … Under the capitalist system, in order that England may live in comparative comfort, a hundred million Indians must live on the verge of starvation – an evil state of affairs, but you acquiesce in it every time you step into a taxi or eat a plate of strawberries and cream. The alternative is throw the Empire overboard and reduce England to a cold and unimportant little island where we should all have to work very hard and live mainly on herrings and potatoes. That is the last thing that any left-winger wants. Yet the left-winger continues to feel that he has no moral responsibility for impe-rialism. He is perfectly ready to accept the products of Empire and to save his soul by sneering at the people who hold the Empire together.[14]

Indeed, following both world wars, the metropolitan working classes saw their living standards rise even further and their political aspirations met to an unprecedented degree, a reward for enduring fealty to imperialism.

In the final years of his life, Lenin came to more clearly perceive the evident shift in revolutionary impetus away from the metropolitan heartlands of capital towards its exploited (then colonial) periphery. As he wrote in 1921, 'The destiny of all Western civilisation now largely depends on drawing the working masses of the East into political activities.'[15] By the time of the First Congress of the Communist International (Comintern), founded by Lenin himself in 1919, all the Communist parties of the time adopted a resolution which stated in unambiguous terms that:

At the expense of the plundered colonial people, capital corrupted its wage slaves, created a community of interest between the exploited and the exploiters against the oppressed colonies – the yellow, black and red colonial people – and chained the European and American working class to the imperialist 'fatherland.'[16]

Paradoxically, however, the Manifesto from the Congress authored by Trotsky, but signed by other leading Bolsheviks, said:

> The workers and peasants not only of Annam, Algiers and Bengal, but also of Persia and Armenia, will gain their opportunity of independent existence only in that hour when the workers of Britain and France, having overthrown Lloyd George and Clemenceau, have taken state power into their own hands.[17]

We will discuss the social imperialism of the communist movement itself in a later chapter. For now, we may refer to several other Marxists who perceived the extent to which imperialism had given the metropolitan working classes a material and ideological stake in capitalism.

MARXISTS AGAINST EUROCENTRIC WORKERISM

Historian Jacques Pauwels notes in his history of the First World War that: 'The profits realised by the systematic and ruthless exploitation of the colonies not only made it possible to remunerate the colonial personnel relatively well, but also offer slightly higher wages to the workers in the metropolis and to finance modest social services for their benefit.'[18] In the process, he writes, much wind was taken out of the sails of the socialist movement at the expense of the people thus plundered.

By 4 August 1914, German, British and French socialist parliamentarians had voted for war credits for their respective governments. Nearly all Socialist parties (with the exception of those in Russia, Serbia and Ireland) insisted that their own state was fighting a defensive war. British socialists, and their European counterparts, had well and truly embraced social imperialism, 'a steadfast defence of the ... national interest combined with a program of social reform helpful to its largely working class constituency'.[19] Russian Marxist Nikolai Bukharin illuminated the material roots of this social imperialist tendency:

> There is an opinion current among many moderate internationalists to the effect that the colonial policy brings nothing but harm to the working class and that therefore it must be rejected. Hence the natural desire to prove that colonies yield no profit at all, that they represent a liability

even from the point of view of the bourgeoisie, etc. Such a point of view is being propounded, for instance, by Kautsky.

The theory unfortunately suffers from one shortcoming, namely, it is out and out incorrect. The colonial policy yields a colossal income to the great powers, i.e., to their ruling classes, to the 'state capitalist trust.' This is why the bourgeoisie pursues a colonial policy. This being the case, there is a possibility for raising the workers' wages at the expense of the exploited colonial savages [*sic*] and conquered peoples.

Such are exactly the results of the great powers' colonial policy. The bill for this policy is paid, not by the continental workers, and not by the workers of England, but by the little peoples of the colonies. It is in the colonies that all the blood and the filth, all the horror and the shame of capitalism, all the cynicism, greed and bestiality of modern democracy are concentrated. The European workers, considered from the point of view of the moment, are the winners, because they receive increments to their wages due to 'industrial prosperity.'

All the relative 'prosperity' of the European-American industry was conditioned by nothing but the fact that a safety valve was opened in the form of colonial policy. In this way the exploitation of 'third persons' (pre-capitalist producers) and colonial labor led to a rise in the wages of the European and American workers.[20]

Undoubtedly, at the time of this writing Bukharin was correct to single out leading German Marxist Karl Kautsky as representative of such views. In an article of February 1906, however, Kautsky himself had correctly laid the relative conservatism of the British working class at the doorstep of Britain's exploitation of the colonial world:

To be sure, English capitalism will suffer a terrible collapse the moment the oppressed lands rebel and refuse to continue paying tribute. If England loses India, Egypt, and South Africa, a mass of surplus-value, which today enriches it, must remain abroad; a higher level of state and community taxation will be shifted onto the shoulders of the working class; industrial capital will win a decisive voice, and immediately sharpen the contradiction between capital and workers to the highest degree. If it does not come even sooner, socialism will then become inevitable in England. Till then, however, it must conduct a harder struggle for supremacy there than in much more backward countries.[21]

At the Second Congress of the Comintern, communists from the colonies began to forcefully attack Eurocentrism in the communist movement. Pak Din Shoon, the Korean delegate at the Congress, criticised the way the colonial question was treated in the First Congress, stating: 'The attention should have been directed to the East, where the fate of the world revolution may very well be decided.'[22] Meanwhile, the Indian delegate Manabendra Nath Roy, Head of the Comintern's Far Eastern Bureau, placed the exploitation of the colonies at the centre of international communist strategy:

> Superprofits gained in the colonies are the mainstay of modern capitalism, and as long as these exist, it will be difficult for the European working class to overthrow the capitalist order ... By exploiting the masses in the colonies, European imperialism is in a position to make concession after concession to the labour aristocracy at home. While European imperialism seeks to lower the standard of living of the home proletariat by bringing into competition the production of the lower-paid workers in subject countries, it will not hesitate to sacrifice even the entire surplus-value in the home country, so long as it preserves its huge superprofits in the colonies.[23]

In the same debate Mirsaid Sultan-Galiev, who came from the Muslim part of the old Russian Empire, and had participated in the revolution of 1917, also recommended that the Comintern give priority to anti-colonial revolutions in the East. He, too, made the correct argument that losing the underdeveloped world to exploit is a precondition for revolution in the West: 'Deprived of the East, and cut off from India, Afghanistan, Persia, and its other Asian and African colonies, Western European imperialism will wither and die a natural death.'[24] Galiev thought that the communist movement had made a serious strategic error by 'giving first priority to the revolutionary movement in Western Europe, and thus had overlooked the fact that capitalism's weak point lay in the Orient'.[25] For Galiev, who was implacably opposed to any and all industrial society, and not simply the capitalist variety, the East may not have a developed working class, but the nations therein were exploited and therefore 'proletarian nations'.[26] A similar point to Galiev's had been made by Li Dazhao, one of the founders of Marxism in China. In January 1920 he described China as 'proletarianized in relation to the world system'.[27]

Unfortunately, Galiev took his correct prognosis about the centrality of imperialist value transfer to the health of world capitalism as the basis for his supposing that the national movements of the poorer Muslim nations within the Soviet Union were intrinsically proletarian, in effect dissolving the internal class dynamics of those nations. Moreover, though justified in his attempt to reconcile elements of Islamic thought with Marxism, Galiev tended to the view that the Islamic fundamentalism espoused by the nationalists of the Caucasus was intrinsically socialist.[28] This led him to pursue an anti-Soviet political agenda in league with imperialist-sponsored landed and clerical elites:

> In April 1923, the center intercepted two conspiratorial letters written by Sultan-Galiev, which revealed he had Basmachi ties [the Basmachi ('brigands') were a right-wing Islamic fundamentalist movement allied with British intelligence] and indicated his willingness to exploit them to further his faction's agenda. With this evidence in hand, Stalin engineered Sultan-Galiev's arrest in May 1923 and his formal denunciation at the June 1923 TsK [Central Committee] conference on nationalities policy.[29]

Both before and after its disagreements with the 'national communism' of the Caucasus (and of the Ukraine), the Comintern began to more forcefully consider the national liberation movements of the Far East. The defeat of the Hungarian Soviet, noted Trotsky, temporarily disagreeing with his earlier suggestion that workers' revolution in the West would free the colonies, showed that British capitalism might be more readily damaged by the Comintern's redoubling its efforts in the oppressed colonies:

> There is no doubt at all that our Red Army constitutes an incomparably more powerful force in the Asian terrain of world politics than in the European terrain ... The road to India may prove at the given moment to be more readily passable and shorter than the road to Soviet Hungary. The road to Paris and London lies via the towns of Afghanistan, the Punjab and Bengal.[30]

SOCIALISM AND THE THEORY OF MASS
EMBOURGEOISEMENT THROUGH IMPERIALISM

The idea that imperialism, value transfer and working class conservatism are closely related is, then, not a new trend within socialist thought. Rather, it has been espoused by thinkers as different as Marx, Engels, Lenin, Bukharin, Kautsky, Stalin and Trotsky. Unfortunately, none of the classical Marxists fully grasped the centrality of colonialism and imperialism to the capitalist mode of production in the metropolitan areas of the world economy. Not only was capitalist crisis (and with it, the prospects for socialist advance) rarely conceptualised by Marxists with regard to the nature and extent of the tribute or rent levied by imperialism in the colonial and semi-colonial areas, but the mass of workers in the developed capitalist countries was usually considered materially insulated from the corrupting effects of imperialist ascendancy. Increasingly, especially following the politically expedient but ideologically damaging Popular Front strategy of the 1930s, the labour aristocracy came to be viewed in ever narrower terms as a special layer of the working class in each and every single capitalist country. As such, it was the allegedly malign influence of a small minority of self-satisfied and complacent trade union bureaucrats or highly skilled professionals that came to earn the epithet 'labour aristocracy' where the term was used by Marxists at all. The original meaning of the concept of the labour aristocracy, denoting as it did the growing division between imperialist nation workers and workers in the oppressed nations, has come to be lost over time.

Undoubtedly, the major reason for the lack of clarity around the issue of the so-called labour aristocracy, and its falling out of favour as a central aspect of global class analysis, is the social and ideological influence of the working bourgeoisie itself. Simply put, as a matter of its own self-preservation, the intellectual champions of the labour aristocracy and other left-wing apologists for global income differentials have preferred to pretend that the labour aristocracy does not exist and need not be accounted for either tactically or strategically. As Orwell again noted, 'It is quite true that the English are hypocritical about their Empire. In the working class this hypocrisy takes the form of not knowing that the Empire exists.'[31] Thus if all workers everywhere have the same 'proletarian' interests, then it follows that gains made by the labour aristocracy cannot possibly have a negative impact on workers anywhere. That false pretence has proved fatal to labour internationalism, as the labour aristocracy has time and time again proved itself to be an unwavering opponent of socialism and national self-determination everywhere.

THE SPLIT WITHIN THE WORKING CLASS: PROLETARIAN VERSUS BOURGEOIS LABOUR

The proletariat is that section of wage-earners that is exploited at the point of production, receiving less value in the form of a wage than it creates during the course of its employment. The labour aristocracy, by contrast, refers to that group of wage-earners whose relatively high wages, regular employment, decent working conditions (what Lenin referred to as 'soft jobs'), realistic prospects for career advancement and/or cordial relations with supervisors and managers sets their living standards far above the mass of proletarians. In political terms, the labour aristocracy spurns labour internationalism in favour of seeking rapprochement with the political and economic institutions of imperialism. Even where economic crisis sometimes impels the labour aristocracy to repudiate this (sometimes tacit, sometimes overt) class compact with employers and the government, it does not acknowledge its material and political debt to the exploited workers of the colonial and semi-colonial countries. Instead, the labour aristocracy prefers to focus on national 'democratic' redistribution of value obtained by means of imperialism (including, especially, colonialism, unequal exchange and capital export to low-wage countries).

The labour aristocracy originated in the craft unions of the early nineteenth century which sought to preserve the wages and working conditions of members by maintaining a monopoly on certain skills and occupations. As the trade union movement matured alongside industrial capitalism, and the working class became a majority of the population, the labour aristocracy struggled to find institutional means to secure its relative labour market privileges. It did so through integration into state structures and through winning legal and industrial recognition for the union movement. Since the labour aristocracy was typically among the best organised section of the workforce, and possessed skills useful in the most advanced sectors of the economy, it was able to effectively confront the capitalist class as the vanguard of the labour movement. At the same time, it was able to widely disseminate its reformist and economistic ideology amongst the wider working class.

Over the past century and more, capital has consolidated its rule on the basis of imperialist expansion abroad and/or internal colonialism domestically. This has afforded the provision of both superwages and generous welfare entitlements to the majority of the metropolitan and/or settler-colonial working classes so that bourgeois ideology has a much wider purchase therein than merely the skilled and unionised component of the labour aristocracy. It is absolutely crucial to understand that the incorporation of the labour aristocracy within established social and political structures could only proceed upon the basis of colonial and neo-colonial oppression. Briefly, wherever the labour aristocracy was able to win enduring material and political gains for itself within its 'own' state boundaries it did so on the basis of colluding or even participating in the enforced dispossession and exploitation of colonised and semi-colonised workers and peasants. As the esteemed English philosopher and activist Bertrand Russell noted, 'To some, the expression "U.S. imperialism" appears as a cliché because it is not part of their own experience. We in the West are the beneficiaries of imperialism. The spoils of exploitation are the means of our corruption.'[32] The growth of imperialism became indispensable to maintaining rising living standards for the metropolitan and settler-colonial working classes. By the beginning of the twentieth century at the latest, the labour aristocracy was concentrated in industries that depended directly upon imperialism for their functioning, and was receiving wages that could only be afforded on the basis of imperialist value transfer and the extreme exploitation underpinning it.

THE NUMERICAL AND GEOGRAPHICAL DIMENSIONS OF THE LABOUR ARISTOCRACY TODAY

The 'Golden billion' (in Russian, 'золотой миллиард') in the advanced industrialised countries of the Western world consume a vastly disproportionate share of the planet's natural and human resources. The advanced capitalist countries have attempted to thwart independent development in all other countries so as to maintain these as suppliers of cheap energy, raw materials and labour. Today, all who live and work legally in the major imperialist countries of Europe, North America and Japan (the First World) are beneficiaries of imperialism and may be referred to collectively as a 'labour aristocracy'. Needless to say, these benefits are not shared equally between the various social groups, classes, class fractions and strata which make up the population of the global North. Enduring patterns of discrimination based on gender, nationality and ethnicity in the metropolitan countries may even lead to the extreme marginalisation of some groups therein (in particular, lumpenised sections thereof) such that these are scarcely capable of consuming transferred value. Such individuals, groups and social layers, however, are distinct minorities. Even where they do constitute a significant social stratum as, for example, with Europe's oppressed national and ethnic minority populations, or the US internal colonial populations, political strategy is typically overdetermined by the influence of the labour aristocracy as opposed to the workers and peasants of the exploited countries.

Whereas there are differences in wages, working conditions, skills and employment opportunities within every country in the world, and whereas regional variations persist within the global South according to levels of industrialisation (these in turn depending upon the nature and extent of land reform and of national sovereignty), the most profound global income variations correspond closely to residence and non-residence in the major imperialist countries. Global income divergence is the accumulated effect of the historical and enduring subordination of Africa, Asia and South and Central America to the requirements of imperialist industry, finance and commerce, and the associated disarticulation of the majority-world's agriculture, industry, consumption and savings. Simply put, the extraversion of these continents' economies in line with imperialist diktat has persistently resulted in an oversupply of labour and a dearth of investment opportunities therein, so that both wage growth and the productivity increase that would sustain it have been drastically curtailed. The labour aristocracy, in consequence, exists primarily in the so-called West (an ideological construct rather than a real geographic or cultural entity) whose economic hegemony in the world market allows for autocentred capital accumulation tending to benefit the broad majority of the population. Meanwhile the overwhelming mass of the world's proletarian, semi-proletarian, peasant and lumpen populations struggle to maintain themselves through their labour.

Nonetheless, even less global imperialist countries such as Russia are able to offer significant benefits to national majorities according to the extent to which imperialist value transfers rely upon differential rates of labour exploitation for 'foreign' and native workers.[33] In sum, the level of privilege attributable to living in a particular country, and the degree to which it is dispersed throughout society depends on a range of factors relating to the dimensions and demographics of the domestic class structure, and the position of a population within the division of labour established by imperialism worldwide.

10
The Metropolitan
Labour Aristocracy

Classical Leninist theories of the labour aristocracy typically understand the phenomenon in terms of the 'bribery' of the upper stratum of the working class and its leadership by the imperialist bourgeoisie, explicitly undertaken so as to secure the political allegiance or, at least, quiescence of the working class as a whole. Writers such as Emmanuel, conversely, emphasise militant class struggle as the key to explaining the wage levels of metropolitan workers. Whether employers provide wage increases as a prophylactic measure against class militancy or, alternatively, whether metropolitan workers are said to have successfully applied pressure on employers to afford higher wages, wage levels are seen as an independent variable in the capitalist economy that is determined by political struggles. While political struggles do play a vital role in the determination of wages and working conditions, however, they are themselves overdetermined by the structural relations pertaining between imperialist countries and exploited countries. The division of the world along these lines had and continues to have profound consequences for the labour market position of both groups of workers.

We define the metropolitan labour aristocracy (MLA) as that section of the international working class whose relative affluence is sustained by the unrequited transfer of value from the exploited countries to the exploiting countries in the capitalist world system. By dint of the imperialist subvention of the advanced economies, the historical ability of the MLA to secure high real wages – disproportionately in the largely unproductive tertiary (finance, retail, public services and real estate) and quaternary (media, consultation, education and design) sectors of the economy – curbs its propensity to struggle for an end to capitalist exploitation, this being ultimately based on the exploitation of both the industrial proletariat and the agrarian semi-proletariat.

The conservatism inherent in the class position of the MLA is reflected in its tendency to adopt, articulate and action a variety of pro-imperialist political positions. To be sure, the bourgeois ideologies of the MLA may be more or less hostile to the domestic political and economic imperatives of monopoly capital and may differ over taxation policy, welfare spending and immigration law. This variance, often hinging on the particular budgetary concerns of different businesses and employers, clearly has strategic and tactical implications for socialists. Nonetheless, given the trend towards mass *embourgeoisement* in the imperialist countries, widespread labour aristocratic disdain for the exploited working class can be most visibly attested to in the record of metropolitan socialism with respect to the colonial and post-colonial world. We will examine this history in a later section. For now, however, we will attempt to outline a structural theory of metropolitan labour *embourgeoisement*.

IMPERIALISM AND THE RESERVE ARMY OF LABOUR

In Marxist terms, the 'reserve army of labour' is the unemployed and under-employed population of capitalist societies. For Marx, the oversupply of labour in relation to its demand depresses the value of wages (which he defines as the value of labour-power). In the early period of capitalist industrialisation in Britain, the reserve army of labour was principally augmented by:

1. Technological unemployment caused by the concentration and development of industry.
2. Outmigration from the rural areas following the relative contraction of petty agricultural production.
3. The ruination of relatively backward (largely artisanal) production in the towns.[1]

In terms of the present analysis, the capitalist centres witnessed a historical decline in the importance of factors (2) and (3) but, crucially, the colonial and semi-colonial countries did not. Rather, the process of separating the producers from their means of production, so-called 'primitive accumulation' and the dispossession of the peasantry, is a more or less permanent feature of underdevelopment alongside the subordination of national to imperialist industry.[2]

Accumulation by dispossession is primarily effected through state and corporate land grabs, typically resulting in proletarianisation or semi-proletarianisation of rural populations.[3] These plantation, mining, energy and infrastructural initiatives are predominantly carried out in the global South, where extractivism is invariably connected to multinational (and allied 'national') capitals' ability to appropriate underdeveloped countries' resources for sale in affluent markets. Imperialism of this kind results in competition among displaced workers for limited jobs in export processing zones and commercial centres, producing constant downward pressure on wage levels. The resultant low wages are reproduced in the low prices of global South exports.

Meanwhile, whereas accumulation by dispossession increases the size of the reserve army of labour, capital scarcity occasioned by the commercial hegemony of business monopolies based in and largely catering to the markets of the global North ensures that the demand for labour in the global South lags behind its supply. The decapitalisation of the exploited countries through the persistent loss of value effected by colonialism, financial imperialism and unequal exchange sets limits to industrial accumulation therein. These limits are further restricted by the meagre basis for domestic sales allowed by the low wages of the working masses. In the imperialist countries, however, the low prices of Third World goods tend to compensate for the globalisation of the reserve army of labour's overall deflationary effect upon wages.

From the 1950s onwards, but especially during the neoliberal period inaugurated in the 1980s, the spread of multinational corporations throughout the Third World in search of low-cost labour-power constituted the internationalisation of capitalist production. It was the vast 'external reserve army' of labour in the underdeveloped countries that created a continuous movement of surplus population into the labour force and weakened labour globally.[4] The 'depeasantisation' of vast swathes of the global South by large agribusiness interests, as well as the integration of the 'actually existing socialist countries' into the world capitalist economy – since the 1980s hundreds of millions of Chinese workers have been displaced from the country's rural areas as a result of agricultural industrialisation – has resulted in the world's workforce increasing from 1.9 billion in 1980 to 3.1 billion in 2007. Today fully 73 per cent of global labour is located in the developing world, with 40 per cent in China and India alone.[5] Currently, the global reserve army of labour (GRAL), not including part-time workers but including unemployed workers aged between 25 and 54, 'vulnerably employed' workers in the informal sector and economically inactive workers consist of approximately 2.4 billion people, compared with 1.4 billion in the active labour force.[6]

Unquestionably, these figures point to a huge surfeit of labour supply within the global economy, holding back development in the agrarian South insofar as massive unemployment in the countryside reduces the bargaining power of the rural workforce to such an extent that landlords can employ hired agriculture wage-labourers for cultivation at a very low cost. As Chandra wrote more than 40 years ago:

We may then infer that labour surplus on a scale that is probably unparalleled in human history is perpetuating the semi-feudal set up. Limited progress along the road to 'modernization' cannot be ruled out. Without vigorous measures to reduce considerably that surplus, we fail to see how one can get out of the vicious circle, or how capitalism can strike deep roots.[7]

In sum, the effects of the GRAL upon the class structure of imperialism are twofold. First, the GRAL induces relative wage stagnation worldwide given an oversupply of labour relative to demand. Second, the monopolisation of world production, distribution and trade, and the attendant negation of price competition by firms based in the developed countries, ensures that the underdeveloped countries' exports are sold at prices reflecting the cheapness of their labour. As a consequence, the working class of the developed countries suffers stagnating wages while, paradoxically, it is able to enjoy increased purchasing power. The working class of the developing countries, meanwhile, suffers both low wages and correspondingly high prices. Paradoxically, its misery is only eased by employment in the low-wage economy; in the absence of a social safety net (see below), exploited wage labour is often less onerous than no wage labour at all.

Global processes of labour stratification are similar to those which created an African proletariat in European- and settler-occupied South Africa, including in the attendant ideological, political and military superstructure. The difference is that neoliberal 'colonisation' typically occurs under the banner of national independence and is advanced by financial as well as agrarian capitalist interests. In both cases, gains for the proletarian and poor peasant majority in the underdeveloped areas are by and large resented by all metropolitan classes.

IMPERIALISM, CAPITALIST EXPANSION AND RISING LIVING STANDARDS IN THE CENTRE

Since the labour market position of the English working class was poor at the time of the industrial revolution due to factors (1)–(3) above, the country's domestic demand did not keep pace with the expanding output of British industry.[8] For that reason, trade with economically backward countries that retained their political independence, especially in Western Europe, grew rapidly, as also did Imperial trade. In addition to another factor that relieved pressure on the labour market in the (metropolitan) capitalist countries and thus allowed for greater wage growth, namely, emigration of masses of workers to North America and overseas colonies, the growth of international trade favoured employment opportunities for workers catering to industrially backward markets.[9]

With the expansion of Britain's overseas markets, the declining significance of domestic underemployment, and political opportunities opened up by intra-ruling class conflict between rural and industrial elites around the repeal of the Corn Laws, the social position and the wages of the British working class began to improve. Initially, imperialist expansion had direct effects only on the export industries of the metropolitan centres, but by improving workers' position on the labour market, by increasing the numbers of employed workers and their real wages, it indirectly stimulated domestic demand for industrial and consumer goods.[10] Colonialism, meanwhile, by at first deliberate, and subsequently laissez-faire means, ensured a massive curtailment of industrialisation and the consequent absence of a working class in the oppressed countries. As a consequence of capitalism's colonial and industrial development, therefore, the situation of the English working class, and that of Europe as a whole, was greatly improved. It meant that the inherent tendency for industrial concentration to cause unemployment was to a large extent annulled (though, of course, by no means entirely). As Sternberg writes:

Let us assume that in a particular period the number of workers engaged in the English textile industry was 300,000, and let us further assume that with the increased introduction of machinery to raise the productivity of labour the same total product could be produced by 250,000 workers. This would mean that machinery had made 50,000 textile workers redundant. However, if at the same time Empire markets offered scope for a greatly increased volume of textile products, and not only for a short transitional period but for generations (because, as we have seen, large-scale textile-production in the Empire was deliberately prevented), so that English textile sales doubled, then there would be work not for 250,000 English textile workers, or even for 300,000, but for twice 250,000. In other words, despite the increased introduction of machinery, the total number of workers employed in the English textile industry would increase by 200,000. That was typical of what happened not only in England but in all other capitalist metropolitan centres in the period of imperialist expansion.[11]

In North America, the even more restricted development of class stratification and working class immiseration had previously been achieved through an expansion that took place within 'its own' territory or, more accurately, the territory of colonised nations with which it shared continental space.[12] Thus, whereas the bourgeois working class that existed in the

United States developed on the basis of capitalist expansion, until the late nineteenth century this expansion did not mainly occur through external or overseas imperialism.[13] Moreover, whereas European workers advanced through the exploitation of a largely foreign 'underclass' of workers excluded from the benefits of imperialism, the majority Euro-American workers of the United States advanced through the ongoing exclusion, marginalisation and oppression of an 'underclass' *inside* the country, made up of dispossessed Black people, Chicano/as and Native Americans. As Boggs argues:

> American radicals have sought to propagate the concept of 'black and white, unite and fight' as if black and white had [only] common issues and grievances, systematically evading the fact that every immigrant who walked off the gangplank into this country did so on the backs of the indigenous blacks and had the opportunity to advance precisely because the indigenous blacks were being systematically deprived of the opportunity to advance by both capitalists and workers.[14]

Class struggle is the effort to remove all obstacles to the political unity of the working class, including hierarchical divisions based on gender, nationality and ethnicity. Unfortunately, the class reductionism endemic to Eurocentric Marxism often derides such struggles as being based on liberal 'identity politics' as opposed to 'revolutionary' class politics. In reality, the economistic 'class struggles' of the labour aristocracy are predicated upon the maintenance of working class disunity.

IMPERIALIST REFORMISM AND THE LABOUR ARISTOCRACY

As ought to be uncontroversial, in the final quarter of the nineteenth century, involvement in trade unions was greater in those establishments where skilled manual workers were better paid.[15] Thus in Germany, Wilhelm Liebknecht (co-founder of the Social Democratic Party with August Bebel in 1869) frankly stated at the Party Congress of 1892:

> You who sit here are also, most of you, aristocrats, to a certain extent, among the workers – I mean in so far as incomes are concerned. The labouring population in the mining regions of Saxony and the weavers in Silesia would regard such earnings as yours as the income of a veritable Croesus.

Britain's trade unions, too, largely represented the labour aristocracy and successfully pursued a reformist course:

[The] mid-Victorian period of trade unionism was essentially that of the definitive national organisation of the 'pompous trades and proud mechanics', the skilled minority of the working class. 'Defence not defiance' became the union motto – to defend the vested interest of the craftsman, not to defy the employing class with the organised might of the whole working class; similarly the line 'a fair day's wage for a fair day's work' implied the full acceptance of the existing order, subject to specific and limited reform, to getting the best that could be got within its framework.[16]

The ability of Britain's rulers to maintain divisions within what were then typically, and quite properly, referred to as the working classes was due to the industrial hegemony Britain had achieved by means of colonialism:

The triumph of Free Trade meant complete freedom for capital. There was an industrial and commercial expansion on an unparalleled scale, 'leaping and bounding' (in Gladstonian phrase), returning profits not of tens but thousands per cent, confirming Britain 'the workshop of the world', in its privileged position of industrial monopoly. Thus it was both possible and necessary for substantial concessions to be made to the two main groups upon whom this prosperity depended, the textile factory workers (who were greatly benefited by the Ten Hour Act of 1847) and the skilled artisans in the metal-working and building trades. The consolidation in this way of an 'aristocracy of labour' over and above the main mass of the working class was fully reflected in the new [reformist and defensist] character of trade unionism.[17]

The growth of new unionism in the final decade of the nineteenth century and beyond broadened the trade union movement. Yet it did so without thereby undoing the stratification of labour and, crucially, without challenging the imperialist social contract. Even the wave of syndicalist unrest in the period leading up to the First World War did not reverse the social chauvinist mentality of most British workers.[18] Rather, throughout the Victorian era we see precisely the kind of social imperialism *avant la lettre* of which the Western left would find itself approving as value transfer has increased:

The domestic Radical programme, like the Fabian program of a few years later, rested on the assumption that home and foreign affairs had in practice very little connection. At home, the task of the radicals was to promote a more even distribution of wealth; but the wealth that was to be redistributed was taken for granted, without any examination of its sources. It was regarded, in effect, as natural and assured that Great Britain, as the leader of world industrialism, should go on getting richer and richer, and should devote her surplus capital resources to the exploitation of the less developed regions of the world, drawing therefrom an increasing tribute which Radical legislation would proceed to redistribute by means of taxation more equitably between the rich and the poor in Great Britain.[19]

The ranks of the labour aristocracy were broadened in the second half of the nineteenth century with the rapid expansion of the capital goods sector and its high demand for skilled workers, new labour aristocrats in the metal trades joining older ones in building and printing in the capitals of England and Scotland. The political moderation of the mid-Victorian labour movement, especially its trade union component, was due largely to the increased dominance of these skilled males therein, those 'moderate and "responsible" men who, whilst laying strong claims to the rights of male citizenship, wished to achieve a stake in society'.[20] Kirk argues that historian Eric Hobsbawm is correct to draw a close connection between the 'distinct if modest' improvement in all but the environmental conditions of the working class in the third quarter of the nineteenth century and increased political moderation. The evidence points to a clear rise in the living standards of a significant section of the British working class from around 1860 and an increasing differential between many skilled and lesser skilled and unskilled male workers during that period.[21]

The rise in British wages was intrinsically connected to growing imperialism. As Hobsbawm has written:

[The] further we progress into the imperialist era, the more difficult does it become to put one's finger on groups of workers which did not, in one way or another, draw some advantage from Britain's position; who were not able to live rather better than they would have done in a country whose bourgeoisie possessed fewer accumulated claims to profit and dividends abroad, or power to dictate the terms of trade with backwards areas. Or, since there is no simple correlation between the standard of living and political moderation, on workers who could not be made to feel that their interests depended on the continuance of imperialism. It is indeed true that the 'benefits' of imperialism, and its promises, were unevenly distributed among various workers at any given time; and that some of the mechanisms for distributing them did not come into full operation until the inter-war years. It is equally true that the growing crisis of the British economy complicated the pattern. But, on the whole, the change remains ... To sum up. The roots of British reformism no doubt lie in the history of a century of economic world supremacy, and the creation of a labour aristocracy, or even more generally, of an entire working class which drew advantages from it.[22]

With some important qualifications and corrections, it is valid to posit 'an overall link between economic improvement and reformism during the third quarter of the century'.[23] Thus, for instance, English cotton operatives were generally much better off in material terms in 1875 than they had been in 1850, with the post-1864 years being a period of substantial, in many cases spectacular, rises in money and real incomes. Given this overall improvement, Kirk argues, '[it] is surely not coincidental that reformism took increasingly deep root in the cotton towns'.[24] Certainly many labour leaders consciously attributed their newfound moderation to the material and institutional gains of the years after 1850. That there had been real improvements in the standard of living of the working class was explicitly vouched for in the analysis of working class reformers and their allies at the time.[25]

Alongside structural changes in the capitalist mode of production, rising living standards brought about by falling prices and the ability of trade union organisations to ensure that wages did not fall concurrently, Kirk accounts for working class conservatism by highlighting conflicts following a massive and unprecedented increase in the level of Irish Roman Catholic immigration into England's cotton districts. In the years after the catastrophic Irish famine of the late 1840s, this led to tensions between sections of the immigrant and host communities. Kirk establishes that a 'working class fragmented [that is, *stratified*] along ethnic (and wider cultural) lines greatly facilitated the (re)-assertion of bourgeois control upon the working class, and helped to attach workers more firmly to the framework of bourgeois politics'.[26] Thus, '[ethnic] conflict operated, against the background of the apparent inevitability of capitalism, to restrict further the potential for class solidarity in Lancashire and Cheshire, and to provide sections of the bourgeoisie with the opportunity to assert their authority, in a fairly direct way, upon workers'.[27]

The extension of the franchise to part of the male working class in Britain with the Reform Act of 1867 (the Second Reform Act) was the means employed by the ruling class to forestall 'an incipient alliance between the casual "residuum" and the "respectable working class", as fear grew on a national level of a possible coalition between reformers, trade unions and the Irish'.[28] This analysis is borne out with the example of Britain's fiscal policy with respect to sugar duties:

Government strategy was driven by a number of different elements, not least the fiscal problems of the state. It was necessary to increase revenues by imposing income tax, beginning to shift the burden of taxation from indirect to direct taxes and, at the same time, keeping income tax low through increasing revenues by lowering duties on consumption goods and thus boosting, in particular, working-class consumption. This has to be seen in the broader context of, on the one hand, dealing with the Chartist insurgency by attempting to attach the working class to the state through encouraging consumption and some measures of social reform and, on the other, of dealing with the interests of manufacturing and the effects of the economic depression of 1837–42 through attacking the Corn Law problem. The latter would also entail addressing the crisis in Ireland by moving towards free trade as the putative solution.

Within the wider framework, [British Conservative Chancellor of the Exchequer and slave plantation owner Henry] Goulburn situated his aims so far as sugar was concerned. Sugar had become an essential element of working-class consumption so his aim was 'to secure to the people of this country an ample supply of sugar.' But he also wished to make that supply 'consistent with a continued resistance to the Slave Trade, and with the encouragement of the abolition of slavery.' Finally, he sought 'to reconcile both with a due consideration to the interests of those who have vested their property in our Colonial possessions'.[29]

However militant the labour aristocracy's struggles against employers over the past century (and these are frequently and routinely exaggerated and whitewashed by the left), they were never directed against the division between oppressed and oppressed nations, against the imperialist system that guarantees the amount of foreign loot to be divided amongst the warring metropolitan classes.

IMPERIAL TRADE UNIONISM

As we have argued, the bargaining power of metropolitan labour improved as the outmigration of the unemployed to settler and non-settler colonies reduced the size of the reserve army of labour, and as the huge inflow of colonial transfers boosted domestically generated productivity, profits, investment and home markets, thus serving to raise mass living standards.

The connection between labour reformism and colonialism was, however, even more direct. As primary wealth-creators, the major producer industries of the Victorian period were agriculture, textiles, coal, iron and steel, and engineering. These industries were also the major employers, the biggest export earners and, in the latter part of the century, the main targets for the newly emerging trade unions. In 1889 trade unions had 679,000 members, the majority of whom were in the primary industries. By 1900 there were over 2 million union members in Britain. Of equal importance was the diversification of industry in this period, along with the ever increasing range of imported products. The majority of the unionised workers in the late nineteenth century were in iron and steel, coal mining, and cotton and woollen textiles (Table 10.1).[30]

The economic and political benefits accruing to the skilled working class of Victorian England organised in these industries were directly attributable to their exceptional position in the international division of labour at the time, that is, to British colonial imperialism:

If we look at the sectors where skilled workers and their organisation were strongest, we find them to be closely connected to Empire: textiles, iron and steel, engineering, and coal. Textiles because of the cheap cotton from Egypt, and a captive market in India; iron and steel because of ship-building and railway exports, engineering because of the imperialist arms industry, and coal because of the demands of Britain's monopoly of world shipping. In a myriad of different ways, the conditions of the labour aristocracy were bound up with the maintenance of British imperialism. And this fact was bound to be reflected in their political standpoint.[31]

The effect of union membership on earnings at this time was of the order of 15–20 per cent and this effect was similar at different skill levels.[32] A broadly similar pattern is observed for industry groups, although the difference in the impact of unions on earnings across industries was greater than across skill groups.

Table 10.1 Trade union membership in Britain, 1882 and 1892

	1888		1892	
	Union Membership	Union Density (%)	Union Membership	Union Density (%)
Metals, Engineering and Shipbuilding	190 000	19.5	310 200	31.9
Mining and Quarrying	150 000	24.2	326 700	52.6
Textiles	120 000	10.5	203 100	17.7
Great Britain	75 000	6.2	1 576 000	13

Source: Hatton et al. 1994. Union membership data for 1888 is from Clegg et al. 1964, p. 1. Membership data for 1892 is from Bain and Price 1980. The union densities were calculated using industry employment data for 1891 from Bain and Price 1980.

IMPERIALISM AND STRUCTURAL *EMBOURGEOISEMENT* IN THE TWENTIETH CENTURY

By the time of the First World War (1914–18), around half the population of the world was subject to colonial or semi-colonial exploitation by the metropolitan capitalist centres. Europe was the centre of a gigantic periphery exploited and politically subjugated by it. This impeded those processes that lead to capitalist crisis (overproduction, underconsumption, a falling rate of profit, stagnant growth) and had profound consequences for the development of class stratification in the metropolitan regions, tending to make it both less polarising and much less unforgiving for the working classes therein.

For Marx, the class polarisation of society and the intensification of economic crisis represent the decisive twin factors that will ultimately lead to the failure and ouster of capitalism and the triumph of socialism.[33] However, the rise in living standards for workers in the metropolitan core of the capitalist world system was not only decisive for the development of capitalism but also for the political course taken by the socialist movement. It led on the one hand to the support of European socialists for their governments in the First World War (US Euro-American socialists were much more isolationist, allowing for a more 'internationalist' approach to the conflagration), while on the other it shaped the revolutionary outlook of Lenin 'which led to the disruption of the politically organized [social-imperialist] working-class movement'.[34]

In the period of capitalist expansion right up to the decade preceding the First World War – when British capitalism entered a period of acute crisis that led to war over preferential trade agreements, tariff barriers, trade routes, protected markets for investments and manufactures, and raw materials sources – the metropolitan working class attained increasingly bourgeois social status. This was despite the destruction of middle class strata that inevitably accompanies capitalism, both because of the increasingly affluent living standards of the workers that accompanied the rise in real wages and, also, because of the process of expansion constantly having created new middle class strata.[35] Unfortunately, though they were unable to ignore its existence altogether, Marx and Engels either failed or refused to recognise the full significance of working class *embourgeoisement*, or to properly explain it in relation to imperialism.[36]

For Engels, the source of the affluence of many English workers was to be found in England's industrial monopoly as well as its colonial Empire. Yet England also had an industrial monopoly in the first half of the nineteenth century no less than it did in the first decades of the second half. Indeed, its advantage in this regard was even more pronounced in the earlier period. Yet the English working class did not receive high wages during the first half of the nineteenth century, while it did do so in the second half. By positing industrial monopoly as the source of rising wages in England, then, Engels had failed to properly appreciate the significance of new factors that led to a rising living standard for English workers, most significantly, their increasingly favourable position on the national and international labour markets. This favourable position came to apply to the entire European and North American working class, and it has lasted until today.[37]

The bourgeois character of the working class in Europe, then, had come about as a result of the relationship between the metropolitan capitalist centres and the colonial and semi-colonial countries, not only in terms of the job opportunities and consumption patterns it had provided for, but also in regard to the favourable position the metropolitan workers occupied within the imperialist labour market thus established. As Sternberg writes:

We cannot satisfactorily analyse the position in England's towns in this period if we ignore the position in India's towns. We cannot adequately analyse the class stratification of the capitalist centres in Europe without at the same time analysing developments in China, the Dutch East Indies and also in Eastern Europe, because the capitalist metropolitan countries were more and more becoming the industrial centre of this vast outer area. Similarly, any analysis of this colonial and semi-colonial periphery must be closely related to a description of the class stratification in the metropolitan centres. Only then can we hope to obtain a really scientific analysis of the whole problem.[38]

The concentration of capitalist industry resulted in a complicated class stratification in the metropolitan centres of the world economy that defied any binary polarisation of bourgeoisie and proletariat. Although a great majority of the population therein were either wage-earners or salaried employees, real wages had risen between 50 and 100 per cent in the second half of the nineteenth century, and the workers had a higher standard of living than that of the former middle classes. At the same time, the system of independent holdings in agriculture had largely remained intact, and the expansion of the service and retail industries had created new independent strata. As the number of employees, officials and professionals also increased with the growth of capitalism, the middle class came to represent an *increasing* proportion of the population. Indeed, the wage-earning working class became little more than 50 per cent of the population of the capitalist metropolitan centres. As the expansion of capitalism through imperialism came into crisis at the beginning and end of the First World

War, the position of the middle class tended to deteriorate. However, by that time, an enduring class structure had begun to develop in the imperialist countries which did not intensify social antagonism but, rather, tended to ameliorate it.[39]

THE IMPERIALIST WELFARE STATE AND THE POSITION OF METROPOLITAN LABOUR

Whereas the size of the reserve army of labour in the metropolitan countries diminished alongside the domestic supply of labour from rural outmigration and ruined artisanal production, its socio-economic significance dwindled as a consequence of the institution of a welfare system with public health, education, pensions and, crucially, unemployment insurance and social security. This latter mitigated the effects of unemployment upon wage levels and bolstered the privileged labour market position of the metropolitan labour aristocracy relative to its counterparts in the Third World.

While there are marked differences in the extent and composition of social expenditure between different states in the global North, even under neoliberalism most liberal and conservative politicians therein remain committed to public welfare. Indeed, between 1980 and 2014, average social expenditure in the Organisation for Economic Co-operation and Development (OECD) countries increased from 15.4 per cent of GDP to 21.6 per cent of GDP. By contrast, of the so-called emerging economies of the global South, whose national incomes are much lower, Brazil is closest to the OECD average at just over 15 per cent of GDP in 2014 (two-thirds of which is spent on pensions in a country with eight persons of working age to one senior citizen). In China in 2009, public social spending amounted to around 7 per cent of GDP, comparable to average social spending in the Asia/Pacific region. Public social spending in India (with spending on labour market programmes at 0.6 per cent of GDP) is around 3 per cent of GDP and around 2 per cent in Indonesia. Public spending in South Africa amounted to around 9 per cent of GDP in 2012.[40]

The idea that the state was responsible for people's social security and welfare gained ground in all Western European countries in the interwar period. The governments of these countries developed and broadened the functions of the welfare state in the late 1950s, throughout the 1960s, and into the beginning of the 1970s. Indeed, throughout the last century, this form of government became increasingly central to the regulation of the capitalist economy; it was the owner of the civil infrastructure, social institutions and even some key means of production, to such an extent that smaller capitalists even complained of being 'crowded out' of the market.

Alongside the development of parliamentary democracy, then, the state ceased to represent the unilateral interests of capital but, rather, capitalist 'society' *tout court*. In terms of class struggle, it became to some extent a third party – a broker – between capital and the working class. Whereas the metropolitan labour aristocracy took the lead in this inter-class compact from the late 1950s until the early 1980s, capital re-emerged triumphant in the ensuing period of neoliberalism. With the current crisis, however, the power struggle between the metropolitan labour aristocracy and the metropolitan bourgeoisie is bound to further intensify.

CONCLUSION

The expansion of capitalism alongside the rise of social democracy and, later, the consumer society generated a typically benign and complacent view of imperialism that was quite oblivious to the chaos that its economy had wrought in those countries subject to exploitation. Before decolonisation, capitalist development and the concentration of industry was not accompanied in the countries exploited by imperialism by any widespread expansion of industry or of a working class as such, by rising wages or by the development of a significant urban middle class. Rather, these countries were dominated by the representatives of foreign imperialism with local landed and comprador elites at their side, while the overwhelming majority of the population was engaged in agriculture and the industrial and plantation proletariat lived lives even more impoverished than those of their Russian counterparts.[41]

Few Europeans knew or bothered to find out what was happening in these faraway places (though, of course, few had the opportunity to do so that most Westerners enjoy today). It therefore seemed obvious that the progress being made in the capitalist countries of Western Europe and North America was independent of capitalist expansion abroad, concretely, imperialism. This common sense view was, of course, bolstered by the fact that an analysis which stressed the centrality of imperialism to capitalist 'progress', to the business cycle, the labour market, wage levels, and the functioning of the capitalist system would have shown the precariousness of the entire edifice of the class structure. The wishful thinking of self-satisfied and complacent conservatism, whether of right, left or centre, found and continues to find its reflection in economic pseudo-science.[42]

Imperialism raised the living standards of all European and European-descended North American workers, particularly those organised, skilled and predominantly male workers poised not only (1) to exploit their advantages in relation to specific training and employment opportunities opened up within the metropoles, but also (2) to secure privileges accruing to 'racial', national and/or ethnic hegemony over colonised peoples at home and abroad. Not only had the bargaining power of metropolitan wage labour improved for the reasons discussed above, but the productivity gains associated with value transfer effected by colonial and neo-colonial trade and investment had allowed for the increasing purchasing power of the average income.

Harvey has distinguished the process of capitalist industrialisation in the most developed capitalist countries and that occurring in the underdeveloped countries:

Primitive accumulation, and other processes of appropriation do not guarantee ... the surpluses can be assembled in time and space in exactly the right proportions for strong capital accumulation to proceed. In eighteenth-century Britain, for example, the strong capital surpluses more than matched the surpluses of labour power. Wages rose, and much of the surplus was absorbed in consumption projects. In contrast much of contemporary Africa, Asia and Latin America is faced with the situation in which immense quantities of labour power has to be dispossessed to release very little capital, creating massive and chronic surpluses of labour power in a context of serious capital shortage. [This is] the hallmark of much of contemporary Third World urbanization.[43]

In the Middle East, as in other areas of the Third World, the value of labour-power is economically negligible. In part, this reflects the diminishing value of human life established through decades of war, siege and occupation to ensure private ownership of natural resources, and associated fiscal, savings and profit advantages to foreign capital. Disproportionately these accrue to globe-spanning Western state, military and industrial concerns, but also to their local suppliers in the 'periphery'.[44] Imperialist ownership of the energy and minerals of the global South is a levy on the wellbeing and sovereignty of the exporting countries. It is also a major stimulus to the production of war materiel and the growth of related industries. Globally, while these have remained largely Western-owned, wars of encroachment occur primarily in the 'developing' countries, and at the cost of millions of lives and livelihoods.

11
The Native Labour Aristocracy

The nativist exclusion of highly exploited foreign workers from the centres of colonial and imperialist accumulation remains the absolute *condicio sine qua non* of metropolitan *embourgeoisement* and the 'place premium' that perfectly encapsulates the labour aristocracy's political economy.[1] In the developed countries, native labour aristocracy (NLA) status is conferred by localised discrimination against ostensible non-nationals from the underdeveloped and oppressed populations. It is typically a product of capitalist *and* working class initiative, collusion and compromise. Nationalist and racist ideologies reproduce themselves in the consciousness and outlook of both workers and capitalists to the extent that both groups receive economic rewards from their capacity to discriminate against 'foreign' nationals. The failure of the labour movement to fight consistently and forcefully against xenophobia and racism is the outcome of the international segmentation and stratification of the labour market rewarding class compromise between 'native' workers and their employers.[2]

At the national level, labour-intensive competitive firms tend to support the inflow of immigrant labour so as to maintain relative overpopulation, labour market competition and a fresh supply of labour-power drawn from the 'industrial reserve army'. At the same time, such firms may support discriminatory measures against foreign workers so as to artificially enlarge the supply of unskilled workers relative to skilled ones by preventing foreign workers from rising into the 'skilled' category. The limited upward mobility of oppressed foreign workers results in the creation of a large pool of unskilled labour, and exerts downward pressure on its remuneration.[3] By assigning skilled and supervisory jobs to native (especially white) workers, a kind of 'caste' hierarchy within the workforce is created, with employers reducing the chances of both sections of workers combining to force wage increases or an improvement in conditions.[4]

Large corporations, meanwhile, particularly those operating on the basis of capital-intensive production and employing greater quantities of skilled labour, may be less straightforwardly supportive of discrimination against foreign workers since this may reduce the supply of skilled labour and create inefficiencies in the use of human resources. Indeed, anti-discriminatory policy may render skilled foreign labour competitive with skilled domestic labour, thus lowering wage costs. However, the restriction of labour market mobility on the basis of nationality may benefit skilled native workers insofar as they can improve their employment and wage prospects if they can insulate themselves from foreign labour competition for the 'best' jobs.[5]

The essence of NLA privilege may be observed insofar as it is not the metropolitan working class facing hostility and discrimination on the part of native metropolitan workers competing for scarce jobs for the simple reason that North-South labour movement in search of better-paying jobs is a very minor aspect of global migration flows. Where it occurs, it is usually to obtain individual employment in sectors wherein there is little competition from native workers, for example, in the state and private 'security' sectors. Therefore, in the developed countries the nativism of the working class has the distinctive feature of being *an attempt to preserve the bourgeois status of metropolitan labour within the imperialist class structure*. This accounts both for its extensive virulence and for its huge political cachet.

To maintain itself economically capitalism must (1) ensure the perpetual expansion of an industrial reserve army of labour willing to work for low wages and whose presence has a depressing effect upon wages *tout court*. At the same time, the political stability of capitalist rule presupposes (2) a privileged layer of workers, a 'labour aristocracy' with a material stake in the system of private property.[6] In the first case, the migration of workers from Southern and Eastern Europe and from the less developed countries of the global South to the countries of the global North, as well as internal migration prompted by increased rural poverty within the less developed countries, acts as a means of expanding the inadequate (from the point of view of capital) reserve army of labour. This explains migration having become a fundamental structural requirement for metropolitan capital. Yet both economic necessity (especially market growth) and political virtue also dictate that the metropolitan bourgeoisie afford better labour market conditions and social status to native workers, thus giving them the 'consciousness of a labour aristocracy'.[7] And not only the consciousness of one!

THE SOCIAL FOUNDATIONS OF
THE NATIVE LABOUR ARISTOCRACY

The native labour aristocracy develops out of the split in the labour market between native and migrant workers. In a split labour market, conflict develops between three classes or class fractions, namely, (1) business, (2) higher-paid labour and (3) cheaper labour.[8] Whereas employers seek to employ as cheap, docile and disenfranchised a workforce as possible so as to better compete with business rivals, higher-paid labour fears the potential of cheap labour to reduce its superior wages and working conditions. If the split labour market is constituted on the basis of ethnicity, as it must be under imperialist and/or settler-colonial capitalism wherein extra profits are accumulated by dint of national oppression, then this class antagonism takes the form of ethnic antagonism. It is important to understand, however, that it is not an oversupply of labour paid at *equal* prices that produces ethnic antagonism but, rather, the price differential accruing to different national sections of labour.[9]

Whereas aristocratic labour will first attempt the *exclusion* of cheap labour from the domestic market, if it is unable to do so it will turn to a caste arrangement based on *exclusiveness* in which higher-paid labour deals with the undercutting potential of cheaper labour by holding it apart from particular occupations. As such, by reserving certain jobs paid at a higher level, and ensuring the restriction of lower-paid labour to a different, typically less skilled set of jobs, the labour market split is annulled insofar as the differentially priced workers rarely occupy the same position in the division of labour.[10]

Xenophobia in imperialist countries functions as a means of protecting "'our' wealth from 'their' poverty' and helps to reinforce the divide between metropolitan labour and the countries oppressed and exploited by imperialist capitalism.[11] The material divisions within the metropolitan working class effected by the subordinate labour market position of immigrant labour relative to native labour are heightened by metropolitan labour's refusal to organise and agitate for migrant labour on an equitable basis. In the context of the social democratic compact between metropolitan labour and imperialist capital that characterises its strategic worldview and praxis, metropolitan labour fears that the presence of surplus migrant labour can only worsen its bargaining position with employers. Metropolitan labour is typically concerned lest migrant labour makes demands on housing and welfare that can only be met at its expense.[12] As such, chauvinistic and xenophobic politics are encouraged by metropolitan labour's refusal to pursue socialist goals from a labour internationalist perspective.

Not only in the United States and other countries founded upon settler colonialism, but anywhere the metropolitan labour aristocracy encounters migration from the oppressed nations, working class organisations typically seek to 'protect their mostly white membership from potential workers, many of whom are black'.[13] Since both the recruitment policies of the dominant capitalist class and the economistic and reformist policies pursued by the native working class organisations militate against active solidarity, the distribution of better-paid, skilled and secure employment within the economy comes to hinge upon nationality and 'race'. As such, the material gains accruing to the metropolitan working class as a whole, and its politico-economic symbiosis with imperialist capital vis-à-vis the subordinate workforce, come to define the behaviour and outlook of even those members of the class who least enjoy the petty-bourgeois status conferred upon their 'native' compatriots.

The metropolitan working class comprises a disproportionately large stratum of employees in the bourgeois occupations, that is, those which are engaged 'more on the mental than the manual side of the mental/manual division of labour, and/or [which are involved] in the reproduction of the political relations of domination/subordination between capital and the working-class'.[14] Though it also includes a lower, less affluent stratum of unskilled and/or underemployed workers, it is a 'bounded working class' insofar as both these sections are socially distinguished from the subordinate wage-earning population of the working class in and, in the case of migrants, of the exploited nations. Within the framework of this bounded working class the central appeal of labour organisations will be towards advancing the interests of the dominant national group. Thus whereas the ability of metropolitan labour to restrict the introduction of a substantially cheaper, subordinated workforce, as well as its effectiveness in collective bargaining depends upon the relative incorporation of subordinate workers under conditions of their numerical growth, there is an inherent tendency within a stratified labour market for trade unions to reproduce skill scarcity, reduce the supply of subordinate workers and promote policies which divide jobs on the basis of nationality.[15] As Greenberg notes, however, the actual strategies pursued by metropolitan trade unions depend upon several variable factors:

But there is little certainty or consistency in the position of industrial and general workers' unions. They may move between two extremes: open industrial unionism against the general thrust of dominant [racist] society and state policy; exclusive industrial unionism with the elaboration of the racial order and state racial apparatus. Which course they pursue and when depend on a mix of factors, by no means idiosyncratic, but with an uncertain relationship to the level of development. Among the factors are the extent of racial integration in industry prior to unionization; the extent of proletarianization of the subordinate population; the degree of skill differentiation in industry; the relative political standing of other groups in dominant society, such as commercial farmers [who have a stake in restricting the proletarianisation of the subordinate population] or primary manufacturers; and the willingness of the state to protect dominant employment, control the movements of subordinate labour, and limit the employer's freedom of enterprise. In combination these factors can yield contradictory results: a high level of integration in an industry, with a continuing influx of subordinate labour and a limited state and societal interest in regulating the industrial labour market, may bring multiracial, open industrial unionism; but the same level of 'mixing' and 'swamping' in the presence of a strong societal interest in safeguarding dominant labour and a strong state racial apparatus may allow an exclusive industrial unionism – with the full panoply of job protections and segregation policies.[16]

Though the strategies pursued by metropolitan labour range variously from a narrow, artisanal approach favouring the preservation of skill scarcity under conditions of limited subordinate working class access to the labour market, right through to a more broad strategy of industrial action involving sections of the subordinate workforce domestically, the preservation of racialised job market privilege is rarely absent altogether.[17] Of course, it is crucial to recognise that despite the long history of 'white' racism in the metropolitan union movements, there is also a history of 'black' labour movement organising in defiance of settler-colonial/imperial institutional structures of which white unionism has historically formed an indispensable pillar. Such metropolitan struggles are the legacy of non-white workers in the metropoles having come to occupy relatively more 'proletarian' positions in the labour market than white workers, typically in historical opposition to white efforts to exclude them.[18] Yet so long as de facto or *de jure* national and ethnic barriers in the labour market remain high, poor or worsening standards for subordinate labour do not necessarily impact adversely those of the dominant workforce. On the contrary, where such policies enhance the 'productivity' of dominant relative to subordinate workers, market mechanisms will tend to buttress racial and ethnic barriers.

Intra-working class inequality derives not only from formal discrimination measures, then, but equally from a combination of economic vulnerability and structural bias against subordinate workers. In fact, oppressive, highly exploitative working conditions for the poorest sections of the working class have not only been accepted by the more privileged sections, but have been actively supported by their organisational vehicles as a means of preserving intact their relative advantages. In the United States, for instance, the 1882 Chinese Exclusion Act had virtually monolithic trade union support.[19] As Castles notes, the 'willingness of more privileged workers to accept inferior conditions for others – whether the criteria are gender, race, ethnicity, nationality, legal status, origins or vulnerability – has been and remains a crucial stabilizing factor for the liberal-capitalist order'.[20]

In an ethnically bounded labour market, entire ethnic groups are ranked according to their supposed possession of particular traits determining their suitability for particular kinds of jobs. As such, *ceteris paribus*, members of the top-ranked group are selected first when employers decide whom to hire, and the other groups follow in terms of rank. Waldinger and Lichter refer to this ordering of job candidates by ethnic or racial origin as a *hiring queue*.[21] This is demonstrably in operation in every labour market where employers aim to extract higher profits from the labour of specially oppressed migrant labour, and where native workers expect to benefit from restrictions placed on the latter's employment opportunities.

Native workers abjure the least desirable jobs where possible, noting that these repeatedly attract stigmatised ethnic outsiders. Thus, where upward job market mobility is made possible by economic expansion, the established native workforce seeks better-paid and higher-status employment in sectors wherein non-nationals are effectively excluded.[22] Replacements for the jobs thus vacated may, of course, be obtained domestically, but it is more profitable for employers to fill them with migrants from low-wage countries having poor working conditions. For employers, immigrant workers may be preferred over native workers who may be accustomed to viewing their job prospects in terms of higher rewards than are available at the bottom of the market.[23] At the same time, as long as conditions in the host country are markedly better than those in the country of origin, migrant workers themselves will place greater value on low-status, relatively low-wage work in the former.[24]

IMMIGRATION, ETHNICITY AND
THE NATIVE LABOUR ARISTOCRACY

In Nazi Germany, the 11 million German working men conscripted for military service left a huge gap in the labour force which came to be filled by *Fremdarbeiter* (alien workers). As German imperialism witnessed its steady decline at the hands of the Red Army, these workers were increasingly recruited by force. The highly exploited foreign workers, particularly those most expendable from a racial point of view, namely, workers from the occupied territories of the East, were housed in barracks under military management, and many died through mistreatment and cruel punishment. While Nazi confidence in imminent military triumph initially ensured that foreign labour recruitment was a secondary concern for the government, it soon became a central bulwark of Nazi production. By 1944, indeed, fully one-quarter of those working within the German economy (leaving aside those countless millions looted and enslaved by German imperialism outside the Greater Reich) were foreigners:

Virtually every German worker was confronted with the fact and practice of Nazi racism. In some branches of industry, German workers merely constituted a thin, supervisory layer above a workforce of which between 80 and 90 per cent were foreigners. This tends to be passed over by historians of the labour movement.[25]

As Castles notes, domestic Nazi exploitation of foreign workers was extreme, but it was essentially predicated on the same sharp division between natives and foreigners as other foreign labour systems wherein a colonialist stratification of the workforce prevails.[26] The capitalist state retains the political ability to deport (sections of) migrant labour as and when necessary, thus exporting unemployment to the home countries of the migrants.[27] Those that remain are given better working conditions than pertain in their home countries, access to metropolitan superwages and opportunities for more permanent settlement. However, as the lowest stratum of the working class typically engaged in unskilled and semi-skilled work in those industrial sectors having the worst working conditions and the lowest wages, these workers still function as a reserve army of labour since they 'have no [or fewer] political rights and may be used as a constant threat to the wages and conditions of the local labour force'.[28]

The labour market position of immigrants allows for the release of large numbers of native workers from inferior working patterns and their advancement to better-paid, skilled, supervisory or white-collar employment. This influences the class consciousness not only of workers thus promoted, but of all native workers who are thereby encouraged in having a sense of entitlement to properly 'white' jobs (white-collar employment in many respects having become the defining feature of whiteness in the contemporary era). Thus, despite the fact that both native metropolitan labour and migrant metropolitan labour to a certain extent share common experiences shaped by a lack of property and the need to sell their labour-power to survive (leaving aside for the moment the extent to which the metropolitan labour aristocracy does, in fact, possess capital), they are part of one deeply divided class.[29]

While all persons who must sell their labour-power are members of the working class (and the operative word here is 'must'), *class fractions* are diverse sections of that class as shaped by distinct economic and politico-ideological relationships with capital and its institutions.[30] The labour aristocracy is just such a class fraction, and substituting its interests for those of the proletariat inevitably produces a reactionary worldview and political practice. Many Marxists recognise that the creation of a segmented and stratified working class composed of various divergent class fractions facilitates the exploitation of the majority of workers and is particularly useful to capital 'as part of an attempt to restore profitability in a context of crisis'.[31] Crucially, however, such perspectives often fail to appreciate how the upper echelons of the global working class (as defined in terms of greater wages, transfer payments, access to developed civilian infrastructure, political representation, leisure time and so forth) typically have less incentive to demonstrate solidarity with the less affluent members of their class than they do to further exclude and marginalise them for the sake of preserving their considerable privileges. As such, the political behaviour of the labour aristocracy bolsters dynamic processes of 'class fractioning'.

IMMIGRATION, IMPERIALISM AND CITIZENSHIP

Shachar refers to the 'birthright lottery' of citizenship whereby the morally arbitrary fact of a person's birthplace conditions their citizenship, which in turn determines their life chances.[32] It is the persistent global inequalities and attendant differences in citizenship rights that bear most heavily on the migratory process. Though some welfare rights have been extended to non-citizens in recent years, citizenship remains a crucial variable in this regard. While contributor benefits are largely insurance-based and accrue through participation in the labour market, non-contributory transfer payments such as income support, disability benefits and housing benefits are very much tied to national status insofar as non-citizens are excluded or entitled only to significantly lower levels of benefit.[33] Many countries place severe restriction on access to such non-contributory social programmes and, moreover, immigrants' rights tend to be highly stratified according to entry categories.[34] Thus immigrants in great demand are enticed with attractive packages of rights; temporary immigrants are offered more limited rights; and unwanted immigrants are deterred by restricting their rights including, for instance, in respect of permanent residency and the right to bring family members.[35]

The subordination of migrant labour relative to native labour is not only observed in the sphere of social rights, but also in terms of employment rights granting access to the labour market itself. Access to private sector jobs is typically restricted according to a person's immigration status with low-skilled immigrants, for instance, only admitted to work in particular sectors or for particular employers. In European countries, employers are legally obligated to conduct a labour market test to show that no domestic worker (a national or a European Union citizen) is available before they can employ a foreigner.[36] In addition, there is great variation between states as to whether they allow members of the migrant's family to work immediately.[37] Meanwhile, national citizenship is a precondition for employment in a range of public sector jobs in countries as different as France (hospitals, postal service), Germany (civil service jobs, including public transport and education) and the United States (public school teachers, state troopers, probation officers).[38]

While political (electoral enfranchisement), social and labour market rights are conditioned by the citizen-alien boundary and stratified according to various statuses within the subordinate category, even in liberal states civil rights, too, are restricted for non-citizens. Since the beginning of the so-called War on Terror – aimed not at restricting political violence against civilians, but at subjecting the energy-producing states of Central Asia and the Middle East to a new round of imperialist discipline – governments in the United States and, latterly, Western Europe have implemented draconian police measures affecting non-citizens. Thus, for instance, in the case of persons imprisoned without charge by US authorities in Guantanamo Bay, Cuba, certain national governments with sufficient political influence in the United States were able to lobby for and in some cases secure the release of their citizens, starkly revealing the hierarchical nature of the right to diplomatic protection and national citizenship.[39] Indeed, the Patriot Act in the United States allows the government to deport or detain non-citizens without a trial if the Attorney General suspects them of 'terrorist activity', while, in the United Kingdom, the Labour government responded to the September 2001 attacks in the United States with legislation that allowed for indefinite detention of non-citizens without trial if the Home Secretary 'reasonably believes' that a person is a terrorist.[40]

Those 'postnationalist' theorists who emphasise the erosion of national boundaries and national legal frameworks for understanding processes of international migration ignore the centrality of citizenship to people's ability to move across state boundaries.[41] Barriers to international mobility are significantly higher for some national citizens than for others and a person's citizenship affects their capacity to travel to another country for a short period of time either for work, tourism or to visit family. Whereas citizens of countries in the global North can regularly travel freely to other such countries without a visa (and sometimes even without a passport), citizens of most states in the global South are required to apply for a visa to enter most states of the global North, with visa management closely correlated with the wealth and citizenship of a country with strong and stable interstate relations.[42]

Crucially, citizenship rights and their relative absence shape people's desire to migrate in the first place, with nominally postnational human rights law having little relation to international reality. Whereas the citizens of highly developed countries enjoy extensive formal rights and institutions capable of upholding these, those of transitional countries have fewer formal rights and less powerful institutions, and persons residing in the poorest countries of the global South 'may be citizens in name but not in reality'.[43] Even were it not to reproduce differential citizenship, however, international migration law restricts the rich as well as the poor from risking their lives to find a home in countries where human life is incomparably easier for the average citizen than it is in much of the rest of the world.[44]

Imperialism today entails the globalisation of capitalist production processes relying on the intensive exploitation of labour in the less developed countries. The globalisation of capitalist production is characterised by increased foreign exchange transactions, international capital mobility, transnational corporate expansionism and the economic ascendancy of financial institutions like the IMF and the World Bank. In part, globalisation was a means for imperialist capital to circumvent the national-social pact it had made with the metropolitan working class within the confines of the nation-state system. Insofar as the metropolitan labour aristocracy had the political and institutional strength to prevent the crisis in profitability affecting its living standards, 'stagflation' followed and contributed to further systemic crisis. Leading sections of the ruling bourgeoisie, particularly in the United Kingdom and the United States, therefore sought to implement a restructuring of global capital that would overturn social democratic, socialist and developmentalist projects throughout the world.[45] The resulting set of policies would become known as *neoliberalism*, an ideology that stresses open markets and private enterprise as the principal engines of economic and political advancement internationally. The massive expansion of accumulation by dispossession accompanying the spread of neoliberalism in the global South has produced a 'virtually inexhaustible' immigrant labour reserve for global capitalism.[46]

There are at least three major benefits that capitalists derive from this immigrant labour. First, it is rendered vulnerable, deportable and, as a result, subject to higher levels of exploitation than pertain for the 'native' working class. Second, the construction of apparatuses of control in the form of private, profit-seeking detention centres, militarised borders, and the military and surveillance hardware necessary to policing immigration has become an important site of accumulation. Finally, anti-immigrant policies designed to create a captive and highly precarious working class necessitate political tendencies that convert immigrants into scapegoats, and distract the attention of the privileged section of the global workforce from the root causes of capitalist decline. The unity of the working class, already fractured as a result of the divergent living standards accompanying the division of the world into exploiting and exploited, imperialist and oppressed nations is further undermined by this ideological effect.[47] The capitalist class is able to secure the optimal conditions for the higher exploitation of immigrant labour by means of (1) the division of the domestic workforce into immigrant and citizen and (2) the racialisation and criminalisation of the former.[48]

Immigrant labour has historically flowed from the exploited countries to the imperialist countries in the capitalist world system primarily, that is, from South and Central America and Asia into North America, and from Africa, the Middle East and South Asia into Europe. In more recent years, however, as export-oriented industrialisation has advanced in parts of the global South, 'from the factories along China's southern coastal belt, to the South African mines and farms, the Middle East oil meccas, and Costa Rica's service industry', immigrants have been drawn to less developed regions of the global economy. In both developed and less developed countries, immigrant labour faces the prospect of low-wage, low-status work, the denial of its rights, political disenfranchisement, state repression, bigotry and nativism on the part of the domestic working class.[49] In the case of workers in the major imperialist countries, however, this nativism is the product not simply of a desire to guarantee a monopoly of jobs for native workers; it is motivated by the at least tacit recognition that the bourgeois living standards these workers enjoy is predicated upon the maintenance of the imperialist subjection of foreign workers.

Although typically experiencing relative economic deprivation and political marginalisation, immigrants in the imperialist countries are nonetheless relatively able to enjoy the wage levels and other benefits accruing to legal residency therein. This has a decisive impact on the political culture of the less developed countries, with members of their middle classes aspiring to migrate to a developed country. In doing so, these groups acquire a greater material stake in the imperialist system, one which is increasingly reflected in a conservative political stance. In the metropolitan countries themselves, meanwhile, the marginalisation and police repression of low-income black and minority ethnic populations provides the material (if not necessarily the ideological) basis for a much more progressive political outlook.

In many instances, the wages of workforces divided along national and ethnic lines within a given economy compare poorly to the wages of more integrated, metropolitan workforces therein (compare, for example, the wages of southern US workers to those of northern US workers, or the wages of workers in Northern Ireland to the wages of workers in Britain). Yet such regional wage differences do not necessarily outstrip those encapsulated by discrimination wages. Moreover, particularly where the ratio between the wages of the mainstream and specially oppressed workforces exceeds or is approaching that between the proportional labour time each group expends within the productive sectors of the national economy (considered abstractly as a self-contained unit), there is a clear class rationale for labour aristocratic contempt for the specially oppressed domestic workforce.[50]

IMMIGRATION, LABOUR STRATIFICATION AND THE RESERVE ARMY OF LABOUR IN EUROPE

Following the Second World War, immigrant labour became increasingly central to accumulation in the metropolitan centres of the capitalist world system, meeting labour shortages in key industrial sectors as well as the peripheral areas to which they had traditionally been confined. Immigrant labour tended to act as a substitute for the reserve army of labour that had been negated as a result of European states' commitment to continuous economic expansion and full employment. As such, the effect of immigration was both to slow the growth in wages in those industries where migrant labour was concentrated and, at the same time, to encourage growth within the economy as a whole.[51]

Immigrant workers contributed to Europe's rapidly developing metal, plastic and rubber industries, where the relative preponderance of shift work, overtime and low wages had encouraged native labour to move to different jobs with better working conditions. White workers were able to move in great numbers into more skilled, supervisory, white-collar and other better jobs, giving apparent credence to capitalist ideologies of meritocracy and upward social mobility. Meanwhile, other groups of immigrants moved into labour-intensive, low-paying and economically marginal employment, replacing the native female labour upon which these had previously relied. As a consequence, the wages of native and migrant labour did not coincide, since the latter were overwhelmingly concentrated in jobs located at the bottom of the occupational hierarchy.

Immigrants' inferior position in the labour market is bolstered by a relative dearth of opportunities for education and vocational training; a high incidence of poverty; substandard, overcrowded and segregated housing; and social welfare and health problems. Fully aware of this stratification of a segmented labour market, native white labour viewed itself as an actually or potentially privileged 'labour aristocracy'. By and large, it has acted to preserve the distinct privileges it possesses vis-à-vis immigrant labour by means of racist political and trade union organisation, with discrimination against immigrants often becoming informally institutionalised in the workplace and in wider society.[52]

By the time of the arrival in London of 492 West Indian immigrants on the Empire Windrush in 1948, the British ruling class had consolidated a national inter-class compact with its workers, cemented by the economic benefits brought by slavery, colonialism and imperialism and ideologically justified by racism and nationalism.[53] In effect, 'the British working class constituted some form of "labour aristocracy" that had rather more to lose than its chains of servitude'.[54] Beginning in the nineteenth century and culminating in the aforementioned establishment of full social democracy following the Second World War, the ruling class successfully incorporated ever larger sections of the working class into the institutions of state and bolstered feelings of national unity with recourse to racist ideology and racial stratification.[55] The imperialist inter-class alliance was embodied in the post-war welfare state. Yet, ironically, an institution established with the express purpose of maintaining the British Empire and 'white supremacy' has only sustained itself by using the skilled and unskilled labour of the 'inferior races' of the former colonies.[56]

In an impressive study of the current features of immigration in the UK economy, Vickers demonstrates how immigration policies implemented by the imperialist state in respect to asylum seekers, refugees and migrant workers (re)produce an increasingly segmented and stratified working class, both nationally and internationally.[57] He emphasises that the reserve army of labour is an indispensable factor of capitalist production and, according to Marx, it can be subdivided into (1) floating, (2) latent and (3) stagnant forms. Each of these allows for differential rates of exploitation from the active labour force and each is integrally related to labour migration.[58] Vickers' research findings apply with as much force to other imperialist countries, and may be summarised as follows: (1) the structural dependency of the imperialist economy on migrant labour; (2) the segmented structure of imperialist labour markets; (3) the polarisation in the rights and class position of different categories of migrants; and (4) the role of state repression in enforcing labour discipline.[59]

In all highly developed countries the majority of immigrant labour is channelled into and subsequently concentrated in the least desirable and most unhealthy, physically demanding, dangerous, monotonous and socially unattractive jobs.[60] In many instances, such as in France's construction industry, certain sections of manufacturing such as clothing and food processing, and service occupations such as cleaning, catering and unskilled health care, employment in such occupations has become socially devalued with native workers typically shunning work therein. In consequence, employers have become increasingly dependent upon foreign (especially female) workers.[61]

Across Europe in recent years, whereas there has been a noticeable trend towards greater inclusion of highly skilled migrants in formal rights, persistent racialised 'real economic and social exclusion' enforces the continued acceptance of low-paid and insecure employment along the lines of nationality and country of origin.[62] In some cases this meets the International Labour Organization (ILO) definition of forced labour as occurring when persons are 'coerced to work through the use of violence or intimidation, or by more subtle means such as accumulated debt, retention of identity papers or threats of denunciation to immigration authorities'.[63] The imperialist capitalism of the European Union and elsewhere has sought to strictly regulate the flow of labour from underdeveloped countries so as to ensure the payment of low wages. In the case of the European Union accession countries of the former Eastern bloc (Czech Republic, Lithuania, Estonia, Poland, Hungary, Slovakia, Latvia and Slovakia as well as Bulgaria and Romania), meanwhile, the imperialist capital of Germany, France and the United Kingdom sought to take advantage of skilled cheap labour.[64]

So-called 'managed migration' concerns itself not with the welfare of the working class, least of all of migrant workers, but with the requirements of capital.[65] In virtually all cases, the residence of migrant labour is legally held dependent on labour market demand, in no small measure explaining the establishment focus on asylum seekers' and refugees' citizenship claims allegedly transgressing this narrow economic relation.[66] Throughout Europe and North America, the mainstream parties from the left to the right wing of the imperialist political spectrum compete for votes in a bid to be the 'toughest' on proletarian immigration.

CONCLUSION

The primary concern of the labour aristocracy has always been its material differentiation from the mass of the working class as a 'bounded' and super-ordinate fraction thereof. Thus, for example, Communist Party chairman Bill Andrews championed an industrial colour bar in South Africa at the Mines Commission of 1908, compelling the Transvaal Native Congress to lobby the colonial-capitalist Chamber of Mines to protect African miners from these policies.[67] As economic historian Bill Freund writes of South Africa's settler-colonial society:

Labour, citizenship, and society were linked in complex ways that reflected a long historical development for the exploitation of black labour. A white working class that was [racially] 'bounded' profited from this system, rather like the classic assessments of worker aristocracies of Lenin and Luxemburg (used to help explain the collusion of worker organizations in policies of imperialism and war in the West), while the poorly paid workers of colour provided the core of profitable value.[68]

Above all, the labour aristocracy has struggled to hold itself apart from the reserve army of labour and its destabilising economic, political and ideological influence on more or less permanent terms. As capitalism has developed into a truly international system of production, the social dimensions of the reserve army of labour have become indissociable from the hierarchical national boundaries established by imperialism. The labour aristocracy has moved from pressing for closed shops to demanding closed borders, with its relative employment precarity determined by its location at the apex of the global labour market. As such, the intent on the part of a great many metropolitan workers to oppress, disenfranchise and exclude immigrants from full citizenship is not merely based on actual or potential competition over just any jobs but, rather, over the very best jobs capitalism has to offer.

The mass xeno-racism of metropolitan labour is an expression of labour aristocratic support for an imperialist system that subjects foreign nations in order to monopolise their natural resources and capital. That global imperialism has found it necessary to admit persons from semi-colonial countries across its borders for economic, diplomatic, political and other reasons has consistently met with the disapproval of the metropolitan workforce. This has only intensified as Keynesian social democracy has been replaced with neoliberal economic restructuring and the accompanying rise of the racialised police state. Indeed, the superwages of metropolitan labour not only depend upon militarised borders and job market discrimination, but also on the degree to which metropolitan workers can influence state policy in their own favour. In the absence of social democratic and trade union vehicles (appropriate to an earlier phase of labour aristocratic organisation), First World democracy finds its *sine qua non* in the same racist national chauvinism increasingly embraced by capital in crisis.

It is crucial to understand, then, that the anti-immigrant sentiment of native metropolitan labour is not solely the product of parochial or racist idiocy, though that assuredly follows. Absent an internationalist and socialist response, the oversupply of labour-power relative to employers' demand for it enhances the bargaining power of capitalists and degrades that of workers. As such, nativism has clear economic dynamics and is rooted in working class attempts to assert authority. Indeed, many on the left argue that immigration from low-wage countries to high-wage countries (the real object of the immigration debate as such) tends to lower wage levels in the latter and is, therefore, a reactionary policy that socialists should oppose. Typically, these critics insist that it is only a tiny plutocratic elite in the global North that benefits from global exploitation, poverty and war and that, therefore, Northern labour ought not to have to suffer any assault on its living standards as a result.

To argue for maintaining wages in the highly developed countries at their current level, however, whether consciously or not, is in fact to demand the continuation of value transfer from the less developed countries. Since it is precisely this which is responsible for mass migration to the global metropoles – the desire to escape the poverty and war wrought by imperialism for the riches brought by imperialism – it is impossible to oppose the migration of workers from the low-wage countries to the high-wage imperialist countries from a socialist perspective. Imperialist depredation is both logically and chronologically prior to mass migration from the oppressed nations, and it is both erroneous and deeply reactionary to treat the latter as a problem that can and should be solved on its own terms, that is, by means of placing restrictions on international labour mobility. Inevitably, 'socialists' seeking to advance the class interests of the metropolitan labour aristocracy are compelled to defend the First World border regimes that cement global wage differentials. Meanwhile, those individuals and groups who combine anti-imperialist rhetoric with anti-immigrant politics simply provide 'left' cover for a profoundly fascistic attack on those workers whose presence endangers metropolitan monopolies on high-waged labour.

A century ago, Lenin described the reality behind the pseudo-socialist nativism of the metropolitan labour aristocracy:

In our struggle for true internationalism and against 'jingo-socialism' we always quote in our press the example of the opportunist leaders of the S.P. [Socialist Party] in America, who are in favour of restrictions of the immigration of Chinese and Japanese workers (especially after the Congress of Stuttgart, 1907, and *against* the decisions of Stuttgart). We think that one cannot be internationalist and be at the same time in favour of such restrictions. And we assert that Socialists in America, especially English Socialists, belonging to the ruling, and *oppressing* nation, who are not against any restrictions of immigration, against the possession of colonies (Hawaii) and for the entire freedom of colonies, that such Socialists are in reality jingoes.[69]

The 'socialism' of the native workforce of the major imperialist countries today, the world's richest by a large margin, is characterised by an imperialist economism that refuses to acknowledge the need to prioritise the struggle for an end to the militarism and neo-colonialism that typifies the capitalist world system. By confining itself to demanding the betterment of its own conditions by any means, including by repudiating solidarity with the world's most exploited wage-earners dispossessed by imperialism, the national socialism of the metropolitan labour aristocracy and its intellectual and political champions is destined to lead it to the social fascist embrace of business nationalists and imperial expansionists.

To summarise, the occupation of indigenous land establishes the basis for *settler land ownership*, the employment of a specially oppressed layer of the metropolitan working class in lower-wage occupations yields *discrimina-*

tion profits, and the enclosure of specially oppressed metropolitan workers in such occupations yields *discrimination wages*. Meanwhile, the imperialist exploitation of foreign labour generates metropolitan *superprofits* and allows for metropolitan *superwages*. We may thus conclude this part of the present work by defining the modern labour aristocracy in the following terms.

As capitalism comes increasingly to form an international system of commodity production, the labour aristocracy is thereby constituted as a superordinate section of the workforce whose relative affluence derives from the politically secured exploitation of subordinate national groups within a system of imperialism. Insofar as it is able to capture or maintain a dominant position in the labour market established by means of the latter, in particular, in the context of militarised borders and relatively exclusive access to training and employment opportunities in sectors dependent upon value transfer, the labour aristocracy guarantees its receipt of superwages, that is, wages incrementally higher than the median value of labour-power internationally. At the extreme end of the scale, superwages are those wages approaching or in excess of the per capita value of labour in the capitalist world system. In other words, superwages are those wages which cost more international labour time than their recipients themselves contribute, and thus represent what Hosea Jaffe called 'negative surplus value'.

Whether or not a group of workers is superexploited is obvious insofar as that involves the payment of sub-subsistence wages. To determine whether a particular group of workers is exploited is more difficult, however, and cannot, of course, be linked to either levels of oppression or to the receipt of wages as such. We argue that determining levels of exploitation for different groups of workers requires comparing the wage bundle (w_1, the quantity of goods and services afforded by the sale of labour-power) of workers in group A to the wage bundle (w_2) of the totality of workers in group B involved in the production of w_1; that is, to determine whether workers in group A are able to purchase with one hour of their labour a greater amount of group B's labour as a condition of institutionally different rates of exploitation, those established by imperialism. We argue that a minority of the world's workers (those living in the developed countries) effectively consumes more of the world's labour than it contributes itself.

Part IV
Social Imperialism
Past and Present

12
Social Imperialism before the First World War

In this part of the book, we present an overview of social-imperialist (or imperialist socialist) political practice in Europe over the last century, demonstrating that anti-imperialism has neither been properly prioritised by the metropolitan left in its political practice nor organically integrated into left class analysis.[1] Whereas Engels had pointed to the existence of a 'bourgeois proletariat' dependent upon the maintenance of imperialism for its relative prosperity, we suggest that this *embourgeoisement* has also produced a 'bourgeois socialism' and even a 'bourgeois Marxism' to justify the maintenance of imperialism's split labour market.[2] In this chapter, we will describe the tradition of social imperialism in the half century and more before the First World War, a watershed moment in labour history when the Socialist parties in each of the major belligerent powers gave in to their pre-existing national chauvinist and racist tendencies in a catastrophic way. Before proceeding, however, we will outline how the social-imperialist attitude of the metropolitan labour movement was reflected in some of the views of its most militant and perceptive progenitors.

ON MARX AND ENGELS' EUROCENTRISM

Karl Marx (1818–1883) was the first person to study human society in a scientific way, explaining how society evolves according to the development of the productive forces (that is, both technology and technical skills); how the development of the productive forces shapes the emergence of social classes defined in relation to their ownership and usage, and their share of value accruing from the same; and how conflict between these classes both conditions the further development of the productive forces and shapes the dominant political, ideological and cultural forms in society. Marx was the first person to apply scientific socialist thinking to the analysis of the capitalist economy, an epochal mode of production that currently encompasses the entire planet. Marx's central contribution to our understanding of capitalism is his theory of value and his understanding of exploitation and economic crisis under capitalism. Crucially, Marx understood the primacy of class struggle in advancing human progress, and how government by the proletariat would ensure the transition from capitalism to socialism, that is, from a lower to a higher mode of production based on production for human need and not for private profit.

Marx's analysis is indispensable to understanding the international political economy today. That Marx was profoundly wrong about the revolutionary character of the Western proletariat (today a full grown working bourgeoisie) does not detract from the aforementioned contributions he made, as well as many others, and nor does the racist and Eurocentric outlook evinced by some of Marx and Engels' writings. Leaving aside those writings of Marx and Engels that point to innate racial differences as explanations for variations in social development across human societies,[3] as well as the authors' use of anti-Jewish and anti-African physiognomic slurs (particularly as used in private to denigrate German socialist Ferdinand Lasalle), Marx and Engels often displayed an indifferent and even contemptuous attitude to those nations they believed stood in the way of capitalist progress. Thus, for instance, in an article published in the *Deutsche-Brusseler Zeitung* of 23 January 1848, Engels wrote:

> In America we have witnessed the conquest of Mexico and have rejoiced at it. It is also an advance when a country which has hitherto been exclusively wrapped up in its own affairs, perpetually rent with civil wars, and completely hindered in its development, a country whose best prospect had been to become industrially subject to Britain – when such a country is forcibly drawn into the historical process. It is to the interest of its own development that Mexico will in future be placed under the tutelage of the United States.[4]

Marx himself had characterised Mexico's Indian population as 'the last of men'.[5] Later, in an article written for the *Neue Rhenische Zeitung* of 15 February 1849, Engels wrote:

> Is it a misfortune that the wonderful California was wrested from the lazy Mexicans, who did not know what to do with it? ... All impotent nations must, in the final analysis, be grateful to those who, obeying historical necessities, attach them to a great empire, thus allowing them participation in a historical development which would otherwise be unknown to them. It is self-evident that such a result could not be obtained without crushing some sweet little flowers. Without violence, nothing can be accomplished in history ... .[6]

In 1848, the French Army under General Bugeaud conquered Algeria, thus initiating more than a century of brutal and exploitative French colonial rule in the country. Following the capture of Algerian resistance leader, the Emir Abdelkader in Algeria and with that the victory of French colonialist forces, Engels wrote

Upon the whole, it is, in our opinion, very fortunate that the Arabian chief has been taken. The struggle of the Bedouins was a hopeless one, and though the manner in which brutal soldiers like Bugeaud have carried on the war is highly blameable, the conquest of Algeria is an important and fortunate fact for the progress of civilisation ... After all, the modern bourgeois, with civilisation, industry, order, and at least the relative enlightenment following him, is preferable to the feudal lord or to the marauding robber, with the barbarian state of society to which they belong.[7]

What was entailed in practice by this bourgeois civilisation, industry, order and enlightenment is starkly revealed in the following passage:

It must be noted that throughout the early period of colonization the Algerian population was forced to provide labour for the construction of roads, the building of *centres de colonisation*, and to perform various other services without any compensation. From 1830 to 1871, forced labour was a standard phenomenon in Algeria; the 'requisition of native manpower for public utility work' was used by army officers in their attempt to oppose the introduction of the Arab workers into the centers of colonization, since they feared they would lose their free labourers to the colonies who offered some sort of wages. But on October 15, 1851, the minister of war, who was in charge of Algeria, rejected the objection of the army in the following terms: 'The introduction, on a large scale, of the Arab or Kabyle manpower into agricultural work is a goal toward which the administration has to concentrate all its efforts and has to pursue by all means in its power. *It is obvious, in effect, that without this powerful auxiliary, cultivation would be for a long time shackled by the high wages and scarcity of European workers*' [Archives Nationales de France, F80443].[8]

The Algerians worked for the French colonial settlers as sharecroppers, and also as wage-labourers on a daily or a monthly basis. In 1851, they were paid between 2 and 2 and one-half francs per day. After studying the wage scaling between Arab and French labourers, a French colonial official observed:

I have indicated what is more important and it is easy to judge the enormous difference in the sum to be paid for the employment of an Arab labourer in contradistinction to that offered to a French labourer ... It is sufficient to ensure that the price paid to the indigenous worker will not ordinarily exceed the fourth of that which we are obliged to give to the European worker [Archives Nationales de France, F80443].[9]

Moore has pointed to Marx and Engels' lack of concern for the struggles of African and African-descended working people around the world, and has suggested that their support for the anti-slavery side in the American Civil War (1861–65) was much less motivated by a concern to uplift the conditions of the slave population of the US South than it was to avoid a victory by the slave states, a victory they feared would lead to the enslavement of the Northern white proletariat.[10] Indeed, other than supporting the Union side in the American Civil War, the First International Workingmen's Association established by Marx, Engels and others in 1869 had

nothing whatsoever to say about the greatest issues of the time – western colonial conquests around the globe, the slave trade, the enslavement of millions of Blacks in the sugar and cotton plantations of the Americas. The 'First International' was concerned *exclusively* with the white proletarian masses of the West; it was a 'White Workers' International' which didn't give a damn about what was happening to the non-white working masses of Africa, Asia, Oceania and the Americas, except when the struggles of these peoples could be harnessed to procure advantages for the Aryan working class.[11]

Indeed, the Paris Commune of 1871, the first time in history that the proletariat as such had conquered state power, albeit briefly, did not for a moment propose to liberate the French colonies. Despite their outrage at some of the 'bleeding practices' employed by British colonialism in India, Marx and Engels were committed to the view that colonial liberation would be a gift bestowed upon the non-white world by the European proletariat. Engels himself had presented such a view when, in his letter to Karl Kautsky of 12 September 1882, he wrote: '[The] countries inhabited by a native population, which are simply subjugated, India, Algeria, the Dutch Portuguese, and Spanish possessions must be taken over for the time being by the proletariat and led as rapidly as possible towards independence.'[12] This view might be charitably described as a 'paternalist social imperialism', were it not for the fact that the European proletariat was already both dependent upon and committed to the maintenance of the system of imperialist plunder. Under the circumstances, it could hardly be expected to be as generous as Engels imagined it would.

SOCIAL IMPERIALISM AND THE INVERSION OF LABOUR INTERNATIONALISM

Social imperialism is the practice of affording all classes in a capitalist country a material stake in the status quo by means of drawing sufficiently great resources from the exploitation of foreign nations that all may share to some extent in the associated economic benefits. Thus, in the period before the First World War, governments began to set unyielding obstacles in the way of socialist internationalism by embarking upon national programmes of social reform and, at the same time, imperial expansion.[13] From the 1880s onward, the policy of social imperialism was pursued as a way of responding to the crisis of the Great Depression.[14]

In Germany, where the practice was most highly developed, intellectuals provided a theoretical justification for Bismarck's social policy, a combination of protectionism and social imperialism.[15] Throughout the Second Reich (1871–1918), vocal appeals were made in support of integrating the increasingly militant German working class into the political life of the nation. Some middle class democratic radicals favourable to liberalism were afraid of losing the support of the proletariat in their endeavours to modernise Germany's semi-feudal society. As what Hobsbawm refers to as a 'prophylactic' against revolutionary class struggle, intellectuals associated with this trend (such as the 'Socialist Professors' – *Kathedersozialisten* – who formed the influential School for Social Policy – *Verein für Sozialpolitik* – in 1872) advocated both imperialism and social reform in favour of the working class.[16]

Leading *Kathedersozialist* economist Gustav Schmoller argued that German imperialism was necessitated and justified by the fact that only three 'world-states' – Britain, Russia and the United States – owned territories so vast and highly populated that they might rely upon internal markets to bring progress to their national citizenry. For Schmoller, capitalism requires export markets to survive and so long as it can expand on this basis, both businessmen and workers have a real interest in imperialism.[17] German Chancellor Otto von Bismark sought to channel burgeoning industrial discontent amidst economic crisis into popular support for German imperialism. This was principally focused on securing markets for the delivery of raw materials, the sale of commodities and the export of surplus labour-power which wealthy lobbyists assured Bismarck could be best achieved by means of imperialism.[18] This would generate great employment opportunities and, at the same time, national pride in a period of otherwise acute domestic class conflict.[19]

In common with their European counterparts, German elites under Kaiser Wilhelm II considered that social cohesion and class peace depended upon their country's strength in the world economy,

> encompassing everything from colonial policy to the arms race and the big navy, export drives and trading policy, the competitiveness of the German economy in world markets, questions of migration and mainte-nance of ties with Germans overseas, German diplomacy and the wider realms of Weltpolitik, and of course the final brinkmanship of the July crisis and Germany's unfolding aims during the First World War.[20]

As early as 1878, a German newspaper had proclaimed the need for the government to organise large-scale colonial migration 'as a safety valve against social problems'. In a different newspaper, an aristocratic colonialist expressed his view that 'German social democracy could not be fought more effectively than by means of colonialism'.[21] Similarly, Austro-Hungarian journalist and Zionist Theodor Herzl considered that the colonisation of Palestine could put a stop to the problem of the rise of revolutionary movements among the poor Jews of Europe.[22]

Colonialism did indeed prove a sure means of quelling the desire for revolutionary change on the part of the European proletariat and petty-bourgeoisie. By offering employment as 'soldiers, employees, and foremen on plantations and in mines (where the natives served as slaves), low-ranking bureaucrats in the colonial administration, and even missionar-ies', Empire offered an escape from misery for the less privileged inhabitants of the metropolitan nations.[23] As eminent German sociologist Max Weber wrote in 1894:

> Only complete political confusion and naive optimism can prevent the recognition that the unavoidable efforts at trade expansion by all civilized [sic] bourgeois-controlled nations, after a transitional period of seemingly peaceful competition, are clearly approaching the point where power alone will decide each nation's share in the economic control of the earth, and hence its peoples sphere of activity, *and especially its workers' earning potential.*[24]

In Britain, meanwhile, social reformer, colonial investor and represent-ative of the Midlands engineering industry Joseph Chamberlain drew widespread support for his campaign to construct preferential Imperial markets. In his role as MP and Colonial Secretary, the avowed social imperialism of Chamberlain impressed upon the working class the view that imperialist economic protectionism would enhance and increase its living standards. While preferential markets for colonial goods would raise their prices, the British working class could be counted on to support the Empire on the basis of better pay and more work, as well as old age pensions, all funded from tariff revenues raised against rival imperialists' imports. Though this system was later implemented by Prime Minister Neville Chamberlain (Joseph's grandson) under the 1932 Ottawa Conference system of imperial preferences, Chamberlain's particular brand of social imperialism based on Tariff Reform aimed at uniting the Empire, providing the revenue for social reform and protecting British steel and agriculture failed because Britain continued to derive benefits from free trade right up until the 1930s. These advantages were based upon Britain's possession of the colonies which provided it with protected markets and opportunities for investment entirely lacking in post-war Weimar Germany.[25]

British social imperialism drew upon the writings of critics of ostensibly laissez-faire (though actually colonialist) capitalism such as Thomas Carlyle (1795–1881), John Ruskin (1819–1900), Charles Dickens (1812–1870) and William James Ashley (1860–1927), a follower of Gustav Schmoller.[26] Perhaps most influentially, social imperialism was advocated by Benjamin Disraeli (1804–1881), who would later become Conservative Prime Minister. 'All is race' wrote Disraeli, 'there is no other truth'. Disraeli's industrial era take on *noblesse oblige* was expressed in his novel *Sybil, or The Two Nations*, the title itself referring to the lamentable gap between the rich and the poor in the England of his day. Like his German counterparts, Disraeli found the solution to this politically portentous class divide in imperialism combined with social reform. Thus in 1867, Disraeli introduced the Second Reform Bill to the Houses of Parliament in England, which reduced property requirements for voting. Once the bill was passed in both Houses, workers above a certain income threshold were given the vote.

Despite its relatively limited scope, working class enfranchisement certainly attracted popular support for the government. Yet Disraeli's imperialist national chauvinism proved still more popular. Indeed, prior to the outbreak of the First World War, European militarism was primarily directed against colonial areas, where brutal wars of conquest and pacification were repeatedly fought. Given that these had been of a limited nature, were cheap and short-lived, with only miniscule losses on the European side, but masses of wounded and killed on the enemy side, and had been widely acclaimed by the mainstream media of the day, they proved to be immensely popular affairs, particularly in Britain where they occurred with greater frequency than anywhere else:

[Although] doubts remain concerning Disraeli's motives in widening the franchise, there was one area where undoubtedly he did win over working-class support to the side of Conservatism. His judgement that imperialism would have special appeal for a large part of the electorate proved remarkably percipient. For all the high-flown rhetoric that so often accompanied Imperialism, the reality was that colonial expansion was an affair of British armies on the ground in foreign lands. Since the rank and file came from the working class, most ordinary families had a father, son or brother for a soldier; they were thus linked in a chain of personal interest in Britain's foreign ventures. It is arguable that, in the last quarter of the century, Imperialism – with its appeal to patriotism – proved as popular as social reform in persuading the bulk of the working class to give Disraeli's new brand of Conservatism a sympathetic hearing.[27]

In England, social imperialism was upheld by influential Labour Party MP and, later, leader of the British Union of Fascists Sir Oswald Mosley who, standing for the Conservative Party in the elections of 1918, explicitly declared his policy to be that of 'socialistic imperialism'.[28] In his 1907 book, *Labour and the Empire*, British Labour Party leader Ramsay Macdonald had also espoused 'socialist imperialism'.[29] While feeling 'the pride of race', Macdonald assured his readers that British socialist imperialism was a quite beneficent species of the genus:

Its imperialism is ... not of the aggressive or the bragging order; it does not believe in the subjection of other nationalities; it takes no pride in the government of other peoples. To its subject-races, it desires to occupy the position of friend.[30]

The 'friendliness' of British socialists' means of governing their 'subject races' was demonstrated, inter alia, by the wave of beatings, shootings, aerial bombardment and imprisonment implemented by them between 1929 and 1931 during the first phase of India's mass civil disobedience movement. This was no aberration, however. For while some individuals within the Labour Party, typically while not in power, did voice anti-colonial concerns, 'Labour governments invariably sought to defend the empire, and even when they promised reform, this was always advocated as a way of making the empire stronger, [along the lines of] an "ethical imperialism".'[31] As early as 1872, with respect to Britain's oldest and last remaining colony, that of Ireland, Engels himself had asked: 'After the domination of the English aristocracy over Ireland, after the domination of the English middle class over Ireland ... must we now look forward to the advent of the domination of the English working class over Ireland?'[32] By the time of the ruling British

Labour Party's introduction of internment without trial in the occupied six counties of northeastern Ireland in 1975, the answer was already crystal clear.

In France, social imperialism was propounded by the monarchist Charles Maurras (1868–1952), who attempted to fuse French national chauvinism and syndicalism to combat liberal democracy, the syndicalist Georges Sorel (1847–1922) who did the same from a 'left-wing' position, and the eugenicist anthropologist and Socialist Worker's Party candidate Georges Vacher de Lapouge (1854–1936). As early as 1879, in a speech commemorating the end of slavery no less, the great French poet, novelist and artist Victor Hugo (1802–1885), who was liberal democratic in his political views, wrote:

> Go forward, the nations! Grasp this land! Take it! From whom? From no one. Take this land from God! God gives the earth to men. God offers Africa to Europe. Take it! Where the kings brought war, bring concord! Take it, not for the cannon but for the plough! Not for the sabre but for commerce! Not for battle but for industry! Not for conquest but for fraternity! Pour out every thing you have in this Africa, and at the same stroke solve your own social questions! *Change your proletarians into property-owners!* Go on, do it! Make roads, make ports, make towns! Grow, cultivate, colonize, multiply! And on this land, ever clearer of priests and princes, may the divine spirit assert itself through peace and the human spirit through liberty![33]

Meanwhile, Maurice Wahl, a high-ranking French colonial official, wrote the following in a book entitled *France in the Colonies*:

> Owing to the growing complexities of life and the difficulties which weigh not only on the masses of the workers, but also on the middle classes, impatience, irritation and hatred are accumulating in all the countries of the old civilisation and are becoming a menace to public order; the energy which is being hurled out of the definite class channel must be given employment abroad in order to avert an explosion at home.[34]

Likewise, French philosopher and Orientalist specialising in the ancient cultures of the Middle East, Ernest Renan declared that colonialism was 'the only way to counter socialism'. 'A nation that does not colonise,' he explained, 'is condemned to end up with socialism, to experience a war between rich and poor.'[35] Left Republican and twice Prime Minister of France (1880–1881, 1883–1885) Jules Ferry was to the fore in implementing colonial policy as a means of expanding the market for French industrial exports. Ferry was plain in admitting the economic motivations behind his country's colonialism, but conveniently decided that plunder of the colonies and the slaughter and exploitation of their inhabitants was also the right and duty of the superior races:

> Gentlemen, we must speak more loudly and more honestly! We must say openly that indeed the higher races have a right over the lower races ... I repeat, that the superior races have a right because they have a duty. They have the duty to civilize the inferior races ... In the history of earlier centuries these duties, gentlemen, have often been misunderstood; and certainly when the Spanish soldiers and explorers introduced slavery into Central America, they did not fulfil their duty as men of a higher race ... But, in our time, I maintain that European nations acquit themselves with generosity, with grandeur, and with sincerity of this superior civilizing duty.[36]

Meanwhile, the most militant sections of Italian revolutionary syndicalism had studiously observed the national chauvinism of the international socialist movement. Demonstrating the unreality behind the rhetoric of proletarian internationalism, many of its leading intellectuals and advocates concluded that national aggrandisement would afford the comparatively backward Italian working class the same economic and political strength that it had the working classes of other European nations. Thus future member of Mussolini's governing Grand Fascist Council Edmondo Rossoni had organised Italian workers in New York before returning to Italy with his syndicalist brand of ultra-nationalism. Reflecting upon his experiences with the ethnic discrimination practised not only by employers, but also by workers in the United States, Rossoni rejected the hypocrisy of socialist internationalist orthodoxy. Similarly, fellow syndicalist and nationalist Alceste de Ambris (who would later become critical of the fascist movement that his ideology had greatly influenced) had described the hierarchy existing within the US industrial proletariat: 'The immigrants from Italy know that the improvement of the salaries of the Italians in the United States is a chimera. There the sons of the Abruzzi and of Sicily empty the garbage and wash the dirty clothes even of the American workers. The Italians are the servants of their American "comrades".'[37]

Whereas the Italian working class had been opposed to their country's ultimately unsuccessful attempt to conquer Ethiopia in 1896, a decade of Giolittian social reforms had convinced them of their common national interest in wresting Libya from Turkey in 1911.[38] Liberal Prime Minister Giovanni Giolitti (1842–1928) had himself averred that Italy's Great Power status could be attained 'not by shooting the workers, but rather by instilling in them a deep affection for our institutions so that we ourselves and not the socialists will be seen as the promoters of progress and as the ones who are trying to do everything possible in their favour'.[39] Advocating Italian participation in the First World War on the side of the Allied powers won revolutionary syndicalist turned reformist Marxist Arturo Labriola (1873– 1959) a place as Minister of Labour in Giolitti's wartime cabinet. In his writings of 1912 and 1915, *La guerra di Tripoli e l'apirlioru socialista* and *La conflagrazione europa e il socialism*, Labriola had attempted to describe the underlying causes of the failure of proletarian internationalism. In the first place, Labriola pointed to the psychological and ideological roots of the problem:

[The] effects which belonging to a political unity predominant in the military and economic sphere have had on the psychology of the working classes. The way the American unions treat foreign workers; the ill-concealed disdain of German workers for Italian immigrants … the international dictatorship of German Social Democracy in the socialist congresses; all this demonstrates that the feelings of hegemony of the upper classes pass even into the working classes, and that it is not probable that their arrival in power would coincide with renunciation of their by-then customary hegemony.[40]

Second, Labriola noted the economic factors leading to division amongst the international proletariat, factors unforeseen either by Marx or his intellectual progeny. Central to these was the protectionism adopted by the leading capitalist powers in the late 1870s which had forged links between consumers and producers in each imperialist country:

Capitalist society … makes the barriers between countries even higher – thanks to the import duties of every kind – and thus the proletariat very well did come to have a fatherland, so that in America the Italians – precisely because of their fatherland – were declared undesirables, and negotiations between national states proved necessary to obtain legal protection for immigrant labour; otherwise those dear proletarians without a country would not have found even a dog that would have concerned himself with them![41]

With the expansion of capitalism's sphere of exploitation abroad, and the implementation of trade and tariff measures favouring export industries and purchasing power in the metropolitan regions, workers in the imperialist countries were given a stake in the successes of their respective ruling classes. It was this common interest of capitalists and workers in the metropolitan countries established on the basis of imperialism that best explains the disdain shown by Socialist parties for the workers of 'backward' countries and led them to support their own governments as they waged imperialist war. Simply put, for Labriola and other Italian syndicalists, 'socialist internationalism could [not] have any practical effect as long as some capitalist countries were more prosperous than others – and as long as protection and imperialism cemented the differences'.[42]

Those Italian syndicalists who turned to imperialist nationalism and fascism criticised imperialism from the perspective of an allegedly 'proletarian nation' facing 'plutocratic nations' and attempting to garner its fair share of the spoils of the redivision of the world amongst the great monopolies. The logic of their politics was one of 'if you can't beat them, join them!' Thus, revolutionary syndicalist and later leading fascist Paolo Orano considered Italian participation in the First World War as an epoch-making vehicle for Italy's national redemption. The industry, discipline and self-confidence to be generated under a wartime economy would finally fit the politically and economically immature Italian working class to found society anew, forging 'the new miracle, that Italy of the labour aristocracy that can be the model of every other people that intends to endure'.[43]

SOCIAL DEMOCRACY AND COLONIALISM
BEFORE THE FIRST WORLD WAR

Renowned social historian and Trotskyist Fritjof Tichelman (1929–2012) has demonstrated that whereas internationalism within Europe itself was a marginal phenomenon, in colonial matters it was even less influential.[44] He argues that British and Dutch labour took a relatively liberal approach to colonial reform compared with the 'nationalist colonialism' of French socialists and the 'nationalist imperialism' of the right wing of German social democracy from around 1907. In all four cases, however, fear of losing international status ensured that the left consistently preferred national conservatism to anti-colonial revolution.[45]

For Tichelman, Marx's view of the struggle leading to world socialist society was inspired by a naive sort of 'liberal economism', the view that the inexorable global expansion of capitalism would erode all national barriers and create a revolutionary working class in all countries.[46] Although Marx's teleological determinism was tempered in later years through his studies of Russian agriculture and the possibility that Russia may be able to bypass strictly capitalist development, as well as by his observation of the negative role colonialism in Ireland played within British working class politics, it was Leninism that first elaborated the prospect that it was the least developed capitalist countries that would pave the way to socialism. For mainstream social democracy, capitalism was seen as a necessary and civilising force for progress in the underdeveloped areas of the world, although its directly colonial form was not necessarily to be celebrated. Accordingly, the First International Working Men's Association (IWMA) did not occupy itself with colonial or non-Western matters and it did not explicitly extend the principle of national self-determination beyond Europe and America.[47]

The growth of powerful labour institutions and organisations, and the wave of strikes witnessed in the final quarter of the nineteenth century did not preclude the 'integration' of leading elites and layers of the working class in the ruling apparatus of bourgeois European and American society.[48] Indeed, in no small measure as a result of its incorporation within imperialist institutions, the labour movement as a whole decidedly failed the test of internationalism, providing little or no support to the national liberation struggles in the colonies and vouchsafing the militarism of Europe's rival ruling classes.[49]

Insofar as the labour movement concerned itself with colonialism at all, the colonial policy of the Second International was largely pacifist and humanitarian, prioritising the prevention of war occurring as the outcome of great power rivalry around imperialist expansion and, secondarily, the ostensibly humanitarian need to protect, educate and 'civilise' the natives of the colonies.[50] Whereas before the Seventh Congress in Stuttgart, August 1907, the parties of the Second International tended to view these broad goals as best achieved under the ambit of moderate anti-colonialism, afterward they shifted their strategy to one of reforming colonial practices.[51] In the case of the SPD (*Sozialdemokratische Partei Deutschlands*) in Germany, this shift may in part be traced to significant parliamentary losses suffered by the party during the so-called 'Hottentot' elections of earlier that year. When the SPD alongside the Catholic Centre Party took a principled stand by denying support for government funding for the suppression of the Nama rebellion in Germany's Southwest Africa colony (modern-day Namibia), it was subjected to a concerted political campaign calling into question its patriotic and democratic credentials. From then on, the liberation of the oppressed non-European peoples was a decidedly subsidiary matter for the party. In fact, only in the cases of *la Semana Trágica* (Tragic Week) in Barcelona, 25 July to 2 August 1909 (precipitated by the Spanish government's calling-up of reserve troops to be sent to Morocco as reinforcements for the Second Rif War), and the resistance in Italy to the conquest of Libya two years later was there any mass resistance in Europe to colonial wars. In both instances, the struggle against colonial expansion was secondary to the struggle against reactionary forces directly threatening the labour movement itself.[52]

The history of British labour is, according to Tichelman, determined by the preponderance of the struggle for 'the direct material and social interests of the [British] workers', much more than by democratic principles. The relative success of this struggle in the context of British capitalism's outward expansion explains the endurance of early to mid-nineteenth-century Liberal and humanitarian ideals on the (centre) left. On the whole, British labour's internationalism was selective, preferring limited practical cooperation to democratic principle.[53] The domestic counterpart of social imperialism, with the national economy bolstered by imperialist capital, was a reformist attempt to integrate the increasingly numerous middle class workers into capitalism's integument.

In the 1880s and 1890s a number of small, newly formed socialist groups in Britain advocated resistance to the 'formal imperialism' of the period. These were anti-expansionist rather than anti-colonialist. They influenced the indifference and hostility of many workers to the Boer War, but they were not always more popular than the jingoism of the 'imperialist lobby'.[54] As Tichelman concludes, '[t]he Empire was accepted virtually by everybody, as became evident after the Boer War'.[55] Nonetheless, the Independent Labour Party (ILP), affiliated to the Labour Party from 1906 to 1932, presented a somewhat more critical social democratic and pacifist view of imperialist policy than either the Labour Party itself or the Trades Union Congress (TUC). Yet it did not achieve great popularity with its stance, and it remained muted in any case.[56]

By the turn of the last century, a pro-colonialist trend had become clearly discernible within the European socialist movement, while an opposite line emerged holding that colonial independence was a precondition for socialism in the metropoles.[57] At the Sixth Congress of the Socialist International held in Amsterdam in August 1904, Dutch social democrats proposed a narrowly defeated resolution espousing the legitimacy of 'socialist colonialism'. While disagreeing with the colonial policies pursued by the Dutch government, addressing the Congress was veteran Dutch socialist Henri van Kol. A year earlier he had described the benevolence of the colonial project as overseen by socialists such as himself in his book *Uit Onze Koloniën* (*From Our Colonies*). 'We must,' he implored, 'lead this people lovingly, augment the riches of the country as benevolent caretakers, and increase the wealth of its inhabitants. In this magnificent country we will support these good people when they stumble in their suffering path to the Sublime!' Though presenting himself as sympathetic to the interests of the indigenous inhabitants of the East Indies, the book's characterisations of them (the 'indolent Javanese', the 'dishonest, self-indulgent Amboinese', the Chinese coolie with his 'revolting [homosexual] habits') reveals a less supportive outlook. At any rate, van Kol generously donated some of the profits from his coffee plantation in Java ... to his home country's markedly liberal labour movement.[58]

13
Social Imperialism after
the First World War

In this chapter, we will describe the tradition of European social imperialism in the period between the end of the First World War in 1918 and the period of the decolonisation of Africa and Asia (1945–60). In this period, the metropolitan workforce, that is, the labour aristocracy supplying a mass base for social democracy, signally failed to demonstrate any significant degree of solidarity with the oppressed working people in the 'developing' countries.

SOCIAL IMPERIALISM IN THE INTERWAR YEARS

The mass mobilisation of labour and the Levée en masse of troops, which the expansion of capitalism overseas in the preceding century had hitherto allowed the ruling bourgeoisies to avoid, meant that the European working class was in a greatly strengthened position during and after the First World War. Indeed, many workers enlisted not only out of a sense of nationalist duty, but also as a means to advance their class interests, in the assumption that the sacrifices they made would bear fruit in the form of higher pay and an extension of welfare reform. As the war dragged on and became increasingly Hellish for its participants, labour militancy spread like wildfire across Europe, particularly in the wake of the Bolshevik revolution in October 1917. After the war, European social democracy enjoyed much greater political influence and living standards, and so again after the Second World War. It did not use its political and social standing to combat imperialism, however. On the contrary, for it was imperialism which allowed the bourgeois elites to incorporate a highly organised and powerful labour movement into capitalist state structures.

Paul Lensch, an early opponent of revisionism in Germany's Social Democratic Party (SPD), wrote a book at the war's end in 1918 that was an open endorsement of Germany as a 'revolutionary' vehicle for state socialism as against the 'bourgeois individualism' of England. Lensch considered that after the war Germany would be enabled to recover by means of an efficient 'socialist' exploitation of the resources of the colonies, something which would equally benefit their 'primitive' inhabitants as it would the German working class:

> After the war, colonial policy will be of the nature of a social policy, for only if the colonial representatives of a government were conscious of their responsibilities as guardians of the interests of the colony, would there be any prospect of making the Colonies what, in the interests of our whole culture and material conduct of life it is essential that they should be: the pillars of that international, or rather intercontinental, division of labour by which the temperate zones are supplied with those indispensable raw materials and fodder stuffs, without which the maintenance of our industrial and agricultural development is impossible ... We cannot in the future allow these productive districts, full of unquarried wealth, to be abandoned to chance or to the money-getting instincts of private capitalists. In order to recover economically from the terrible catastrophe of the war, we need to develop all the productive powers at our disposal. Just because in the Colonies, the cream has already been skimmed off the surface, the tropical zone will in future only yield up its treasures as the white man undertakes the prodigious work of the opening up and cleansing of the Tropics.[1]

The reconstituted Second International was established in Berne, Switzerland, in February 1919. When in 1920 the headquarters of the Second International were placed in London, the British Labour Party effectively took charge of the moribund organisation's affairs.[2] Unsurprisingly, the post-war Second International's first priority was not to advocate self-determination for the colonies, to India or to Ireland but, rather, to relentlessly insist on its utmost urgency for Georgia, where the country's Menshevik government had distinguished itself by putting down peasant revolts (especially amongst national minorities), suppressing the Communist Party and waging war with Armenia over disputed territory.[3] At its Brussels Congress of 1928, the Second International adopted a social democratic programme for the colonies favouring the extension and intensification of the League of Nations' mandate system (essentially a pseudo-democratic form of imperial annexation); protection of native labour and living conditions; and gradual socio-economic and political reform in the direction of 'home rule' government other than for China, Egypt, Iraq and Syria, which should become independent. However, given its increasing rightward and anti-communist drift, even this was to become a dead letter.[4] Indeed, the more left-wing successor organisation to the defunct Second International, the Labour and Socialist International generally supported colonialism, with partial exceptions.[5]

Although some cooperation at the trade union level did take place, hostility towards radical nationalist movements in the colonies was strong in the European labour movement before the Second World War, preventing solidarity between the Socialist parties of the imperialist countries and the socialist and nationalist organisations of the colonial world. During the interwar period in France, government policy became to transform overseas possession into colonies, a shift in policy which may be attributed to the rallying of socialists to colonialism.[6] In 1925 Leon Blum, the leader of the Socialist Party in France (SFIO, *Section Française de L'Internationale Ouvriere*), who introduced labour legislation designed to protect native rights in 'French' India, stated: 'We recognize the right and even the duty of superior races to draw unto them those which have not arrived at the same level of culture.'[7] None of the three parties composing the French Popular Front government of 1936–38, namely, the Radical Party, the Socialist Party and the Communist Party, was 'unconditionally anti-colonial' and their devotion to reform was 'at best equivocal'.[8] When out of government all three parties opposed particular colonialist policies, especially military expeditions, but abandoned their critical stance when entering government.[9] Despite earlier opposition to colonialism, by the turn of the last century, the majority of France's Radical Party favoured colonial empire, albeit a reformed one ostensibly more attuned to the interests of the native population.[10] At the same time, although French socialists before the First World War had 'generous explosions of indignation … it was difficult for them to avoid being accustomed to colonialism, to accept the empire implicitly'.[11] Whereas the leading force within the Popular Front, the SFIO tended to urge a conservative approach to colonial policy, 'even encouraging repression', the Radical Party actively supported repression.[12]

French Jacobin nationalism and perceptions of French cultural superiority did not provide a fertile ground for internationalism. The overwhelming majority of French socialists came to identify French wellbeing with the fate of mankind – France's *mission civilisatrice* – with only a minority current voicing largely rhetorical opposition to colonialism.[13] In relation to Algeria, for instance, the great majority of French socialists and the French labour movement were unambiguously colonialist, with both social democratic and communist branches in the colony thoroughly infused with settler-colonial ideology and exerting considerable conservative pressure on the respective metropolitan parties. Class and national questions surrounding land ownership, labour conditions, political representation and cultural advancement for the majority Arab population were elided in favour of the assimilation through the education system of a narrow Arab elite.[14]

In Britain, the Labour Party, though struggling to obtain and keep power for much of the last century – forming a government briefly in 1924, between

1929 and 1931, 1945 and 1951, 1964 and 1970, 1974 and 1976 and between 1997 and 2007, a total of 27 years – received a plurality of working and middle class support for its agenda, having over 380,000 members in 2016. Though Tichelman is perhaps correct that British labour was more accommodating to anti-colonial demands than its influential French or German counterparts, its class basis in the metropolitan labour aristocracy denied it genuine democratic potential. Defence of imperialist capitalism has proved to be a more pressing and less distant imperative for British labour to pursue than the construction of socialism. If anti-colonialism is defined as a commitment 'first, to the basic equality of European and non-European peoples and cultures and to the right of all nations to self-determination; and secondly to political action aimed at eradicating colonialism in one's own country as well as in others, and to international as well as national work', then there was very little of it displayed by the European labour movement before the Second World War.[15]

Whereas the British labour movement was more tacitly than actively supportive of Empire before the 1920s, afterwards it developed its own colonial policy.[16] British labour's interest in the colonies in the interwar years was primarily motivated by two concerns. First, there was apprehension that the British Empire might completely collapse as a result of the rise of national liberation movements throughout the colonies. Second, the example set by Bolshevism and the anti-imperialist Communist International it had founded also provoked realistic fears of the Empire's disintegration.[17] Since many anti-colonial activists came to identify increasingly with communist internationalism as a force for national liberation, the British Labour Party (particularly when in power in 1924) began to belatedly focus on the prudent formulation of colonial policy.[18]

While it is important to recognise the efforts of minority sections of British social democracy to advocate 'greater self-reliance' for the colonial countries, even veteran left Labour notable Fenner Brockway, despite being considered a prominent opponent of colonialism on humanitarian grounds, had denounced the anti-colonial, peasant 'Mau Mau' rebellion in Kenya, and later became a member of the House of Lords.[19] In fact, the prevailing concern of the Labour Party has been and continues to be the profitability of British capital. It is worth quoting British Marxist historian Robert Clough at length:

This is the real story of the Labour Party: how it used the RAF to defend the British Empire against the Kurdish and Indian people; approved the use of battleships against the Chinese people to maintain the gains of the Opium Wars; used headhunters against Malayan freedom fighters;

later on tortured and interned Irish nationalists, approved the torture and internment of Muslims and defends the Zionist occupation of Palestine.

It is the story of Labour's racism; its description of Africans as 'non-adult people'; its decades of connivance with South African apartheid; its continuous support for racist immigration controls and asylum laws.

It is the story of a left wing which constantly sanctioned such terror because it saw its membership of the Labour Party as of greater importance than the fate of millions suffering the iron heel of Labour imperialism.

It is the story of a Party which, representing a small, privileged section of the working class, has constantly betrayed the interests of the mass [though surely not a majority] of the working class: unemployed workers, black, Asian and Irish people, all those engaged in a struggle against the British state.

It is the story of a Party which has made a mockery of the words 'freedom', 'democracy' and 'socialism'.[20]

All of this without, of course, mentioning the Labour Party's prosecution of the bombing of Yugoslavia in 1999, the catastrophic invasion and occupation of Afghanistan in 2001, or the equally criminal, genocidal war and sanctions the Labour government waged against Iraq, killing over a million and displacing many more so as to maintain the petrodollar financing of the neoliberal economy and with it the institutional foundations of imperialist globalisation.[21]

In Germany, the only party in the Reichstag that was to oppose the demand for the restitution of all German colonies after the First World War was the small Independent Social Democratic Party (USPD, *Unabhängige Sozialdemokratische Partei Deutschlands*), which attempted a middle course between Bolshevism and social democratic revisionism. With some exceptions, however, the German left did not overly preoccupy itself with colonial matters.[22] In the Netherlands, a large number of people found work or settled in its large and lucrative Southeast Asian colonies, and many more had direct material and personal ties with colonialism. This reality exerted a formidable colonialist influence on public opinion, affecting the parliamentary reformist Social Democratic Labour Party (SDAP, *Sociaal-Democratische Arbeidersparti*) and the labour movement more broadly.[23] However, since the Dutch colonies were not the object of fierce inter-imperialist rivalry and did not, therefore, become a major electoral issue, there was some scope for left-liberal criticism of colonial policy in Indonesia albeit within the parameters of support for colonialism and opposition to the national liberation of the colonies.

SOCIAL DEMOCRACY AND COLONIALISM
AFTER THE SECOND WORLD WAR

After the break-up of the international war coalition and the development of the East-West conflict, by 1947 none of Europe's Socialist parties (with the exception of the German and Italian) had a foreign policy that was any different from that of the centre and centre-right parties.[24] Neither British nor French socialists had given colonialism serious consideration, with their attitudes to the colonies best summarised as 'hold on to them if you can'.[25] For the French, perhaps even more than for the British, the preservation of Empire was a means of strengthening France's weakened role globally.[26] Accordingly, the French government, even when it contained both socialists and communists, did not remotely approximate an anti-colonialist force.[27] Despite a recognition that reform of the Empire was imperative (nationalist movements had to be placated and so did the US anti-colonialism), decolonisation was not the objective of the French government or the French left.

Just as the French left did not mention the colonies in their manifestos for the general election of October 1945, the British Labour Party's election manifesto of 1945 was equally silent on the subject of Britain's Empire, despite the monumental tide of decolonisation that was to sweep the world in the ensuing two decades.[28] Indeed, judging by its Conference resolutions and other statements, the Labour Party opposed withdrawal from the colonies. British Empire socialism, like its European counterparts, had always exercised an entrenched commitment to Empire as a protected field of investment, a protected source of raw materials, a protected market for their country's exports and a means of protecting the value of the national currency.[29] Thus the Labour Party favoured the preservation of the 'white' Commonwealth based on the Ottawa system of imperial preference, with India to be allowed an indigenous government with exceptionally close economic and military ties to the United Kingdom.[30]

Between 1939 and 1945, India's trade surplus with Britain was worth £1.3 billion (British overseas investment amounted to £659 million between 1948 and 1951) and there was an impending run on the pound.[31] Britain was finally forced to devalue its currency, and it used the sterling balance of its colonies to help pay off the debts it had incurred with the United States in the previous decade. Thus, for instance, after the Second World War net dollar earners such as the Gold Coast (now Ghana) and Malaya were prevented from purchasing outside of the sterling area, in effect forcing them to hold a large surplus of sterling, the entirety of which was to be held in London. In practice, this amounted to their lending to Britain at low rates of interest.[32] As conservative British historian David K. Fieldhouse described events:

The British, while having to devalue the pound against the dollar in 1949, kept the pound strong against all colonial currencies (in most cases at par) by devaluing them at the same time and to the same extent. In short, the sterling area was used after 1945 as a device for supporting the pound sterling against the dollar ... At the same time, the pound was kept strong against the colonial currencies to avoid an increase in the real burden of blocked sterling balances [that is, Britain's current account deficit with its colonies]. In both ways, the colonies were compelled to subsidise Britain's post-war standard of living. [The] Labour government used the colonies to protect the British consumer from the high social price which continental countries were then paying for their post-war reconstruction. Consciously or not, this was to adopt 'social imperialism' in an extreme form.[33]

In 1948, to protect the profits of Britain's rubber and tin industries and thus ensure the solvency of sterling, the country's Labour government launched a massive counter-insurgency operation against the communist-led Malayan independence movement.

As a result of colonialism, Malaya was effectively owned by European, primarily British, businesses, with British capital behind most Malayan enterprises. Most importantly, 70 per cent of the acreage of rubber estates was owned by European (primarily British) companies, compared to 29 per cent Asian ownership. Malaya was described by one Lord in 1952 as the 'greatest material prize in South-East Asia,' mainly due to its rubber and tin. These resources were 'very fortunate' for Britain, another Lord declared, since 'they have very largely supported the standard of living of the people of this country and the sterling area ever since the war ended.' 'What we should do without Malaya, and its earnings in tin and rubber, I do not know.' The insurgency threatened control over this 'material prize.'[34]

The repression of Malaya's communist movement by the British Army resulted in thousands of Malayan deaths from the use of fragmentation bombs, chemical warfare and massive forced resettlement programmes later used by the United States in Vietnam (with the covert support of the ruling British Labour government).[35]

The secretary of the Fabian Colonial Bureau formed in 1940,[36] South African-born economist Rita Hinden was conscious of the contradiction between Labour's avowedly developmentalist policies for Britain's colonies and its domestic welfare agenda. For not only were there clear capitalist imperatives at stake in maintaining the colonies in a state of semi-feudal dependence, but the British electorate desired cheap food and cheap colonial imports at the direct expense of colonial living standards.[37] The Labour government's priorities from 1945 to 1951 were dictated by the needs of the British economy and the 'urgent necessity' of procuring raw materials and foodstuffs and earning precious dollars from its colonies.[38] As a consequence, the Labour government tended to prioritise colonial issues only when it was imperative to do so in the face of effective national liberation struggle.[39]

In those colonies where neither communist nor national liberation forces were particularly strong (India was written off as a colony due to the strength of both tendencies there), the Labour movement sought to either delay independence or, in the worst case, ensure that the 'independent' country retained exceptionally close political and economic ties to Britain. The Caribbean was considered particularly promising for such a strategy, since it was thought that communist influence was weak there. In the case of Africa, the Labour Party expressed its view in the 1943 pamphlet *The Colonies*, wherein it was argued that its African colonies were inhabited by 'backward people' of 'primitive culture' who were simply 'not yet able to stand by themselves'. British rule was to be munificently maintained 'as a trust for the native inhabitants' until they could be deemed suitable to govern themselves.[40] Meanwhile, the exploitation of colonial labour and the export of cheap goods and huge profits it made possible were to continue apace, as a fitting reward for British labour's carrying the white man's burden. The true intent behind Labour's 'positive' colonial policy (as opposed to mere 'negative' anti-imperialism) was announced to an unshocked House of Commons by Labour's Secretary of State for Foreign Affairs and, later, founder of Britain's National Health Service, Ernest Bevin in 1946: 'I am not prepared to sacrifice the British empire,' he said, '[because] I know that if the British empire fell it would mean that the standard of life of our con-stituents would fall considerably.'[41]

Needless to say, Labour's record of social imperialism, of ameliorating the living conditions of Britain's population by oppressing and exploiting the peoples of Africa and Asia, is of scant concern to those 'old-style socialists' yearning for the return of the post-war welfare state. Although the domestic policy of the first majority Labour government of 1945–51 is considered to have been radical, the presumption has also been that its foreign policy was also progressive, particularly in light of India's achievement of inde-pendence in 1947. However, Labour was not anti-imperialist; other than India, only Israel, Burma and Ceylon managed to wrest their independence from Britain during that period. Labour's main concern was to either preserve the Empire or, failing that, to guarantee that the post-colonial world remained safe for British capital investments. Its strategy was to kill colonial independence by kindness, that is, to provide the minimal reforms necessary to prevent the grievances of the colonised from being 'exploited' by communists and radical nationalists.[42]

At the same time, the policy of the Trades Union Congress (TUC) in Britain was just as conservative and colonialist as that of the Labour Party. Between 1945 and 1951, the period of the third Labour government, very little was done to substantiate trade unionist rhetoric of colonial self-government. Davis summarises the attitude of Britain's union movement to colonialism:

Implicit racist thinking overtly nurtured in the previous seventy or so years [before 1945] continued to influence the labour movement's views. The use of trade unionism to discourage the development of a pro-communist political movement, which might take advantage of the much delayed voting rights granted in most colonies after 1945 was partially successful. Where it did not deliver compliance, the movement was crushed as in the Malayan Federation and in Kenya. But for the most part, British-inspired trade unionism, working with the Colonial Office and through trade union labour advisors, began to take hold. Supplemented by a major programme of government-funded trade union education and later by the resources of the ICFTU, the colonial world was left safe for neo-colonialism once independence had been won.[43]

SETTLER-COLONIAL LABOUR AND METROPOLITAN SOCIALISM

The white nationalist ideology of British workers in Australia and South Africa exerted tremendous influence on British trade unionism in the late nineteenth century.[44] As Hyslop writes:

The white working classes in the pre-First World War British Empire were not composed of 'nationally' discrete entities, but were bound together into an imperial working class, by flows of population which traversed the world. [The] labour movements based on this imperial working class produced and disseminated a common ideology of White Labourism. In this ideology, the element of the critique of exploitation and the element of racism were inextricably intermingled. This was an era of radical labour militancy, of profound ideological hostility to capitalism, of widespread influence of syndicalist doctrines in the unions. But these trends fused with the notion that employers were attempting to sap the organised power of white workers internationally by subjecting them to the competition of cheap Asian [and, in South Africa, African] labour. This internationally constructed synthesis of militant labour and racist visions was a major cultural source of the rise of working class racism in turn of the century Britain, of the beginning of South African industrial segregation, and of the politics of the 'White Australia' policy. These phenomena were not separate, but rather, part of a single story … The political concerns of white labour were carried around the empire by persons, by newspapers, and by organisational links.[45]

Indeed, the largest British labour demonstration of the early twentieth century occurred on 1 March 1914 when around half a million workers turned out in a 7 mile-long column in London's Hyde Park to demonstrate solidarity with nine South African trade unionists who had been deported from their country for demanding the exclusion of Black and Chinese workers from skilled jobs.[46] Settler-colonial trade unionism and metropolitan trade unionism were deeply rooted in the politics of Empire. Similarly, the great majority of French socialists and the French labour movement were unambiguously colonialist, with white socialists and communists in the Algerian colony having been thoroughly infected with settler colonialism.[47] Although the left in Britain did sometimes present positive, if patronising, images of African and Asian people, often proffering a view emphasising the fundamental equality of all 'races' (of which, in fact, there is only one, the human race). Yet even the most antiracist and anti-imperialist sections of British left opinion stopped far short of advocating the dismantling of the British Empire. Indeed, during the 1920s and 1930s the Independent Labour Party was more consistent and committed in its anti-imperialism than either mainstream Labour supporters or communists.[48] Earlier, the late Victorian British left's anti-imperialism was motivated by its anxiety about the actual and potential domestic consequences of the 'new imperialism', namely, 'militarism and conscription, the swollen and parasitical state, the suppression of dissent, the "growth of executive power", the "weakening of party government," and the "undermining of the independence of the electorate"'.[49] That the outlying left of such putative anti-imperialism couched its arguments in continued support for the rights and interests of the indigenous inhabitants of the colonies does not diminish the reality that there was virtually zero support on the left, even on its fringes, for decolonisation and national self-determination for the colonies.[50]

As Kirk acknowledges, 'the language of aggressive and unapologetic racism was most pronounced among white settler socialists, often of British origin'.[51] While not so openly racist as their white-settler counterparts,

British socialists not only often adopted superior chauvinistic and paternalistic attitudes towards colonial subjects, they frequently elaborated their derogation of the right of self-determination for the colonial peoples in the evolutionary language of 'stages of development' and 'higher' and 'lower' forms of civilisation.[52] Unquestionably, since the same concern was not extended so fulsomely to the inhabitants of India or Ireland, the impassioned pleading by British socialists on behalf of the natives of South Africa against the racist and exploitative depredations of the Afrikaner state in Natal was driven by opposition to its independence from the British Empire. One 'socialist', the prominent Fabian and Labour Party MP Sydney Olivier, who had been colonial secretary to Jamaica between 1900 and 1904 and later served as governor there for five and a half years, ignored its well-established white supremacy and held that country up as a fine example of a successfully colour 'blended' society.

While taking care not to depict the Chinese and other Asiatic people as 'racially inferior', even the most egalitarian British socialists nonetheless criticised the

employment of the Chinese in South Africa ... [not] upon [the basis of] opposition to the Chinese labourers *per se*, but upon their employment as 'cheap' and 'forced', or 'unfree' and 'slave' labour – the poor and largely unwitting victims of the real culprits, the unscrupulous mine-owners of the Transvaal and the imperial and colonial governments.[53]

British socialists who advocated white labour's solidarising with non-white colonial peoples did so only insofar as doing so would not disturb the privileged position of white labour: 'In keeping with their class based, inclusive philosophy [*sic*], British socialists generally offered a hand of friendship to Asiatic labour on the condition that it did not pose a threat to the existing conditions and future prospects of other workers.'[54] In other words, British 'anti-imperialist socialists' wished to avoid at all costs the proletarianisation of the native populations of white-settler or any other colonies. Rather, colonised societies were to be maintained in their predominantly agrarian form with the subsistence peasantry barred from taking jobs held rightfully by white workers. Thus although some British socialists did defend existing imperial practices, especially as against the allegedly more brutal and rapacious methods of Germany, most criticised 'the predatory and irresponsible imperialism of the Boer war, and the individualist and hierarchical, if more enlightened and responsible, radical Liberal view of Empire' on the basis of an ideal 'higher' imperial form.[55]

British socialists in general considered existing imperialism as a method of class domination which was increasingly racialised in character. None, however, considered imperialism in and of itself wrong, but instead aimed to place the working class, in cooperation with the colonial peoples themselves, at its head. Socialists like Kier Hardie held up nineteenth-century Cobdenite liberalism as the ideal form of free-trading and peace-loving Empire. Even socialists opposed to imperialist militarism and jingoism at the time of the South African War, emphasised their support for the 'honest', 'decent' and 'loyal' British 'Tommy', while identifying the 'autocratic and bullying "Prussian Goth"'... as the main threat to world peace'.[56] In sum, concerted opposition to employers' use of non-white 'scab' and 'blackleg' labour against the white worker elite in Australia and South Africa was intended to bolster the class privileges enjoyed by members of all-white labour unions.

LEFT-WING SOCIAL DEMOCRACY TODAY

In recent years, and particularly since the onset of the Great Recession in late 2007, the entire political spectrum of the global North has moved right, to the point where there are now essentially three major trends therein, namely, (1) neoliberal social democracy; (2) right populism; and (3) national leftism. None of these responses to increasing social precarity on the part of the metropolitan and native labour aristocracies is focused on preventing the costs of economic retrenchment from falling to other, oppressed nations. We will examine here the contention that the current Jeremy Corbyn leadership of the British Labour Party represents a fresh turn towards socialism and a genuine alternative to what Hosea Jaffe has aptly termed 'tributary capitalism'.

As with his predecessors, Corbyn promotes a national chauvinist version of socialism that aims to share among the British people more of the wealth accumulated through Britain's imperialist exploitation of dependent countries. The mechanisms for this exploitation are varied, but they function to such an extent that Britain and all of the classes and class fractions therein (albeit to varying degrees) are net consumers of value created elsewhere. Corbyn has been a consistent long-term critic of the neoliberal restructuring of Britain's welfare state, and that is where his mass appeal undoubtedly lies. He has also been less supportive of Britain's wars around the globe than many elected members of his party. Yet neither Corbyn nor his supporters have concerned themselves with stopping the flow of surplus value from the exploited countries. Doing so would require the radical restructuring of British society as we know it, that is, an end to British economic and military imperialism. So long as the absolute priority for British socialists is merely to maintain or extend current British living standards and/or British transfer payments, very few Britons would see any short-term gains in effective anti-imperialism. More importantly, the fundamentally bourgeois class structure of Britain means that there is no mass basis for British people to act as agents of such change.

Whereas Corbyn is on the left of the imperialist project, his 'anti-establishment' bedfellows Le Pen, Farage, Trump and other race-baiters are to the right of it. In Western Europe, the vast majority of far right parties combine racist culturalism with social democratic economism based on welfare chauvinism and nativism (that is, British hospital beds for British people, British jobs for British workers, British dole for British unemployed and so forth). By feeding the grossly one-sided view that globalisation has been straightforwardly disastrous for British workers, by blaming high immigration levels for stagnant wages, and by studiously ignoring Britain's role as a parasitic drain on the countries of the global South, Corbyn's social democratic nationalism legitimises and promotes a self-pitying British nationalism. This imperialist left nationalism is not an antidote to the imperialist right populism that is responsible for rising racist hate crime across the United Kingdom. On the contrary, it provides right populism with a pseudo-socialist patina of democratic respectability. Indeed, in purporting to oppose the upsurge in popular xenophobia and racism, the mainstream of the British left (and its European and US counterparts) is indulging in rank hypocrisy. The long-running Islamophobic campaigns waged by nominal leftists appealing to cultural liberalism, atheism and feminism to justify wars of depredation (in the process negating the progressive content of each), as well as the anti-immigrant and anti-free trade campaigns indulged in by protectionist metropolitan labour, have found fertile ground among a right-wing electorate that fears above all the dissolution of white supremacy as a condition of its caste-class status.

In relation to the rise of populism, both left and right, whereas the consumer boom brought about by the globalisation of capitalist production based on the exploitation of Third World labour has afforded the workers of the global North unprecedented purchasing power at the expense of the world majority, it has failed to arrest capitalism's long-term tendency to stagnation. In recent years, the unfolding crisis of profitability in the major imperialist countries has brought with it pressures on wages, housing and welfare provision, squeezing the number of middle paying jobs while increasing the number of both low-paying and high-paying jobs. The social base of the winning side in the Brexit vote (the popular referendum taken as to whether the United Kingdom should leave the European Union) consisted primarily in those sections of the population that prosper least from globalisation, namely, small businesses and agricultural communities unable to compete in continental European markets; 'native' British workers facing competition from migrant European labour; and property owners from England's rural shires resentful of the tax burdens necessary to maintain British ties to Europe. Pitted against these groups are the minority of workers organised in unions (not least those producing for European export); the public sector salariat; the intelligentsia in the academies and the professions; immigrant and minority ethnic communities; and the metropolitan elite. Thus the Remain vote was strongest among the upper or upper middle class (company directors, surgeons and professionals), intermediate managerial layers (bank managers, head teachers, accountants and lawyers) and, less categorically, the lower middle class (shop managers, bank clerks, sales representatives, nurses and so on). The Leave vote, by contrast, was based largely on semi-skilled (machine-operators, drivers, call centre employees), unskilled (cleaners, porters) and skilled (electricians, heating engineers, mechanics) white workers.[57]

Despite its 'working class' basis, however, the Brexit vote was much more a protest against neoliberal globalisation in the European context than it was a protest against capitalism as such. Working class citizens in the imperialist countries have voted for Eurosceptic and fascist parties as a rearguard action against globalisation by (1) asserting their national privileges vis-à-vis immigrant labour, and (2) allying with those sections of national capital promoting protectionist and classically colonialist strategies to reverse the global decline of their monopolies and reap the attendant superprofits. As such, the turn to populism in the West is primarily an attempt to maintain superwages by reasserting Western pre-eminence at the expense of the rest of the world.

Opposition to war should be the number one task of socialists in the West today: nothing else is more important, or more conducive to developing an understanding of the imperialist world system that both necessitates war for the structural maintenance of its value flows and which depends upon the military industrial complex as a principal source of accumulation. Tellingly, as well as promising more police on British streets, in its 2017 Manifesto the Corbyn-led Labour Party promises to maintain British imperialism as a first tier military power. The Manifesto boasts that the last Labour government consistently spent above the North Atlantic Treaty Organization (NATO) benchmark of 2 per cent of GDP and commits Labour to doing so again if re-elected. It supports the renewal of Britain's Trident nuclear weapons system, and assures British voters that Labour will maintain the UK's 'defence' industry in its world-leading position so that British jobs in steel, arms manufacture and suppliers can be protected.[58]

Needless to say, such fealty to British imperialism is diametrically opposed to internationalism and to real socialism. Rather, the political line of the Labour Party and its supporters confirms the view in 1960 of French journalist and anti-imperialist Marcel Péju that the Western left wishes 'to construct a socialism *de luxe* with the fruits of imperialist rapine'.[59] A year earlier, poet, politician and socialist first President of Senegal, Léopold Senghor, correctly observed that 'the proletarians of Europe have benefited from the colonial regime; therefore they have never really – I mean effectively – opposed it'.[60] As British geographer Keith Buchanan has written,

[This] absence of any really effective aid cannot be laid solely at the door of the great monopolies or a greedy group of capitalists; the working class has forced up its standard of living in very large measure at the expense of fellow-workers in the colonial world and, in the opinion of Moussa, these efforts of Western workers to raise their standards of living have contributed more to the deterioration of the position of the underdeveloped countries than has the profit motive of industrial or commercial leaders. Having tasted the delights of affluence, European workers have tended to become 'embourgoisé' and ever more Europe-centric and parochial in their attitudes. A Fanon may cry that the well-being and progress of Europe have been built with the sweat and corpses of black man and yellow man, Indian and Arab – but the cry is unheard amid the distractions of a new and delightful opulence.

The record of the political leaders of the left in Europe ... has been one of defection and treason, of resounding phrases and empty gestures. Preoccupied with the redistribution of wealth within their own countries (with 'the sharing of the booty' as Péju puts it) they have consented to a token embellishment of the ghettoes of the Third World, but have never dreamed of showing their solidarity with the workers who live in these ghettoes by formulating measures to redistribute wealth on a global scale. Since many of us believe that one of the main forces behind socialism is its morality and its human decency, it may well be that much of the impotence of the left in Europe today derives from the neglect of these primary virtues, from the bankruptcy of its ideas and its leaders when confronted with the problems of a global socialism. Equally, it may well be that a courageous confrontation of the political and moral issues posed by the Third World – a real rejection of and active opposition to all forms of economic and political domination, the formulation and adoption of a massive policy of genuine redistribution of wealth between the affluent nations and the proletarian nations – it may be that such a confrontation will restore to the left the drive and idealism which it possessed when confronted with these problems at a national level.[61]

In the following chapter, we will describe how Western Marxism has signally failed to meet the challenge of all-round opposition to imperialism.

14
Social-Imperialist Marxism

In this chapter we will describe social-imperialist currents in European communist and Trotskyist movements. Both political trends have exhibited a profound ignorance of the transfiguration of the class structure of the developed countries by imperialism, and both have revised their Marxism according to the interests of their would-be constituencies in maintaining the imperialist world economy.

EUROCENTRIC COMMUNISM

During the interwar period, the foreign policy of the Soviet Union shifted its focus from fomenting and consolidating revolutionary momentum in the imperialist countries to forging ties with national revolutionary movements in the colonial world and neighbouring states in the East. This helped to inspire and consolidate militant internationalism and a break from the colonialist reformism characteristic of social democracy, which very largely left the field open to communist forces in the colonial world. The Comintern (Communist, or Third International) was established in 1919 by the minority of Marxists who considered that the old parties of the left had thoroughly discredited the cause of socialism by supporting the imperialist policies of their own capitalist governments before, during and after the First World War. However, after an initial period in which it paid much greater attention to the revolutionary liberation movements in the colonial and semi-colonial countries, the Comintern reverted to standard Marxian Eurocentrism.

By the end of the First World War, the metropolitan labour aristocracy had not overthrown capitalism as many Bolsheviks had anticipated, and had left the Soviet Union isolated to fend for itself in an extremely hostile international environment. Under the circumstances, the Soviet aim of averting an imperialist invasion of its borders ensured its willingness to uphold the spheres of influence of the imperialist powers of the time. Referring to Comintern support for imperialist country 'social patriotism', Redfern summarises the Soviet strategy following the 1933 Nazi electoral victory in Germany: 'If the workers of Britain and France would not embrace communism, why not mobilise their patriotism in the cause of the defence of the Soviet Union?'[1] Thus, for instance, on the occasion of the twentieth anniversary of the October Revolution, the Comintern urged the working class of Britain and France to demand that their governments defend their colonial empires in the East, 'menaced by Japanese imperialism'.[2] Contrastingly, the Chinese revolution of 1949 was achieved by a Communist Party that flouted the line propounded by the Comintern as it became imperative to break the United Front with the Chinese Nationalists.[3]

To put it mildly, the workers of the imperialist countries did not respond with alacrity to the 1920 Second Comintern Congress' insistence that they take up the cause of the national liberation of the colonies. Indeed, a few months after the Congress, V. I. Lenin reported that he had instructed a delegation of English workers on this obligation, but 'they made faces ... They simply could get not into their heads the truth that in the interests of the world revolution, workers must wish the defeat of their government.'[4] The record of Western European Communist parties shows that despite their being far to the left of mainstream Social Democratic parties on the question of opposition to imperialism, they fell short of consistent internationalism. Although compared with its First, the Second Comintern Congress definitely witnessed a 'qualitative leap'[5] in its appreciation of the significance of the colonial question, this was not 'reflected in any sustained effort by the Comintern either on the theoretical plane or that of practical activity. The "Eurocentrist" viewpoint continued to predominate in the leadership of the Comintern and in the Communist parties of the metropolitan countries.'[6]

Indeed, from its foundation onwards, the Comintern tended to grossly overestimate the revolutionary potential of the European working class, which supported Conservative and Social Democratic parties in its great majority.[7] Despite considerable attention paid by the Comintern to the revolutionary movement in the East, its preoccupation throughout the 1920s, 1930s and 1940s was with Europe, and increasingly so as the years rolled on.[8] Thus, in 1924 Vietnamese communist Ho Chi Minh noted:

As for our Communist Parties in Great Britain, Holland, Belgium and other countries – what have they done to cope with the colonial invasions perpetrated by the bourgeois class of their countries? What have they done from the day they accepted Lenin's political programme to educate the working class of their countries in the spirit of just internationalism, and that of close contact with the working masses in the colonies? What our Parties have done in this domain is almost worthless. As for me, I was born in a French colony, and am a member of the French Communist Party, and I am very sorry to say that our Communist Party has done hardly anything for the colonies ... It is the task of the communist newspapers to introduce the colonial question to our militants to awaken the working masses in the colonies, win them over to the cause of Communism, but what have our newspapers done? Nothing at all.[9]

In August 1936, the Italian Communist Party (PCI) newspaper *Stato Operaio* (Workers' State) published its leader Palmiro Togliatti's 'L'appello Ai Fascisti' ('Appeal to the Fascists') in which he signally condemned the invasion of Ethiopia a year earlier not for the misery it had caused to Ethiopians (the war had resulted in around 760,300 Ethiopian deaths),[10] but for the disappointing paucity of benefits the war actually brought to, amongst others, the volunteers who fought there and the Blackshirt rank and file. Togliatti, indeed, declared that 'Communists [rather than Mussolini's government] do justice to the fascist program of 1919, which is a program of freedom'. A decade later, in 1946, as Minister of Justice, Togliatti passed an Amnesty for all Italian fascists. The PCI led by Palmiro Togliatti enthusiastically participated in the post-war Italian government despite its being an imperialist one.[11] In the same year, the PCI demanded the restitution of Italy's colonies and the reoccupation of Eritrea, Somalia and Libya since, according to Togliatti and Pietro Nenni, the National Secretary of the Italian Socialist Party, Italy had a popular front government, not an imperialist one, and the Italian proletariat was destined to lead the colonies into independence. In 1949, the PCI openly supported Italy's joining NATO.

SOCIAL-IMPERIALIST MARXISM IN BRITAIN

In Britain, no organisation represented at the Communist Party of Great Britain's (CPGB) founding Unity Convention in 1920, no delegate present, nor the provisional committee, which convened the Convention, considered it necessary to discuss the colonial question.[12] British communists did, however, deem it imperative that alcohol prohibition be discussed (a resolution calling for prohibition was referred to the provisional Executive Committee).[13] In fact, according to Soviet Communist leader Karl Radek, CPGB member Tom Welch had during discussions on the colonial commission, in an often quoted remark, justified his party's inactivity on the colonial question on the grounds that 'the ordinary British worker would regard it as treachery if he was to help the dependent peoples to rebel against English domination'.[14] The riposte of an Irish delegate to Welch was 'the faster English workers learn to commit such treason against the bourgeois state, the better it will be for the revolutionary movement'. Radek himself suggested that the Comintern would judge British communists not for the number of articles written denouncing colonial outrages, 'but by the number of Communists who are thrown into jail for agitating in the colonial countries'.[15]

Throughout its history, unfortunately, the CPGB found colonial work a low priority. There were, however, occasional signs that the leadership would begin to prioritise anti-imperialist work. Thus in 1921, the party's executive committee issued a statement deploring the failure of British workers to support anti-colonial struggles: 'we have betrayed them, and, in so doing we are betraying the whole working-class movement ... For us, if we were to connive at these things, to claim for our motto "workers of the world unite" would be to merely add hypocrisy to treachery.'[16] The *Communist Review* of June 1921, moreover, had stated that the British Empire was 'the knot which socialism in this country will have to unravel if it is to succeed'. Yet, as Redfern is forced to conclude, there is little evidence of any sustained attempt by the party to match words with deeds in this crucial respect.[17]

Sometime between 1919 and in 1921, in a document entitled 'The Inapplicability of Third International Principles to Britain', Indian member of the CPGB Rajani Palme Dutt had cast serious doubt on the prospects for a revolution in Britain. In contrast to Russia, he argued, there were 'strong non-revolutionary working-class institutions in the Labour Party and the trade unions ... [There is also] a large middle class of undoubted white sympathies and ... a large parasitic loyalist proletariat which would form a considerable reservoir for dependable soldiers and White armies.'[18] Yet despite Comintern interventions instructing it to strengthen its understanding of imperialism, the British Communist Party 'continued [throughout the 1920s] to ignore the role of Empire in permitting rising living standards in Britain'.[19]

Indeed, in 1924, the Comintern had complained that the CPGB had never 'demanded clearly and unequivocally the secession of the Colonies from the British Empire'.[20] After 1928, however, and the adoption of the 'Class Against Class' strategy said to be appropriate of the 'Third Period'[21] – to which many Marxists today impute all of the failures of the German working class to overthrow capitalism and to have resulted in the single greatest defeat of the working class in world history – the Comintern came to promote the view of the impending downfall of capitalism at the hands of a European workers' revolution. At its Sixth Congress, it was asserted that only a tiny minority of the working class benefited from imperialism: the labour aristocracy was defined as 'the leading cadres of the social democratic parties'.[22] In this view, it was only necessary to remove social democrats from power before capitalism would collapse. Imperialism, and anti-imperialism, was rendered a moot point. Indeed, after 1935 the CPGB 'worked more vigorously to help defend the British Empire against its imperial rivals than it ever had to support anti-colonial movements in the Empire'.[23] Redfern writes:

> In 1937 the London DPC [District Party Committee of the CPGB] reported that it was to hold a 'Save China, Save Peace' meeting (the CP was by now leading a vigorous campaign in support of China against Japanese aggression) whilst Manchester and Salford mentioned only the work of the China Campaign Committee. Teresa Hunt, then a rank-and-file member in Manchester, recalls lively discussions of the means test, Abyssinia, the Spanish Civil War, anti-fascism and the Soviet Union among Party members, but has no recollection of discussions of the British Empire.[24]

With regard to Ireland, CPGB leader Harry Pollitt dutifully explained to the Central Committee in 1936 that the main task of communists was to help Irish comrades by explaining the alleged falsity of the Irish nationalist dictum 'England's difficulty is Ireland's opportunity'. Pollitt's desire to 'help' his Irish comrades was an expression of the Communist Party's post-Seventh Congress view that 'the most important anti-colonial work was that directed against Britain's imperial rivals',[25] specifically, Italy, Germany and Japan (the campaign to support the beleaguered Spanish Republic being the CPGB's largest concerning foreign affairs). Between 1936 and 1939, as British forces in Palestine were engaged in massive violent repression of an anti-imperialist uprising in which the Palestinian Communist Party played a leading role and during the course of which over 5,000 Palestinians were killed, the CPGB was wholly silent.

SOCIAL-IMPERIALIST MARXISM IN FRANCE

Meanwhile, due to their abject failure to show genuine solidarity with anti-colonial movements throughout the French Empire, and the refusal of communist union organisers to approach workers with anti-imperialist as opposed to purely 'bread-and-butter' economic issues, Comintern leaders denounced the leaders of the French Communist Party (PCF, *Parti Communiste Français*) as 'incorrigible social democrats' and the party's Algerian members as 'possibly excellent Frenchmen but very indifferent Communists'.[26] Given the minority position of the working class in the Third Republic (1870–1940) and the dependence of Marseille on colonial trade and Lyon on raw silk imports from Indochina, it was little wonder that French socialists 'pulled their punches' when it came to criticising France's role in the underdeveloped countries.[27] One of the more militant members of the SFIO and a member of their commission on colonial affairs, Daniel Guerin observed that the PCF, especially in the Popular Front period, sought to preserve France's colonial Empire for fear that its dissolution would favour the fascist enemies of both France and the USSR.[28] Its rhetoric, in fact, dovetailed with that of the SFIO which regularly denounced national liberation movements in the colonies as 'fascist' and 'racist'. However, at discussions held in Paris in August 1936 with the Third Reich's Finance Minister, Hjalmar Schacht, the leader of France's Popular Front government, Leon Blum insisted on his willingness to meet Nazi demands for a redistribution of the colonies.[29] Their inhabitants, presumably, were to be 'civilised' according to the tender mercies of openly genocidal and racist fascist German imperialism. Overall, for the French left, whereas capital export to the colonies was periodically criticised as draining the metropolis of needed investment, as were the deleterious effects of military conscription upon the French working class, colonial policy per se was not consistently denounced, nor was national self-determination upheld as the best solution for its associated problems. In her autobiography, feminist philosopher Simone de Beauvoir wrote about the PCF's social chauvinism:

[The PCF] made no effort to combat the racism of the French workers, who considered the 400,000 North Africans settled in France as both intruders doing them out of jobs and as a sub-proletariat worthy only of contempt ... What is certain is that by June [1955] all resistance to the war had ceased ... the entire population of the country – workers, employees, farmers and professional people, civilians and soldiers – were caught up in a great tide of chauvinism and racism ... .
... Provided it was properly costumed for them, the people of France were prepared to accept this war with a light heart ... I was not at all upset when the ultras demonstrated ... They were just ultras. What did appal me was to see the vast majority of the French people turn chauvinist and to realize the depth of their racist attitude ... I was even more stupified and saddened when I learned with what docility the youth soldiers sent to Algeria became accomplices in the methods of pacification.[30]

Likewise, the eminent French philosopher Jean-Paul Sartre accused the PCF of tailing the Socialist Party, which was the main force behind prosecuting the war on Algeria of the 1950s and 1960s.[31] In an interview, Sartre suggested that colonialism to some extent protected the French working class from unemployment and immiseration, allowing it to enjoy a higher standard of living than it would in its absence. He also suggested that colonialism fostered a political collusion between the metropolitan working class and the imperialist bourgeoisie and 'un certain paternalisme de la classe *ouvrière envers le sous-prolétariat* ('a certain paternalism of the working class towards the sub-proletariat'). Sartre also considered that the '*surexploitation*' (superexploitation) of Algerians forced many to seek work in France where French workers perceived them as competitors for jobs.[32]

The PCF, in relative terms embodying the most anti-imperialist sentiments of the French working class, 'tempered its anti-colonialism in order to establish its credentials as a patriotic party and thus declared, in January 1944, that the French people, with its metropolitan and overseas territories, is "one and indivisible"'.[33] The PCF remembered its anti-colonialism only when in opposition and at odds with the Socialist Party, the French Section of the Workers (SFIO), that is, before 1936, between 1939 and 1941, and after 1947. The SFIO, meanwhile, justified its hostility towards the Vietnamese national liberation struggle with the excuse that it went against the principles of internationalism. Indeed, at its 1944 Congress, Vietnamese (though not French) nationalism was stigmatised as an ideology which 'would keep the overseas peoples in the grip of backward feudalism or agitators in the pay of foreign powers', presumably Soviet, and, at the 1947 Congress, as a straightforwardly reactionary creed.[34]

The 'national colonial consensus' pervading virtually the entire French polity was built up through the colonialist campaigns of the later part of the nineteenth century. In spite of militant demonstrations from 1917 onwards against the war and against conquest and intervention in Russia, the early absorption of the labour movement in the colonialist bloc was further consolidated after the First World War.[35] Moreover, although the PCF was less conservative around the issue of colonialism, and launched a quite vigorous campaign in 1925 against Spain and France's war against the Berbers of the Rif mountains in Morocco, 'the PCF's policy remained one of militant liberalism until the end of the French Empire'.[36] Within the Labour and Socialist International, the French socialist movement constituted the colonialist right wing, insisting on assimilation to French state structures as the path to the emancipation of France's colonies. The Popular Front government lasting from 1936 to 1938 and including the PCF, the SFIO and the Radical Party actually strengthened the grip of colonial conservatism on the labour movement and ensured the enduring continuity of left and right on the issue.[37] Even after the Second World War, the SFIO and the PCF persisted in their national-colonialist positions vis-à-vis Algeria and Indochina. Thus in 1963, Chairman of the Communist Party of China Mao Zedong was forced to conclude: 'For the past ten years and more, the leaders of the French Communist Party have followed the colonial policy of the French imperialists and served as an appendage of French monopoly capital.'[38] As noted, during that period the French Socialist Party in government was the main force behind the violent repression of the national liberation movement in Algeria, while the PCF simply tailed it, opportunistically divaricating when it came to whether independence should be granted and vocally opposing Algeria's FLN (*Front de libération nationale*). The PCF was quite realistically concerned that it would lose the support of the patriotic French workers if it came out as a genuinely internationalist party. To its partial credit, the PCF did condemn the mass torture that French imperialism was using to terrorise Algeria into submission. Moreover, after the rout of French occupying forces in Vietnam at Dien Bien Phu, the PCF became more vocal in its opposition to colonialism with its perspective best summarised as 'quit while the going is good'.[39]

It would be wrong, however, to single out the Leninist parties of the far left for their ideological and organisational capitulation to the class interests of Europe's metropolitan labour aristocracy. Their Trotskyist opponents operated as the militant wing of imperialist social democracy, and were historically even more Eurocentric than the pro-Soviet parties.[40]

TROTSKYISM AND IMPERIALIST SOCIALISM

Trotskyism is generally characterised by nominally Marxist opposition to actually existing socialism in any form. In the underdeveloped countries, where it has always been a distinctly minority trend (having failed to secure power anywhere), Trotskyism is typified by economism, workerism and anti-nationalism, and tends to be preoccupied with reformist methods of political agitation. Trotsky's conceptions of 'permanent revolution' and 'uneven and combined development' are his major contributions to revolutionary theory as pertaining to the exploited countries of the global South.

Uneven and combined development is defined as the 'dialectic of international competition in which the industrialization of some countries prompted others to hothouse industrial development'.[41] Thus, according to Trotsky, economically backward capitalist countries are forced to bridge the gap in development that exists between them and the more advanced capitalist countries. As Trotsky describes the process, while backward countries may skip 'a whole series of intermediate stages' of development, they invariably do so by combining new economic forces and relations of production with outmoded and archaic ones within the same national economy (combined development).[42]

Although there are some exceptions, the absolute impossibility of the construction of socialism in one country for any sustained time period is a central shibboleth of Trotskyism, as is hostility to national liberation struggle. This reflects Trotskyism's faith in the possibility of simultaneous global proletarian revolution. As such, Trotsky's theory of combined and uneven development provides a theoretical rationalisation of his erroneous belief that (a) capitalist expansion leads to international economic, social and cultural convergence, so that socialist revolution may emerge simultaneously across the entire industrialised world, and (b) that the Russian proletariat could and should 'skip stages' and take power in Russia by and for itself alone, so that it might completely ignore, and even ride roughshod over, the class interests of the peasantry. Absent this understanding of Trotsky's is the idea that imperialism emanating from the centres of the capitalist world system could superimpose capitalist social and production relations on the semi-feudal economies of the underdeveloped countries and thereby relatively hold back their ability to supersede outmoded economic forms. That is to say, the 'uneven' development of capitalism in Trotsky's theory is due principally to the 'anarchy' inherent to the capitalist production, as opposed to its being an ineluctable result of the world's most powerful capitalisms having converted large parts of the global economy into extraverted dependencies of the imperialist core.

Aside from a few neo-Trotskyist groups proclaiming their ideological adherence to the 1959 revolution in Cuba, for Trotsky and his followers both national liberation from colonialist and neo-colonialist oppression and the construction of socialism in particular countries are consistently denounced as reactionary. Arguing for the fundamental similarity of all countries within the capitalist system (despite the unevenness of their development, backward countries might easily catch up with the advanced ones), in 1928 Trotsky made the following erroneous claim:

> In contrast to the economic systems which preceded it, capitalism inherently and constantly aims at economic expansion, at the penetration of new territories, the surmounting of economic differences, the conversion of self-sufficient provincial and national economies into a system of financial interrelationships. Thereby it brings about their rapprochement and equalizes the economic and cultural levels of the most progressive and the most backward countries. Without this main process, it would be impossible to conceive of the relative levelling out, first, of Europe with Great Britain, and then, of America with Europe; the industrialization of the colonies, the diminishing gap between India and Great Britain, and all the consequences arising from the enumerated processes upon which is based not only the program of the Communist International but also its very existence.[43]

Contrary to the above sanitised view of the benefits brought to the Third World by capitalist expansion, it is abundantly clear that there is no general convergence of capitalist countries to the same level of economic development. While imperialism did ameliorate the problems of capital accumulation caused by an excess of supply over effective demand, buoyed the rate of profit by lowering the costs of constant and variable capital, and created profitable markets and investment opportunities in the colonies, this did not lead to the development of a form of capitalism there as in Western Europe. Rather, imperialist capitalism is 'a new synthesis of extended capitalist social relations that also changes the conqueror's mode of production'.[44] Capitalism in the colonies was not a mirror image of capitalism in Europe, but the other side of the imperialist coin. In terms of the resulting international class structure, some countries contain proletarian majorities, others peasant majorities and still others petty-bourgeois majorities. As such, the class struggle and its immediate tasks diverge greatly from country to country and from region to region.

Crucially, for example, imperialism depends upon the maintenance of income deflation in the peripheral countries so that petty producers there consume less of their output and do not push the prices of primary commodities up, thereby threatening metropolitan industry and investment. So-called 'fiscal responsibility' as well as the shift in agricultural earnings to favour multinational distributors over direct producers are two means by which such income deflation has been achieved under neoliberal globalisation; onerous taxation was another such means in the colonial era. Resolution of the land question in favour of domestic consumers is, therefore, a major way in which the class struggle in the global North differs from that in the global South, where agrarian revolution is still very much the order of the day.

Trotskyism has a long history of preferring imperialism to nationalism or to socialism in the underdeveloped countries. Trotsky himself always considered Europe the centre of world revolution, and believed that European workers would bring liberation and socialism to the rest of the world. As late as 1940, Trotsky made the following strikingly incorrect prediction:

A socialist Europe will proclaim the full independence of the colonies, establish friendly economic relations with them and, step by step, without the slightest violence, by means of example and collaboration, introduce them into a world socialist federation ... The economy of the unified Europe will function as one whole.[45]

This faith in the capacity of European workers to bestow liberty on the colonies was, however, ignored by communists in Asia and elsewhere who went on to lead socialist revolutions without the aid of the metropolitan labour aristocracy or its leaders. Likewise, the Soviet Union did not heed Trotsky's advice with respect to the international balance of class forces during the Second World War. In January 1940, Trotsky had mistakenly averred that the Soviet government would side with Hitler in the war, but that this treachery would be prevented by the revolutionary challenge posed to the Hitler regime by the German working class:

His probable participation in the war on the side of the Third Reich, Stalin covers with a promise to 'sovietize' Germany ...

The idea of Stalin's sovietizing Germany is as absurd as Chamberlain's hope for the restoration of a peaceful conservative monarchy there. Only a new world coalition can crush the German army through a war of unheard-of-proportions. The totalitarian regime can be crushed only by a tremendous attack on the part of the German workers. They will carry out their revolution, surely, not in order to replace Hitler with a Hohenzollern or Stalin.

The victory of the popular masses over the Nazi tyranny will be one of the greatest explosions in world history and will immediately change the face of Europe.[46]

In fact, it was not the German workers who defeated the Nazi regime; they did not even mount any significant challenge to it. Even more detached from reality was Trotsky's presumption in 1940 that the soldiers of the German Wehrmacht would feel such sympathy for the Soviet people that they would become a revolutionary vehicle in the occupied Soviet territories and in Germany itself:

Hitler's soldiers are German workers and peasants ...

The armies of occupation must live side by side with the conquered peoples; they must observe the impoverishment and despair of the toiling masses; they must observe the latter's attempts at resistance and protest, at first muffled and then more and more open and bold ...

The German soldiers, that is, the workers and peasants, will in the majority of cases have far more sympathy for the vanquished peoples than for their own ruling caste. The necessity to act at every step in the capacity of 'pacifiers' and oppressors will swiftly disintegrate the armies of occupation, infecting them with a revolutionary spirit.[47]

Trotsky, blinded by Eurocentrism, workerism and social chauvinism, was wrong to anticipate such proletarian consciousness from the Nazi Army; in the Second World War, German soldiers probably massacred more civilians than had any previous army in history. It is at least fortunate, nonetheless, that Trotskyists have not resurrected this specious argument to suppose, for instance, that the 'working class' British soldiers in Iraq might rise up against their command and liberate the grateful Iraqi masses.

15
Conclusion: Imperialism and Anti-Imperialism Today

Our conclusion to the present work examines some of the major issues facing anti-imperialist labour internationalism at the present historical conjuncture. In particular, we will argue that even as US hegemony faces great challenges worldwide, there is little possibility of authentic anti-imperialism gaining ground in the major imperialist countries where the population continues to benefit from consumption levels and occupational structures established by imperialism. Moreover, any potential that does exist for genuine anti-imperialism has been squandered insofar as putative 'anti-imperialism' has become dominated by metropolitan nationalism of both the left and the right, both sides being fully committed to the maintenance of imperialism's hierarchy of nations.

THE RISE OF THE GLOBAL SOUTH
AND THE CRISIS OF IMPERIALISM

Whereas the countries of the global South remain subject to massive value transfer predicated upon the economic predominance of European, North American and Japanese financial, industrial and retail monopolies in world markets, what Amin has called 'the imperialism of the triad' is currently in a weakened position globally.[1] The share of the developed countries in global industrial 'value added' (that is, market value as opposed to value in the Marxist sense) dropped from 68.3 per cent in 1971 to 51.9 per cent in 2008, while the share accruing to Brazil, Russia, India and China rose from 2.6 to 16.5 per cent over the same period (with similar figures applying to capital spending). Having around 11 per cent of the world's population, the G7 countries' (Canada, France, Germany, Italy, Japan, the United Kingdom and the United States) share of global GDP has, however, fallen less dramatically from 70.5 per cent in 1971 to 61.1 per cent in 2008.[2] As British economist Stephen D. King surmises, the developed countries have moved away from manufacturing while the 'developing' countries have become dependent upon it. Whereas the 'periphery' produces increasingly more of the world's value and surplus value under globalisation, then, the major imperialist countries have managed to maintain their position as consumers of value by means of preserving their monopolistic position in global trade and finance. It is, however, crucial to understand the international political economy behind today's crisis of imperialism.

The ongoing capitalist crisis that began in 2007 has its origins in the globalisation of capitalist production and, in particular, the relocation of production to low-wage, low-consumption countries in the decades since 1980.

The series of financial heart attacks that first struck on August 9, 2007 were provoked by adverse side effects of two principal factors that allowed capitalists in Europe, Japan, and the U.S. to escape from the systemic crisis of the 1970s – an enormous expansion of debt, domestic, corporate, and sovereign, which propped up demand, contained overproduction, and maintained GDP growth; and the globalization of production and the shift of much of it to low-wage countries, enabling capitalists to cut costs and restore sagging profits by replacing relatively expensive domestic labor with cheap foreign labor.[3]

The 'long boom' that occurred in the United States between 1993 and 2000 was largely the result of an exceptional infusion of capital from across the global South and, in particular, from industrial 'socialism with Chinese characteristics'. Cheap labour-intensive imports from the newly industrialising countries temporarily allowed the imperialist bourgeoisie to offset its inability to sell as much as it could produce domestically. As such, 'overcapacity in southern labour-intensive production processes, through its effect on repressing the prices of consumer goods, intermediate inputs etc., has played a key role in helping the imperialist economies to contain and alleviate their domestic overcapacity'.[4]

As Smith argues, inflationary pressure associated with the US trade deficit was offset by the falling prices of outsourced intermediate inputs and consumer goods. China and other manufactures-exporting global South countries returned surplus export earnings to the US government 'as loans at zero or negative real rate of interest', concerned as they were to prevent their currencies appreciating against the dollar, thereby making their exports more expensive and scuppering export-oriented industrialisation.[5] In 2007, 11 per cent of China's GDP was invested in US treasury bonds, an amount equivalent to one-third of its personal consumption.[6] As such, despite expanding trade deficits, interest rates in the United States stayed low while volatility in the prices of financial assets was subdued.

Outsourcing and global labour arbitrage have, therefore, provided 'the necessary conditions for continued GDP growth, for the "excessive" leverage and risk-taking now being widely blamed for the crisis, and for the explosive growth of financial derivatives over the past decade'.[7] Put simply, the cheap inputs and consumer goods imports from semi-industrialised states from the early 1980s, alongside the huge trade deficits sustained by interest-free 'loans' from these same states, allowed monopoly capital to postpone the crisis resulting from its inability to sell as much as it could produce. In first selling their exports at bargain-basement prices reflecting historical under-development and the ongoing legacy of imperialism, and then loaning the United States money so that it might buy more of them, the countries of the global North were effectively allowed, as Lenin put it, to 'skin the ox twice'. The resultant value transfer helped to temporarily stabilise the impe-rialist economy as the surfeit of dollars in the global economy ensured low interest rates and facilitated the turn towards financial speculation as an especially lucrative profit-making enterprise. Capital income became the predominant form of accumulation under neoliberalism, but the hegemony of finance helped generate a series of bubbles in the US economy that in 2007 culminated in the collapse of the US property market and a major crisis in the entire system of banking.

CRISIS, WAR AND RIVALRY IN TODAY'S IMPERIALIST ECONOMY

The fall in the rate of profit attendant to the Great Recession has occurred alongside a longer-term decline in the global position of the US economy. China is now the world's second largest economy, and may even overtake the United States over the next decade if its high average growth rates of between 9 and 11 per cent can be maintained. From having held almost half of the world's FDI stock in 1960, the United States currently has 20 per cent, with that of the European Union (the world's largest source of FDI outflows) having remained constant at just over 50 per cent. The expansion of the European Union and the consolidation of its currency, the euro, pose a major challenge to US imperialist dominance.

Likewise, China's rise within the global economy, though heavily circum-scribed by its own dependency as manifested by a net transfer of labour and finances to the major imperialist countries, has increasingly come to be viewed as a potential competitor to US neo-colonialism worldwide, particularly in high 'value-added' technology sectors. Countries in Africa and Asia increasingly look towards semi-imperialist China as a substitute for the lagging investment and markets of the United States. Russian imperialism, meanwhile, has to some extent countered US militarism and neo-colonialism in Central Asia, consolidating the interests of its own more localised monopolies therein. Finally, the position of the export-dependent states of the global South as centres of manufacturing, outsourcing and sub-contracting has afforded them greater influence and manoeuvrability within the global system of capital accumulation.

In short, new political alignments based on movement away from unfettered US domination of financial and trade networks have been forming over the past decade and more. The United States has attempted to meet the challenges posed by this evolving system of international relations with recourse to increased aggression against sovereign states in the global South judged to be insufficiently attuned to the commercial and military needs of US banks and corporations. Since 1999, through invasion and by proxy the United States and its allies (especially the United Kingdom) have waged devastating wars on Yugoslavia, Afghanistan, Iraq, Libya, Syria, Yemen and many other countries. These wars have left millions dead and whole regions in ruins. However, the spiralling costs of US militarism, the massive destabilisation produced by US-initiated wars in Africa and the Middle East, instability in Eastern Europe traceable to US attempts to undermine Russian influence, American exceptionalist unilateralism in international relations, and the increasingly protectionist measures undertaken by the US government have heightened inter-imperialist tensions between the United States, the European Union, Russia and China. Undoubtedly, the United States hopes to resolve these conflicts on its own terms, and its capacity to dictate these terms depends in no small measure upon its control of global energy supplies.[8]

The means of eliminating poverty around the world is to implement an international strategy to (1) end the monopolisation of land, technology and finance capital; (2) equalise wages for equally productive work; (3) share productive employment; and (4) provide for a decent standard of living for the planet's population in an ecologically sustainable way. With these measures in place the purchasing power of labour in all countries will even out and ensure a distribution of wealth to all of society as efficiency increases and as more wealth is produced.[9] As Amin writes:

Any society (state power and people) which aims at 'emerging' cannot avoid 1) entering into a long process of building a modern integrated industrial system centred on the internal popular demand as far as possible, 2) modernising family agriculture and ensuring food sovereignty, and 3) planning the association of the two targets identified above through a consistent non-liberal policy. That implies to imagine moving gradually on the long road to socialism.[10]

The de-linking of the exploited countries from the current system of imperialist value transfer would allow for higher rates of industrial development in the world 'periphery'. This would provide the indispensable economic and political conditions for the growth of democratic and socialist forces globally. With the rise of the newly industrialising countries, the potential emerges for a more international consumer base for the world's surplus. A far more likely scenario, however, is a drive towards another cataclysmic inter-imperialist war, one which a social-imperialist left is hopelessly ill-equipped to prevent.

LEFT NATIONALISM, RIGHT POPULISM
AND THE 'RED-BROWN' CONVERGENCE

The new international division of labour associated with transnational corporate capitalism – as made possible by technological developments in automation, transportation and information – has imperialism as its foundation no less than did capitalism in its earlier colonial and national monopoly phases. This form of imperialism based on the globalisation of monopoly under US hegemony (also known as the Dollar Wall Street Regime) is experiencing profound instability as it has succumbed to its own internal contradictions in a massive crisis of overproduction and financial ruin.

As Petersen has argued, the rapid and visible weakening of established ethnic and national status hierarchies creates resentment on the part of the traditional superordinate group, which tends to assume its dominant position to be part of the natural order. Feelings of resentment impel its members to attempt to reduce the position of that group which is perceived as furthest up the ethnic status hierarchy but which might be most surely subordinated through violence.[11] As he writes, 'Fear prepares the individual to take action to reduce dangers in the environment; Hatred prepares the individual to attack previously identified enemies; [and] Resentment prepares the individual to rectify perceived imbalances in group status hierarchies.'[12] In recent years, increased immigration, the greater visibility of ethnic minorities in public life, and the outsourcing of previously well-paid industrial employment to low-wage countries has encouraged the perception that the white section of the metropolitan labour aristocracy has lost or is losing its hitherto privileged social position. This, in turn, has inspired a white backlash, a 'whitelash', against those forces said to be responsible for the (in reality very partial) shift in metropolitan status hierarchies.

The nativist resentment that has so far gifted the world President Trump and Brexit is a convergence around *metropolitan populism*. The basis of the de facto left nationalist-right populist, 'red-brown' alliance most visibly apparent in anti-US interventionist circles is common opposition to neoliberalism and globalisation (or, in the language of the far right, to liberalism and 'globalism'). Opposition to neoliberalism is taken to be the high water mark of democratic politics by both the far left and the far right in the imperialist countries. The major difference between the two sides of this reactionary unity is in their respective views on already settled ethnic minorities (both sides are staunchly opposed to new immigration), but anti-globalisation, anti-interventionist populism unites many on both the left and the right. In the major imperialist countries the anti-interventionist left has completely failed to draw a clear line of demarcation between itself and the anti-interventionist right for the simple reason that both sides seek to garner the support of the petty-bourgeois majority for a similarly national chauvinist agenda.

All mass politics in the major imperialist countries is necessarily geared towards representing and advancing the interests of non-proletarian classes and class fractions in receipt of (a share of) the value transferred from the global South proletariat, semi-proletariat and peasantry. Paradoxically, the material demands of the popular classes in the global North for wealth redistribution are typically upheld by leftists therein as advancing the cause of socialism when, in fact, these demands can only be met by means of imperialism, settlerism, nativism and/or fascism. In the global South, where the ruling strata are effectively subcontractors for imperialism, economic populism has a progressive democratic content (albeit with the abiding potential of inflaming intra-proletarian tensions on the basis of ethnic or national chauvinism conducive to local capitalist interests). In the major imperialist countries, however, populism primarily serves to enhance the feelings of entitlement of the *haute* petty-bourgeois majority, that is, the wealthiest fraction of the petty-bourgeois classes at the world level. In short, the 'liberal' left, the 'radical' left and the radical right in the major imperialist countries are each populist and social imperialist as a condition of their popularity with non-proletarian working bourgeois and *haute* petty bourgeois strata with vested interests in imperialism.

It is, or should be, readily acknowledged that there is a pseudo-left component to all fascism. While preserving capitalism, fascism aims to broaden its base of support by means of the *embourgeoisement* of the working classes, this to be achieved at the expense of the 'inferior' nations or 'races'. Thus fascism is not opposed to the provision of welfare to all members of the '*Herrenvolk*', or to 'national comrades' having a monopoly on relatively well-paid and comfortable employment. Indeed, the Nazi regime was experienced very differently by 'Aryan' workers in Germany, Polish immigrant workers in Germany, Jews in and outside the 'Greater Reich', and the working masses in the German-occupied territories of the Soviet Union.

The 'socialist' or social-imperialist aspect of Nazism certainly explains why 'proletarian passivity against, if not acceptance of the Nazi-takeover in 1933 was widespread', and why there was at least tacit German support for Nazi imperialism thereafter.[13]

What is not so commonly understood, however, is that Nazism not only presented itself as socialist, it also presented itself as 'anti-imperialist' both at home and abroad, and not only when it was trying to convince the Arab people that it was their ally in the struggle against British colonialism. The Nazis portrayed their society as being in direct opposition to the pluto-cratic, ('Jewish') finance capitalism of Britain and the United States. The Italian fascists, likewise, presented both Italy and Germany as 'proletarian nations' exploited by usurious cabals of foreign bankers. Similarly, today's fascists present their politics as a struggle between populist ethnocentrism and neoliberal multiculturalism, with globalisation representing the victory of imperialism over nationalism. Of course, despite some fascists pretending respect for the national and 'racial' integrity of all nations, and not just 'white' ones, the putative anti-imperialism of the fascist movement was, is and can only be a fraud, since the preservation and extension of labour *embourgeoise-ment* is possible only on the basis of monopoly capitalist property relations (albeit with the financial sector temporarily abased and with a significant element of labour imperialism) and with that the exploitation of 'foreign' territories or peoples.

On the populist right today, the ideology of the 'ethno-state' expresses the revanchist desire to return to the racialised politics of the pre-globalisation era when the state was more or less openly white nationalist in both met-ropolitan and settler-colonial countries. By contrast, both left nationalism and neoliberal social democracy generally uphold a form of domestic mul-ticulturalism which purports to be internationalist, but like right populism displays complete indifference to the imperialist nature of First World (British, French, German, Japanese, US and so on) economy and society, the taproot of which is global monopoly combined with international wage divergence.

Meanwhile, the 'revolutionary' *anti*-anti-imperialist left in the metro-politan countries has demonstrated a marked preference for neo-colonial globalisation abroad and social democracy at home, thus aligning itself firmly with US imperialism. Conversely, the 'revolutionary' 'anti-imperialist' metropolitan left very often makes common cause with the forces of fascist reaction on the basis of a common 'anti-establishment' nationalism aimed at bolstering the global standing of the metropolitan working- and petty-bourgeoisie by curbing the power of 'transnational' finance. Some met-ropolitan leftists even go so far as to echo far right opposition to so-called 'identity politics', condemning the resistance of colonised New Afrikan/

Black and Chicano/a populations, women and minority ethnic populations to patriarchal, white nationalist revanchism as little more than a culturalist abdication of pure 'class struggle'. The putative 'anti-imperialist left' appears content to work alongside the far right, and to indulge in similar rhetoric about elites, globalisation and white working class victimhood, thus adding fuel to the fires of social chauvinism, populism and, ultimately, imperialism itself.

To some extent, left nationalism, right populism and neoliberal social democracy represent distinct configurations of popular classes and class fractions in the geographic centres of global capital formation. Regularity of employment, career prospects, wage levels and working conditions vary according to occupation and levels of cultural capital, and in relation to the business cycle. Moreover, national, 'racial' and gender divisions underlie all class formations and alliances. Broadly speaking, right populism is reflective of the declining power of the traditional white labour aristocracy in the imperialist countries, those whose social position has been or risks being undercut by the relocation of industry to and immigration from the global South; left nationalism appeals to the more precarious strata of educated youth, public sector workers and minority ethnic populations in the capital cities; and neoliberal social democracy (and its 'centre-right' permutations) appeals to those sections of the population who continue to benefit from globalisation's prevailing property and labour market dispensation, particularly skilled workers in dynamic sectors of export-oriented industry and services.

The unionised metropolitan workforce tends to vacillate between neoliberal social democracy and left nationalism. Yet the metropolitan trade union movement can swing sharply to the right where immigration appears to threaten the labour market advantages of its members. In Germany today, for example, large unions have come out in support of the right populist Alternative for Germany (AfD, *Alternative für Deutschland*), a party very much in the Nazi mould.[14] The lumpen populations of the ethnically/nationally dominant majority in the metropolitan countries, meanwhile, tend to gravitate politically towards the ideology of the traditional (pre-neoliberal) labour aristocracy, and are regularly enlisted as the enforcers of its authority.

It is a mistake to suppose, however, that today's left nationalism and right (fascist) populism have radically different class constituencies. Clearly, this was the case in the 1920s and 1930s, despite *embourgeoisement* accompanying the success of the fascist project in Germany at least having led to significant overlap in the state's support bases. At that time, as it is today, fascism was primarily a movement of the petty-bourgeoisie, specifically, small shopkeepers, farmers and white-collar workers, the latter

highly conscious of their material privileges relative to the industrial proletariat, albeit with some support from sections of the industrial working
class. As Glazebrook argues:

Fascism is a mass movement, predominantly rooted in a middle class
whose privileges are being undermined by capitalist crisis, and whose
'national pride' has been wounded by national decline and military defeat
and humiliation. It is based on a promise to restore these privileges and
national pride through, on a domestic level, purging 'impure elements'
within the polity blamed for national weakness, and on an international level, restoring military prowess and 'great power' status. It is a
'pseudo-revolutionary' movement inasmuch as, whilst it adopts much in
the way of imagery and policies from the socialists, it does not threaten
fundamental property relations: rather, it redirects popular anger away
from powerful elites and towards vulnerable scapegoats in a way that
actually serves the 'elites' it claims to oppose. It is sponsored and helped
to power by powerful elements of the dominant political and economic
classes. It opposes liberalism on the grounds that liberalism is unable or
unwilling to deal effectively with those internal and external enemies
weakening the national polity.[15]

With imperialist mass *embourgeoisement*, right populism and left nationalism come to have intersecting social bases as opposed to having rigidly
distinctive constituencies. In the richest countries no group of workers as
such has an objective interest in anti-imperialist socialism; a socialist redistribution of internationally produced value would leave the metropolitan
workforce materially worse off, even insofar as its welfare provisions are
cemented. Both metropolitan right populism and metropolitan left nationalism make a foundational appeal to national chauvinism, that is, to the
strengthening of national privileges grounded in imperialism. Left nationalism can easily elide into left ethnocentrism, particularly when issues of
migration and citizenship come to the fore. The putative 'anti-imperialism'
of sections of the far right is found at the intersection of left nationalism
and right populism; it combines welfarism and protectionism with ethnocentrism and what Marx called 'petty-bourgeois socialism'.[16] Up to the last
decade or so, the state has been the site of rapprochement by hegemonic
sections of metropolitan labour and capital, respectively. The crisis of globalisation, the Great Recession has eroded the social class partnership
underlying social democracy in both its Keynesian and neoliberal phases,
however, and both the right and left populists hope to retrench labour aristocratic ascendancy, whether on a tacitly or explicitly social-imperialist basis.

A net recipient of wealth produced by the exploited workforce of the global South, the insecure middle class majority in the imperialist countries, mostly composed of workers, reacts against the erosion of its national privileges. It fights a rearguard action against the neoliberal imperatives of the hegemonic imperialist class using national parliamentary democracy as its weapon to guarantee exclusive entitlement to the spoils of superexploitation and plunder. Yet as markets become more uncertain, rivalry with the rising powers of the global South deepens, and the most marginalised youth of Western society become more restive, it is likely that the ruling classes in Britain and elsewhere will have increasing recourse to the populism of the traditional labour aristocracy and petty-bourgeoisie. Those sections of metropolitan capital which do not have the global reach of the leading financial and multinational concerns, which are unable to take advantage of global labour arbitrage and outsourcing, and which cannot compete in free markets with the traditional or rising imperialist powers look to protectionism, business nationalism and militarism as the surest guarantors of their continued rule.

In opposition to the aforementioned tendencies, internationalist, feminist, labour anti-imperialism observes that private property in the major means of production is only compatible with 'democracy' where the exploitation of especially oppressed foreign or domestic labour is the central node in the circuit of capital. In other words, metropolitan workers who wish to remove the yoke of capital from their shoulders can do so only in circumstances where additional surplus value extracted from oppressed populations ceases to allow for the *embourgeoisement* of the majority workforce in their countries. As Patnaik and Patnaik correctly argue, given the huge differences in material conditions and consciousness between workers and farmers at the centre and at the 'periphery' of the global economy forging common bonds of labour solidarity poses formidable problems for the left at the present time.[17] While the crisis of imperialism places internationalism on the political agenda once more, it is only the most marginalised and precarious minority sections of the working populations of the major imperialist countries who may be ready to act as its champions. By contrast, particularly if the left therein is ready to take up the challenge of reforming characteristically pre-capitalist agrarian relations, the workers and farmers of the global South are economically predisposed to lead the global struggle against imperialism and for socialism.

Appendix: Physical Quality of Life in Capitalist and Socialist Countries

Using World Bank data (especially the 1983 *World Development Report*), Cereseto and Waitzkin compared the physical quality of life (PQL) measures of capitalist and socialist countries at similar levels of economic development in the early 1980s. The level of economic development was measured according to gross national product (GNP) per capita of the sampled capitalist and socialist countries, respectively. The designators 'socialist' or 'capitalist' were applied according to whether the World Bank had classified them as market economies or as centrally planned economies, respectively. The capitalist countries surveyed comprised approximately 62 per cent of the world's population at the time; the socialist countries, approximately 32 per cent; and the then 'post-revolutionary' countries, about 3 per cent. Examining infant mortality rates, life expectancy and literacy rates, the authors computed composite measures of PQL so as to compare the respective performances of capitalist and socialist countries.[1] The authors summarised their findings as follows:

The data revealed major associations of PQL with both level of economic development and political-economic system. All the measures showed marked improvements as level of economic development increased. However, at the same level of economic development, the socialist countries showed more favorable outcomes than the capitalist countries in nearly all the PQL variables. The more favorable performance of the socialist countries was evident in 22 of 24 comparisons. Differences between capitalist and socialist countries in PQL were greatest at lower levels of economic development. The discrepancies between capitalist and socialist systems tended to narrow at the higher levels of development, although differences in PQL persisted even at those levels.[2]

In reality, by the early 1960s at the latest, the socialist countries of the Eastern bloc had embarked upon a process whereby their economies would become increasingly based upon state monopoly capitalism under the command of corrupt and unaccountable 'Communist' Party elites. By the early 1980s all of the socialist countries including China had economies where production was 'planned' according to market profitability criteria applied at the level of the industrial sector or individual firm. The covert restoration of capitalism in the socialist countries was massively undermining the social and economic basis of socialism. Nonetheless, in all cases there continued to be high levels of state involvement in the economy and provision of generous welfare entitlements to the population. The continued application of socialist redistributive norms throughout the 'socialist' world ensured that citizens of poor socialist countries were far better off physically than those of poor capitalist countries.

The following list presents the classification of countries that was used in the study. Within each category, the ordering of countries corresponds to that of the World Bank.

CAPITALIST COUNTRIES

Low-income: Bhutan, Chad, Bangladesh, Nepal, Burma, Mali, Malawi, Zaire, Uganda, Burundi, Upper Volta, Rwanda, India, Somalia, Tanzania, Guinea, Haiti, Sri Lanka, Benin, Central African Republic, Sierra Leone, Madagascar, Niger, Pakistan, Sudan, Togo, Ghana, Kenya, Senegal, Mauritania, Yemen (Arab Republic), Liberia, Indonesia.

Lower-middle-income: Lesotho, Bolivia, Honduras, Zambia, Egypt, El Salvador, Thailand, Philippines, Papua New Guinea, Morocco, Nigeria, Cameroon, Congo, Guatemala, Peru, Ecuador, Jamaica, Ivory Coast, Dominican Republic, Colombia, Tunisia, Costa Rica, Turkey, Syria, Jordan, Paraguay, South Korea, Lebanon.

Upper-middle-income: Iran, Iraq, Algeria, Brazil, Mexico, Portugal, Argentina, Chile, South Africa, Uruguay, Venezuela, Greece, Hong Kong, Israel, Singapore, Trinidad and Tobago, Ireland, Spain, Italy, New Zealand.

High-income: United Kingdom, Japan, Austria, Finland, Australia, Canada, Netherlands, Belgium, France, United States, Denmark, West Germany, Norway, Sweden, Switzerland. High-income-oil-exporting: Libya, Saudi Arabia, Kuwait, United Arab Emirates.

SOCIALIST COUNTRIES

Low-income: China.
  Lower-middle-income: Cuba, Mongolia, North Korea, Albania.
  Upper-middle-income: Yugoslavia, Hungary, Romania, Bulgaria, Poland, USSR, Czechoslovakia, East Germany.

RECENT POSTREVOLUTIONARY COUNTRIES

Low-income: Kampuchea, Laos, Ethiopia, Afghanistan, Vietnam, Mozambique, Yemen (People's Democratic Republic), Angola, Nicaragua, Zimbabwe.[3]

Table A.1 Physical quality of life comparison, socialist and capitalist countries at similar level of development

Infant mortality (per 1,000, 1981)	Capitalist Countries	Socialist Countries
Low-income	131	71
Lower-middle-income	81	38
Upper-middle-income	42	22
High-income	10	–
High-income-oil-exporting	73	–

Child death rate (per 1,000), 1981	Capitalist Countries	Socialist Countries
Low-income	25.7	7
Lower-middle-income	11	2.3
Upper-middle-income	4	1.1
High-income	(<1)	–
High-income-oil-exporting	8.2	–

Population per nursing person, 1980	Capitalist Countries	Socialist Countries
Low-income	4 763	1 890
Lower-middle-income	1 646	303
Upper-middle-income	692	210
High-income	142	–
High-income-oil-exporting	518	–

Daily per capital calorie supply (% requirement), 1980	Capitalist Countries	Socialist Countries
Low-income	94	107
Lower-middle-income	106	117
Upper-middle-income	122	137
High-income	131	–
High-income-oil-exporting	134	–

Crude birth rate (per 1,000), 1981	Capitalist Countries	Socialist Countries
Low-income	46	21
Lower-middle-income	38	28
Upper-middle-income	26	26
High-income	13	–
High-income-oil-exporting	40	–

Population per physician, 1980	Capitalist Countries	Socialist Countries
Low-income	19 100	1 920
Lower-middle-income	5 832	638
Upper-middle-income	1 154	488
High-income	524	–
High-income-oil-exporting	965	–

Higher education (% age group), 1980	Capitalist Countries	Socialist Countries
Low-income	1.7	1.0
Lower-middle-income	12.1	11.7
Upper-middle-income	15.7	18.6
High-income	28.3	–
High-income-oil-exporting	7	–

PQLI, 1980–81	Capitalist Countries	Socialist Countries
Low-income	35	76
Lower-middle-income	62	83
Upper-middle-income	81	92
High-income	98	–
High-income-oil-exporting	60	–

	Life expectancy (years), 1981		Adult literacy rate (%), 1980		Crude death rate (per 1,000), 1981		Secondary education (% age group), 1980	
Low-income	48	67	34	69	18	8	15	34
Lower-middle-income	60	68	63	87	11	6	38	74
Upper-middle-income	69	72	81	97	9	11	59	74
High-income	75	–	99	–	10	–	86	–
High-income-oil-exporting	61	–	50	–	9	–	56	–

Note: For further discussion of the statistical analysis and significance testing see Appendix therein. P values reported here were computed by two-tailed t-test for the difference of means between capitalist and socialist countries at the same level of economic development.

Source: Cereseto and Waitzkin 1986, pp. 650–1.

Notes

Preface

1. Çelik 2017.
2. Linder 1985, p. 37.
3. Engels 1962 [1858], p. 537.
4. Hobsbawm 1970, p. 208.
5. Foster 1974.
6. Gray 1976.

1 Value Transfer

1. Patnaik 1995, p. 84. 'Periphery' is in parentheses here to indicate the paradoxical fact of underdeveloped world labour's economic centrality to patterns of global capital accumulation, albeit alongside enormous divergences in associated gains. Smith (2013) notes how the term 'periphery' is particularly anachronistic in the context of 80 per cent of the world's industrial workforce today residing in the global South.
2. Higginbottom 2015, p. 23.
3. Amin 2015a, p. 14.
4. Bieler et al. 2015, p. 4.
5. Swanson 2017, p. 24.
6. Lenin 1970 [1916].
7. Freeman 1998, p. 4.
8. Hickel 2017, p. 18.
9. Baran and Sweezy 1966, p. 178.
10. Schumpeter 1951, p. 96. Former World Bank economist Professor Branko Milanovic has convincingly argued, however, that Schumpeter realised that monopoly capitalism does indeed have very good reasons to prefer imperialist foreign policies, namely, so that the monopolist firms 'can use cheap native labor ...; they can market their products even in the colonies at monopoly prices; they can finally invest capital that would only depress the profit at home and that could be placed in other civilized countries only at very low interest rates' (Schumpeter, *The Economics and Sociology of Capitalism*, pp. 201–2). To the extent that Schumpeter considered monopoly capitalism the most efficient and innovative form of capitalism, Milanovic argues that his theory of imperialism comes very close to the Marxist and Leninist theory that considers imperialism inseparable from capitalism at a certain monopoly phase of its development.
11. Marx 1977 [1885], Chapter 19.
12. Day 1981, pp. 9–12.
13. Sweezy 1949, pp. 97–100.
14. Wood 2003.
15. Addo 1986.
16. Hadjimichalis 1984, p. 338.
17. Ibid., pp. 340–1.
18. Marx 1977 [1894], Chapters 9–11.
19. Hadjimichalis 1984, pp. 341–2.
20. Warren 1973, p. 41. See also Warren 1980.
21. Kiely 2009.
22. See especially Amin 1974; Emmanuel 1972; Frank 1966; Rodney 1989 [1972]; Cardoso and Faletto 1979. For 'orthodox' Marxist criticisms of Dependency theory, see Bettelheim 1972; Brenner 1977; Weeks and Dore 1979.

23. Dos Santos 1970, p. 231.
24. Bello et al. 1999, p. 7.
25. Ibid., p. 3.
26. Smith 2010, p. 49.
27. Raffer 1987, p. 10.
28. Yoshihara and Veneziani 2016; Slaughter 2001.
29. Suwandi 2015, p. 47; see also Niño-Zarazúa et al. 2017.
30. Nolan 2012, p. 66.
31. Kerswell 2012. With reference to World Bank and United Nations data, King (2018, p. 447) has shown that there has been no convergence in prosperity or developmental levels between rich and poor states during the neoliberal era. Almost all states (98.6 per cent by population) are either rich or poor, with 85 per cent defined as poor, and there has been a widening of the income gap between these two extremes. King demonstrates that rising average Chinese income over the period to a level similar to other large relatively developed poor states such as Mexico and Brazil does not challenge this polarisation. He concludes that what has transpired in China and some other regions is a new relative level of development among still poor states.
32. Kadri 2015; Liberti 2011.
33. Tausch 2002, p. 235; cf. Braun and Topan 1998, pp. 35–7.
34. Tausch 2002, pp. 247, 252.
35. Sogge 2002, p. 34.
36. Hickel 2017, p. 27.
37. Watkin 2001.
38. Krooth 1980, pp. 76–7.
39. Aristide 2001, pp. 11–12; cf. Sogge 2002, p. 35.
40. World Bank 2001, p. 246; cf. Sogge 2002, p. 35.
41. IMF 2000, p. 263; cf. Sogge 2002, p. 35.
42. Hickel 2017, p. 26.
43. Cope 2015, p. 303; cf. Prebisch 1950; Singer 1950.
44. Heintz 2003, p. 8.
45. Wood 1997.
46. Gelb 1999; cf. Sogge 2002, p. 36.
47. Tripathi 2000, p. 6.
48. Raman 2005.
49. Raffer 1987, p. 74; cf. Braun 1977. Amin disputes Braun's periodisation of North-South economic exploitation arguing that the period of unequal exchange as the dominant form thereof must be dated from the time when double factoral terms of trade became especially significant, that is, from around the beginning of Braun's third phase. For Amin (1976, pp. 148ff.), unequal exchange in terms of double factoral terms of trade is defined as occurring when 'labor of the same productivity is rewarded at a lower rate in the periphery'. From the 1880s onwards, he argues, wage increases in the metropolitan areas have sustained enhanced autochthonic reproduction at the same time that conditions for unequal exchange were established. Nonetheless, whereas Braun argues for the centrality of capital flows from the metropolis to the periphery in this third period, his view that there were then insufficient outlets for investment in the centre does not necessarily contradict Amin's view that wage increases would establish the conditions for domestic outlets for investments, or that they had already done so in some measure even at that time (Raffer 1987, p. 90).

2 Colonial Tribute

1. Blaut 1987, p. 105.
2. Ibid., p. 181.
3. Acemoğlu et al. 2002.
4. Barnes 1939.
5. Kittrell 1965, p. 49.

6. Habib 2002, pp. 8–9; cf. Gallagher and Robinson (1953) and Macdonagh (1962) for discussion on the concept of 'free trade imperialism' as practised by the British Empire in the mid-Victorian age.
7. Thomas and McCloskey 1981.
8. Tucker 1960, p. 135.
9. Ibid., p. 141.
10. Mill 1972 [1861], p. 72.
11. Ibid., p. 73.
12. Losurdo 2011, pp. 225–6; cf. ibid., p. 198.
13. Mill 1963–91, p. 247.
14. Mill 1909, p. 739; cf. Tucker 1960, p. 136.
15. Porter 1984, p. 142.
16. The advanced capitalist economies of imperialist Europe and North America became increasingly thoroughly dependent on securing sources of cheap raw materials in the colonial and semi-colonial world. By 1925, the Caribbean, South Africa, Asia and Oceania (furnishing about 73 per cent of colonial produce) produced some 54–60 per cent of all oil seeds, 50 per cent of all textiles, 34–5 per cent of all cereals and other foodstuffs, 100 per cent of rubber, 24–8 per cent of all fertilisers and chemicals and 17 per cent of all cereals alone (an average increase of 137 per cent of 1913 levels of raw material production) (Krooth 1980, pp. 84–5).
17. Deane 1965, pp. 66–8; cf. Frank 1978, p. 227.
18. Anievas and Nişancıoğlu 2015, p. 143.
19. Hickel 2017, p. 19.
20. Ibid., p. 71.
21. Anievas and Nişancıoğlu 2015, p. 145.
22. Ibid., p. 147.
23. Schumpeter 1960, pp. 64–6.
24. Engerman 1972.
25. Blackburn 2011, pp. 105–6.
26. Hickel 2017, p. 74.
27. Weber 1981 [1927], p. 298.
28. Marx 1977 [1867], p. 925.
29. Jevons quoted in Kennedy, p. 194.
30. Kennedy 1989, p. 194.
31. Anievas and Nişancıoğlu 2015, p. 151.
32. Patnaik 2011.
33. Anievas and Nişancıoğlu 2015, p. 151.
34. Ibid., p. 152.
35. Hickel 2017, p. 74.
36. Anievas and Nişancıoğlu 2015, p. 164. See also Beckert and Rockman (2016) for an exploration of the ways in which slavery contributed to capitalist development in the United States, and how capitalism profoundly shaped American slavery.
37. Bagchi 1982, pp. 22–3.
38. Ibid., p. 24.
39. See Tharoor 2017 for an in-depth account of British colonial parasitism in India.
40. Bagchi 1982, p. 24.
41. Ibid., pp. 26–7.
42. Ibid., p. 31.
43. Böröcz 2016, pp. 57, 63–4, 68.
44. Patnaik and Patnaik 2017.
45. Hickel 2017, p. 21; cf. Rodrik 2001.
46. Smith 2002, p. 43.
47. Ibid., p. 7.
48. Cope 2013, pp. 118–21.

3 Monopoly Rent

1. Amin 2014, pp. vii–viii.
2. Bukharin 1973 [1915 and 1917], pp. 104–6.
3. Amin 2011, p. 11n.
4. Pal 2005, pp. 395–6; cf. Kalecki 2008 [1935].
5. Amin 2012. See also Higginbottom 2015.
6. Amin 2012, p. 85.
7. Clelland 2016, p. 1032.
8. Crooks 2004.
9. Mangum and Philips 1988, p. 10.
10. Emmanuel quoted in Raffer 1987, p. 38.
11. Smith 2002, p. 9.
12. Ibid., p. 288.
13. Ibid., p. 15.
14. Ibid., p. 15.
15. Brown 2012.
16. Smith 2002, p. 15.
17. Makhijani 1992, p. 163.
18. Smith 2002, p. 16.
19. Ibid., p. 22.
20. Bieler et al. 2015, p. 4; Chang 2006.
21. Wallerstein 2000 [1988], p. 338.
22. Norfield 2016, p. 118.
23. Nolan 2012, pp. 20–1.
24. Ibid., pp. 48–50.
25. Ibid.; cf. BERR 2008.
26. Patnaik 2007 [2000], p. 25.
27. EcoNexus and Berne Declaration 2013.
28. Ibid.
29. Menon 1982, p. 8.
30. FAO 2004, p. 31.
31. Chossudovsky 2003, p. 80.
32. Jaffe 1985, p. 140.
33. Wong et al. 2011, p. 10.
34. Ibid.
35. Folfas 2009.
36. Wong et al. 2011, pp. 10–11.
37. Folfas 2009.
38. Menon 1982, p. 15.
39. Ibid.
40. Hickel 2017, p. 26.
41. Eaton 1949, p. 147.
42. Barnet and Müller 1974.
43. Roxborough 1979, p. 58.
44. Harvie and de Angelis 2008.
45. Cope 2015, pp. 261–3.
46. Raffer 1987, p. 12.
47. Ibid., p. 53.
48. Clelland 2016, p. 1030.
49. Ibid., p. 1029. See also Lauesen and Cope 2015.
50. Clelland 2016, p. 1037.
51. Ibid., p. 1030; cf. Fröbel et al. 1980.
52. Clelland 2016, p. 1031; cf. Gereffi et al. 2005.

53. Heintz 2003, p. 3.
54. Patnaik and Patnaik 2017, p. 75.
55. Heintz 2003, p. 5.
56. Ibid., p. 3.
57. Ibid., p. 2.
58. The term 'commodity chains' was invented by sociologists Immanuel Wallerstein and Terence Hopkins to highlight the fact that capitalist production processes have always crossed multiple geographical boundaries, each containing within them multiple modes of controlling and utilising labour. For Wallerstein and Hopkins, this insight allows us to establish how surplus value is distributed among its appropriators internationally and, thus, how the system of unequal exchange works in practice (Wallerstein rarely, if ever, uses the term 'imperialism' to describe this system, but that is surely implied) (Wallerstein and Hopkins 2000 [1986], p. 221).
59. Heintz 2003, p. 1.
60. Clelland 2016, p. 1032.
61. Ibid., p. 1033.
62. Ibid.
63. Ibid., p. 1037.

4 Unequal Exchange

1. Andersson 2006, p. 120.
2. Emmanuel 1972, p. 64.
3. Brolin 2007, pp. 1–2.
4. Marx 1977 [1867], p.574.
5. Zarembka 2015, p. 107.
6. Roberts 2017.
7. Raffer 1987, pp. 19–20.
8. Ibid., p. 75.
9. Ibid., p. 43.
10. Smith 1976 [1776], p. 142.
11. Marx 1963 [1863], p. 569.
12. Raffer 1987, p. 14; cf. Lin Biao 1965.
13. Braun 1977, p. 49.
14. Raffer 1987, p. 78.
15. Braun 1977, p. 54.
16. Raffer 1987, p. 80.
17. Braun 1977, p. 114; cf. also p. 111.
18. Amin 1976, p. 148n.
19. Webber and Foot 1984, p. 939.
20. Li 2016, p. 73.
21. Ibid., p. 75.
22. The World Trade Organization (WTO 2017) states that poorer exporting countries such as Cambodia and Bangladesh face tariffs 15 times higher than those applied to wealthy nations and oil exporters, while consumers and governments in rich countries have paid US$350 billion per year supporting agriculture – enough to fly their 41 million dairy cows first class around the world one and a half times.
23. Sau 1982, pp. 119–20; Shaikh 1979, pp. 301–2.
24. Shaikh 1979, pp. 298–9.
25. Sau 1982, p. 120.
26. Ibid.
27. Sau 1978, pp. 164–5.
28. I am indebted to Gernot Köhler for providing this example in private correspondence.
29. Raffer 1987, p. 266.

30. Ibid., p. 267.
31. 'Maxwell's Demon' is a term from thermal and statistical physics referring to James Clerk Maxwell's thought experiment imagining the possibility of refuting the Second Law of Thermodynamics. 'In the thought experiment, a demon controls a small door between two chambers of gas. As individual gas molecules approach the door, the demon quickly opens and shuts the door so that fast molecules pass into the other chamber, while slow molecules remain in the first chamber. Because faster molecules are hotter, the demon's behaviour causes one chamber to warm up as the other cools, thus decreasing entropy and violating the Second Law of Thermodynamics' (Wikipedia). International value transfer has curbed capitalism's entropy only insofar as it has been relatively capable of displacing its most heated contradictions to its 'periphery'.
32. Martinez-Alier 2002, p. 204.

5 Imperialism and Its Denial

1. Finger 2017, p. 135.
2. Ibid.
3. John Smith, private correspondence.
4. Jedlicki 2007.
5. Marx 1977 [1867], p. 53. It is important to note that similarly skilled workers in sectors as diverse as education, transportation, retail, information technology, engineering and many others earn highly divergent wages internationally.
6. Raffer 1987, p. 42.
7. There are several pressing reasons why the *haute bourgeoisie* in command of the heights of the global capitalist economy pays its domestic working class superwages, even where it is not forced to by militant trade union struggle within the metropolis. *Economically*, the *embourgeoisement* of metropolitan workers has provided oligopolies with the secure and thriving consumer markets necessary to capital's expanded reproduction. *Politically*, the stability of imperialist polities with a working class majority is of paramount concern to cautious investors and their representatives in government. *Militarily*, a pliant and/or quiescent workforce furnishes both the national chauvinist personnel required to enforce global hegemony and a secure base from which to launch the subjugation of Third World territories. Finally, *ideologically*, the lifestyles and cultural mores enjoyed by most First World workers signifies to the Third World not what benefits imperialism brings, but what capitalist industrial development and parliamentary democracy alone can supposedly achieve (Cope 2015, p. 76).
8. Smith 2016, p. 220.
9. See, for example, Szymanski 1981, especially pp. 465–92.
10. Emmanuel and Bettelheim 1970, p. 18.
11. Green and Sutcliffe 1987, p. 46.
12. Sutcliffe 1980, pp. 324–5.
13. Amin 1977, p. 211.
14. Roxborough 1979, p. 60.
15. Kohlmey 1962; cf. Raffer 1987, p. 26.
16. Finger 2017, p. 128.
17. Marx 1968 [1863], Chapter IV. Theories of Productive and Unproductive Labour; cf. Marx 1977 [1885], pp. 135, 136, 299, 376.
18. Marx 1977 [1867], pp. 518–19. My emphasis.
19. Finger 2017, p. 128.
20. I am indebted to Scott Horne for the four sentences following the quotation.
21. Maddison 1994, p. 47.
22. Nolan 2012, p. 95.
23. United Nations (2012), Figure III.5. 'External Debt Service-To-Exports Ratio, 2005–2010', p. 91. See Knauss (2015) on the statistical manipulation involved in World Bank calculations

that determine the size and earnings of the 'global middle class'. World Bank economist Nancy Birdsall (2010) considers only those who earn at least US$10 a day as part of the global South's middle class. By this standard, a mere 3 per cent of China's urban population, and only 1 per cent of its rural population are middle class. In South Africa, this standard puts the middle class at 8 per cent of the population, in Brazil at 19 per cent and in Mexico at 28 per cent. If the same criterion were used for the United States, the middle class would consist of fully 91 per cent of the population.

24. Personal email correspondence between author and Torkil Lauesen.

25. Emmanuel 1972, pp. 376–8.

6 Measuring Imperialist Value Transfer

1. Amin 2011.

2. Hickel 2017, p. 30.

3. Global Financial Integrity 2016, p. 4; Global Financial Integrity 2017, Table X-1. 'Estimated Illicit Financial Flows, All Developing Countries, 2005–2014', p. vii.

4. Global Financial Integrity 2016, p. 2.

5. Ibid., Table 3. 'Recorded Transfers (RecT) to and from All Developing Countries, 1980–2012 (billions of U.S. dollars)', p. 11.

6. Global Financial Integrity 2017, p. iii.

7. Ibid.

8. Global Financial Integrity 2016, p. 3.

9. Global Financial Integrity 2017, p. viii.

10. Ibid., p. iii.

11. UNCTAD 2016, p. 2.

12. Baker 2005, p. 30.

13. Christian Aid 2009. See also Sikka and Willmott 2010.

14. Christian Aid 2009, p. 8.

15. Bettelheim 1972, p. 271.

16. Lauesen and Cope 2015, p. 54.

17. This formula is a modification of the one set forth by Köhler 2002, p. 13.

18. OECD 2017.

19. We follow here the World Bank's classification of countries into 'high-income' as those with a Gross National Income per person at market prices of US$11,906, and 'low and middle-income' countries as below this level (World Bank 2010, p. xxiii).

20. ILO 2017.

21. Moyo and Yeros 2007, p. 176.

22. Gowan 1999, p. 56.

23. Pallares-Miralles et al. 2012.

24. Towers Watson 2015, p. 28.

25. ALFI 2015.

26. Johnston et al. 1987, p. 242.

27. Hobson 1968 [1902], p. 314

28. Lenin 1968 [1915–16], p. 420; ibid., pp. 194–5.

29. Davies 1973, p. 49.

30. Jaffe 1980, p. 63.

7 Measuring Colonial Value Transfer

1. Jaffe 1980, p. 113.

2. Ibid., p. 102.

3. Ibid., p. 111.

4. Karmakar 2001, p. 69.

5. Frank 1966.

6. Baran 1957, p. 163.
7. Karmakar 2001, p. 67.
8. Edelstein 1994, p. 203.
9. Ibid., p. 204.
10. Patnaik 2006, p. 36.
11. Ibid., p. 41.
12. Braudel 1982, p. 279.
13. Stavrianos 1981, p. 171.
14. Bagchi 1972.
15. Patnaik 2006, pp. 49–50, quoted in Cope 2014, pp. 276–8.
16. Williams 1944, p. 142.
17. Hira 2014, p. 19.
18. Ibid., pp. 19–20.
19. Jones 1974, p. 170.
20. Robinson 1970, pp. 64–6.
21. See, for instance, Lane 1987.
22. Jones 1981, p. 67.
23. Davis 1979, p. 52.
24. Hersh and Voth 2009.
25. McCants 2007, p. 436.
26. Ibid., p. 446.
27. McCants 2007.
28. Higginbottom 2015, p. 24.
29. Baran 1957, p. 247.

8 Comparing Value Transfer to Profits, Wages and Capital

1. Lenin, V. I. 1970 [1916].
2. United Nations Development Programme 2011, p. 100.
3. This measure of determining the size of the developing country workforce employed in developed country industrial concerns has been simplified in certain respects. First, as is in fact the case, where the foreign-owned sector in the developing countries is expanding because of increased FDI, and the size of domestic capital there is dwindling due to foreign competition, then the relative absolute sizes of foreign-owned versus domestic-owned capitals cannot be definitively inferred from the ratio of FDI to GFCF. Indeed, it is likely that the export-industrial sector of developing country industry is larger than 15 per cent of the whole. Second, many direct investors outsource the hiring of direct labour as well as the production of intermediate inputs, and it is therefore difficult to disentangle these 'hybrid forms' of labour arbitrage from those corresponding to FDI as opposed to the arm's length relationship. This measure of the FDI-weighted workforce is, therefore, correspondingly conservative, favouring social chauvinist arguments, while nonetheless refuting their conclusions about the insignificance of capital export to capital accumulation in the First World. Finally, there is a risk of overestimating the FDI-weighted industrial workforce insofar as more workers are employed per dollar invested in mining and other extractive industries than in manufacturing. I am indebted to Dr John Smith for pointing out these limitations, but I consider that the calculation provides a sound overall picture of the matter.
4. Harvie and de Angelis 2008.
5. Eurostat 2017. Gross Operating Rate by NACE Rev. 2. %. Online: http://ec.europa.eu/eurostat/tgm/table.do?tab=table&init=1&plugin=1&language=en&pcode=tin00155 (accessed 17 November 2018).
6. World Bank 2017. GDP (current US$). Online: https://data.worldbank.org/indicator/NY.GDP.MKTP.CD (accessed 17 November 2018).
7. ILO 2011b, p. 56.
8. Rosenthal and Martin 2008.

9. OECD 2016.
10. UNESCO 2013.
11. Alexander 1996, pp. 59–70.
12. Cope 2015, pp. 265–66.
13. Amin 2018, p. 30.
14. See, for example, Harvie 2005.
15. Köhler 2007, p. 55.
16. The idea for Figure 8.2, a graphical comparison between global consumption and global production, was suggested to me by Dr John Smith in private correspondence. I am indebted to Dr Smith for the use of the idea herein.
17. Clark 1899, p. 3; cf. Baran and Sweezy 2012, p. 29.
18. Marx 1977 [1867], p. 53.
19. Engels 2010 [1884], pp. 181–2.
20. For a Marxist view on productive and unproductive labour, see Amin 1976, p. 244; Cope 2015, pp. 231–8; Marx 1963 [1863], p. 157; Marx 1977 [1867], pp. 518–19; Resnick and Wolff 2006, pp. 206–20; Shaikh and Tonak 1994, p. 25.
21. Köhler 2005, p. 9.
22. Piketty and Saez 2004.

9 Anti-Imperialist Marxism and the Wages of Imperialism

1. We define the bourgeoisie as that group in society which directly (through full or part ownership of the means of production) or indirectly (through being paid superwages) depends upon the exploitation of workers for all or part of its income. Superwages are wages above the level whereby an hour's worth of concrete labour can purchase on the market more than the product of an hour's abstract labour.
2. Settler colonialism is generally recognised as distinct from colonialism. Fieldhouse (1982, pp. 11–13), for example, usefully distinguishes between pure settler colonies, mixed colonies, plantation colonies, occupation colonies, and trading settlements or naval bases. The construction of social and economic systems which perpetually marginalise indigenous peoples and oppressed nations residing upon indigenous land, thus reinforcing settler domination are critical to settler-colonial regimes of accumulation. As such, the dynamics of class struggle in societies where indigenous land is directly occupied by a settler-colonial population are markedly different from those where the land remains occupied by the indigenous population but is held by a metropolitan elite.
3. For analysis of settler-colonial labour and its characteristic politics in the United States, see Sakai (2014 [1983]); for South Africa, see Davies (1979); for the northeast of Ireland, see Clayton (1996); and for Israel, see Duke (2018).
4. Sinclair 1994 [1935], p. 109.
5. The often superficial and identitarian nature of disputes involving rival leftist factions is well illustrated in the following example. In a case concerning alleged 'entryism' (that is, the infiltration of an organisation by another group's members who intend to change its policies) by the Communist Party of Ireland (CPI), in July 2016, a Northern Ireland employment tribunal criticised the trade union NIPSA (Northern Ireland Public Service Alliance). The tribunal found that two members of the CPI had been unjustifiably expelled by the Trotskyist-dominated union, but said they had not shown that the two factions actually have any substantive political differences. It added that name-calling or trolling on social media is not sufficient to show political difference, and nor is 'alleged adherence to Trotsky's 1938 Transitional Program'. Despite the claimants having said that they suffered stress, insomnia and reputation damage as a result of their expulsion, the tribunal said it had seen no evidence of this, adding that neither 'the claimants nor any representative of the respondent trade union evinced any degree of stress or upset during the hearing ... To the contrary everybody involved, and their supporters, showed every sign of enjoying the process' (Campbell 2016).
6. Lenin 1964 [1916].

7. Marx 1962 [1862], p. 538.
8. Engels 1962 [1858], p. 537; Engels 1962 [1885], p. 351.
9. Lenin 1964 [1916], p. 105.
10. Lenin 1970 [1916].
11. Lenin 1969, p. 64.
12. Foster 1976, p. 31.
13. Polan 1984, p. 172.
14. Orwell 1958 [1937], pp. 159–60.
15. Lenin 1971 [1921], p. 369.
16. Degras 1956 [1919], p. 18; cf. Cope 2015, p. 77.
17. Lenin et al. 1980 [1919], p. 32.
18. Pauwels 2016, p. 64.
19. Redfern 2005, p. 22.
20. Bukharin 1973 [1915 and 1917], pp. 164–5.
21. Kautsky 2009 [1906], p. 663. In 1921, British Intelligence, then engaged in compiling a dossier on alleged Soviet infractions of the Anglo-Soviet Trade Agreement of 16 March that year – which committed the USSR 'to restrain all persons under its direct or indirect control from any act endangering the tranquillity and prosperity of Great Britain, or intended to embitter the relations of the British Empire with other countries' – was informed that Stalin had made a similar point to Kautsky's in a speech, namely: 'The problems connected with the class struggle in the West will be incomparably easier of solution if the external power of England can be undermined.' When confronted, Georgy Chicherin, the People's Commissar for Foreign Affairs, protested that Stalin had been away from Moscow on 1 June when he was reputed to have made the speech. US military intelligence later revealed the likely source of the information to have been a Volga German employee of Soviet state security, the Cheka (Cave Brown and Macdonald 1981, pp. 190, 194–5).
22. Quoted in Bashear 1980, p. 13.
23. Roy 1984, p. 219.
24. Sultan-Galiev 1979 [1919], p. 136.
25. Bennigsen 1958, p. 404.
26. Roberts 2007, p. 39.
27. Meisner 1970, p. 401.
28. Renault 2015.
29. Martin 2001, p. 230. See also Baker (2014, p. 590), who finds that Sultan-Galiev 'did indeed violate party discipline in a number of ways, and was engaged in developing conspiratorial ties outside of the party' and concludes that 'the party leaders, and Stalin in particular, treated him less severely than they could have'. Though critical of the right wing of the party whom he said had failed to become 'a reliable bulwark against the nationalist trend ... which is growing and strengthening due to NEP [New Economic Policy]', Stalin remained strongly committed to *korenizatsiia* (that is, the policy of indigeneisation of Soviet political and industrial authority) and its promotion through *smenovekhovsto* (or 'National Bolsheviks') (Martin 2001, p. 231). Galiev's activity was alleged to have been in direct opposition to the Soviet government's policy of variously avoiding the extremes of, first, arrogance towards the needs and requirements of the non-Russian nationalities within the USSR and, second, 'the excessive claims of the bourgeois upper stratum of those nationalities, directed against the Russians, and even more, against weaker neighbour-nations' (Galiev's Pan-Turkism was itself accused of being chauvinistic in respect to the Bashkir region) (Schlesinger 1956, p. 19). Galiev was subsequently arrested and sentenced to imprisonment for nationalist deviationism and for conspiracy against the Soviet government. In 1923, even after Sultan-Galiev's expulsion from the Communist Party of the Soviet Union (Bolshevik), Stalin stated that propaganda in favour of Pan-Turkist and Pan-Islamist views within the party might be tolerated, and theoretically criticised by the party ranks; only its practice in collaboration with Basmachi anti-Soviet insurgents was to be outlawed. Stalin went so far as

to pay compliments to the Tatar leaders ('splendid practical workers in spite of their lack of ideological stamina') who had expressed solidarity with Sultan-Galiev (ibid.).

30. Trotsky quoted in Read 2009, p. 180.

31. Orwell 1970 [1941], p. 81.

32. Russell 2013 [1966], p. 394.

33. Russia is a semi-peripheral, dependent and export-oriented capitalist economy, but one dominated by national monopolies with regional reach. A handful of these lead firms constitute Russia as a minor imperialist power globally and a marginal net consumer (as opposed to producer) of value generated in the world economy according to the global production/consumption index outlined above. Russia's energy and arms companies vie with European and US rivals for control of markets and value chains in Eastern Europe and Central Asia. Its political system is a form of authoritarian neoliberalism (barely) functioning on the basis of systemic corruption and ties to organised crime. Whereas Russia is the victim of encirclement and attempted subversion by the United States, it has so far successfully rebuffed the US attempts post-Yeltsin to convert it into a straightforwardly peripheral part of the world economy. Though Russia is currently dependent upon Western markets, and largely seeks to maintain rather than overturn its subordinate position within global value chains established according to the 'Washington Consensus', aggressive US rollback is pushing Russia in the direction of inter-imperialist conflict. Russia is at the forefront of pushing far right nationalism and anti-immigrant chauvinism in Europe as a means of undermining its European Union rival insofar as the latter is seen to implement policies detrimental to Russian interests, or is perceived as being overly subservient to a hostile United States. Though Russia is a minor imperialist power, just as with Germany in the early twentieth century, it is a country whose monopoly capitalism constantly pushes it in the direction of conquering foreign and internal colonial markets. While Russian intervention may be justified when solicited by governments fighting to retain their national unity and sovereignty in the face of US regime change operations, it must be opposed where it is either illegal or unwanted by those nations hosting its military. Whereas any efforts to move away from US global hegemony should be critically supported, we should be under no illusion that Russia represents anything other than an Empire of the periphery (Kagarlitsky 2007).

10 The Metropolitan Labour Aristocracy

1. Sternberg 1951, p. 59.

2. Von Werlhof 2000.

3. Harvey 2004.

4. Foster et al. 2011.

5. Ibid.

6. Ibid. Neilson and Stubbs (2011) estimate a GRAL of 2.9 billion people.

7. Chandra 1974, p. 1309.

8. Sternberg 1951, p. 59.

9. Ibid., p. 62.

10. Ibid., p. 68.

11. Ibid., p. 66.

12. Ibid, pp. 83–4.

13. As Torkil Lauesen has noted in private correspondence, this statement requires qualification. From the seventeenth century, the United States developed a burgeoning trade with the Caribbean and Central and South America. Gradually, it was able to assert its economic hegemony over its British rivals in this its 'back yard'. In the Spanish-American War in 1898, the United States captured Puerto Rico, Cuba and the Philippines from Spain's decadent Empire. Spain had effectively lost control of these colonies before the war with the United States, partly because of its own weakness, and partly because of the bourgeois-led national liberation movements in the colonies. Indeed, despite the Monroe

Doctrine opposing European colonialism in the Americas, national uprisings proved more bothersome for the US imperialists than did the Spanish. In the Philippines, after a national revolution had successfully evicted Spain from the country, the United States had to engage more than half of its army of 1.2 million men in a brutal counterrevolutionary war lasting more than three years in order to defeat the Filipino guerrillas. Over 200,000 Filipinos lost their lives in the war against the United States. So while the European powers divided Africa among themselves, the Caribbean and Central and South America became, in the words of US Secretary of State Henry Stimson, 'our little region over here which has never bothered anyone' (quoted in Hoffman 2001, p. 140).

14. Boggs 2011 [1967], p. 173.
15. Prandy et al. 1983, p. 54.
16. Hutt 1975, p. 24.
17. Ibid., pp. 24–5.
18. Holton 1976.
19. Cole and Postgate 1949, pp. 411–12.
20. Kirk 1985, p. 11.
21. McClelland 2000, p. 104.
22. Hobsbawm 1964, pp. 324, 341.
23. Kirk 1985, p. 81.
24. Ibid., p. 82.
25. See, for example, Ludlow and Jones 1867.
26. Kirk 1985, p. 310.
27. Ibid., p. 335.
28. Stedman Jones 1971, pp. 241–2.
29. Hall et al. 2014, p. 145.
30. Clegg et al. 1964.
31. Clough 1993.
32. Hatton et al. 1994.
33. Sternberg 1951, p. 91.
34. Ibid., p. 97.
35. Ibid., p. 96.
36. Ibid., p. 97.
37. Ibid., p. 99–100.
38. Ibid., p. 102.
39. Ibid., pp. 112–14
40. OECD 2014, p. 3.
41. Ibid., p. 120.
42. Ibid., p. 115.
43. Harvey 1989, p. 25.
44. Kadri 2015.

11 The Native Labour Aristocracy

1. Clemens et al. 2009.
2. Macheda and Nadalini 2018.
3. Ibid., p. 5.
4. Ibid., p. 2.
5. Ibid., p. 5; cf. Shulman 1990.
6. Castles and Kosack 1972.
7. Ibid.
8. Bonacich 1972, p. 553.
9. Ibid., pp. 553–4.
10. Ibid., p. 555.
11. Vickers 2013.

12. Quinoa 1982.
13. Knowles and Prewitt 1970, p. 274.
14. Davies 1979, p. 11.
15. Greenberg 1980, p. 285.
16 Ibid., p. 287.
17. Ibid., p. 277.
18. In the 1960s, the US AFL-CIO's belated stands for civil rights, according to Herbert Hill, the NAACP's Labor Secretary, was extremely limited (especially given the lengthy and egregious history of racism exhibited by the US labour movement) and functioned largely as a means of boosting the fortunes of the union movement and the Democratic Party. The AFL-CIO is today a major vehicle for labour imperialism.
19. Milkman 2015.
20. Castles 2016.
21. Waldinger and Lichter 2003, p. 8.
22. Ibid., p. 9.
23. In this regard, Black/New Afrikan workers may suffer a 'double disadvantage' in the labour market, 'sharing the liabilities of the native-born American worker – that is, a sense of entitlement greater than the employer thinks appropriate – but few of the social advantages that accrue to native whites' (ibid., p. 17). In consequence, when employers select from a range of candidates, Black/New Afrikan workers may be relegated to the end of the queue. The historical lesson for immigrants, meanwhile, points to the advantages of adopting the perennial Euro-American hatred and disdain for Black/New Afrikan people.
24. Ibid., p. 9.
25. Burleigh and Wippermann 2011 [1991], p. 296.
26. Castles et al. 2014, pp. 93–9. For an extensive study of the foreign labour regime in Nazi Germany, see Homze 1967.
27. Castles and Kosack 1972, p. 3.
28. Ibid.
29. Ibid.
30. Phizacklea and Miles 1980, p. 6.
31. Vickers 2016.
32. Shachar 2009.
33. Hampshire 2013, p. 113; cf. Howard 2006.
34. Morris 2002.
35. Hampshire 2013, p. 113.
36. Ibid., p. 114.
37. Joppke 2010, pp. 86–8.
38. Hampshire 2013, p. 114.
39. Ibid.
40. Ibid.; cf. Hampshire 2008.
41. Hampshire 2013, p. 115. See, for example, Soysal 1994.
42. Hampshire 2013, p. 115.
43. Castles 2005, pp. 690–1; cf. Hampshire 2013, p. 115.
44. In 1894, Anatole France wrote: 'In its majestic equality, the law forbids rich and poor alike to sleep under bridges, beg in the streets and steal loaves of bread.'
45. Robinson et al. 2014, p. 5.
46. Ibid., p. 1.
47. Ibid.
48. Ibid., p. 6.
49. Ibid., p. 3.
50. Cope 2015, pp. 265–6.
51. Quinoa 1982.
52. Ibid.
53. Gilroy 1992; cf. Kyriakides and Virdee 2003.

54. Kyriakides and Virdee 2003, p. 286.
55. Ibid.
56. Ibid.
57. Vickers 2016.
58. Ibid.
59. Ibid.
60. Castles and Miller 2003 [1993], p. 191. See also Orrenius and Zavodny 2009.
61. Castles and Miller 2003 [1993], pp. 191–2.
62. Schierup and Castles 2011, p. 23; Strikwerda and Guerin-Gonzales 1998, p. 20; cf. Vickers 2016.
63. ILO 2014.
64. Vickers 2016.
65. Ibid.
66. In Australia, for example, the Subclass 457 temporary work visa ties the migrant to their employer and requires that if she or he loses their job they have 30 days to find a new employer or leave. The H-1B visa in the United States has a similar scope, and following the onset of the financial crisis beginning in 2008 there was an outflow of Indian software engineers back to India as a result.
67. Jaffe 1994, p. 145.
68. Freund 2013, p. 495.
69. Lenin 1974a [1915]. Emphases in the original.

12 Social Imperialism before the First World War

1. For an overview of social imperialism in the United States, see Rubin 2018.
2. Bonacich 1972.
3. Bober 1950, pp. 67, 69.
4. Moore 1977, p. 19.
5. Ibid., p. 17.
6. Ibid., p. 20.
7. Frederick Engels, 'French Rule in Algeria', The Northern Star, 22 January 1848, quoted in Avineri 1968, p. 43.
8. Bennoune 1981. My emphasis.
9. Ibid.
10. Moore 1977, pp. 26–8.
11. Ibid., p. 29. Emphasis in the original.
12. Engels 1965 [1882], p. 351.
13. Stråth 2016, p. 226.
14. Ibid.
15. Ibid.
16. Hobsbawm 1999, p. 139.
17. Stråth 2016, pp. 226–7.
18. Wehler 1970. By the turn of the twentieth century, however, many German statesmen looked less towards the construction of a vast sea-based empire and its associated Weltpolitik than to the creation of a 'land-based empire built in the east at the expense of a defeated Russia', a theme later taken up explicitly by Hitler in his Mein Kampf: 'Therefore we National Socialists have purposely drawn a line through the line of conduct followed by pre-War Germany in foreign policy. We put an end to the perpetual Germanic march towards the South and West of Europe and turn our eyes towards the lands of the East. We finally put a stop to the colonial and trade policy of pre-War times and pass over to the territorial policy of the future. But when we speak of new territory in Europe today we must principally think of Russia and the Border States subject to her' (Hitler 1939 [1925], p. 360; cf. Eley 2015, pp. 45–6.
19. Stråth 2016, p. 227.

20. Eley 2015, p. 28. See also Cope 2016a.
21. Pauwels 2016, pp. 65–6.
22. Ibid., p. 66; Losurdo 2013, pp. 163–4.
23. Ibid., p. 63.
24. Weber quoted in Hobsbawm 1994 [1987], p. 56. My emphasis.
25. Cope 2015, pp. 146–7.
26. Stråth 2016, p. 227.
27. Lynch 1997, p. 24.
28. Semmel 1968 [1960], p. 241. Amongst Mosley's early followers was post-war architect of Britain's National Health Service, Labour's Aneurin Bevan.
29. Newsinger 2010, p. 146.
30. Macdonald quoted in Newsinger 2010, p. 146.
31. Newsinger 2010, p. 146.
32. Engels 1978 [1872], p. 419.
33. Rist 2002, p. 51. My emphasis.
34. Wahl quoted in Pauwels 2016, pp. 65–6.
35. Renan 1947–1961, p. 390.
36. Ferry 1897 [1884], pp. 199–201, 210–11, 215–18.
37. Roberts 1979, p. 108.
38. Stråth 2016, p. 227.
39. Davis 1989, p. 191.
40. Roberts 1979, p. 109.
41. Ibid.
42. Ibid.
43. Ibid., p. 154.
44. Tichelman 1998, p. 87.
45. Ibid.
46. Ibid., p. 90.
47. Ibid.
48. Ibid., pp. 91–2.
49. Ibid., p. 92.
50. Haupt and Rebérioux 1967, p. 44n, cited in Tichelman 1998, p. 91.
51. Tichelman 1998, p. 92.
52. Ibid., p. 93.
53. Ibid., p. 94.
54. Ibid., p. 95.
55. Ibid.
56. Ibid., p. 96.
57. Brun and Hersh 1990, p. 18.
58. Schrevel and Schwidder 2009.

13 Social Imperialism after the First World War

1. Lensch 2013 [1918], pp. 200–1.
2. Cole 1958, pp. 329–30.
3. In September 1918 Georgia's Menshevik President Noe Zhordania had declared to the German commander: 'It is not in our interests to lower the prestige of Germany in the Caucasus.' By January the following year, following Germany's rout, however, he was praising the British commander General Walker as 'the first person that understood the state of affairs in our country'. Quoted in Trotsky (1975 [1922], pp. 24, 45); cf. Clough (2014 [1992], pp. 53–4).
4. Tichelman 1998, p. 94.
5. Derrick 2008, pp. 156, 180.
6. Geetha 2008, p. 83.

7. Cited in Aldrich 1996, p. 115.
8. Cohen 1972, p. 368.
9. Ibid., p. 370.
10. Ibid., p. 369.
11. Olivesi 1964, p. 65. See also Slavin 1991.
12. Cohen 1972, p. 390.
13. Tichelman 1998, pp. 97–8.
14. Ibid., p. 98.
15. Owen 2007, p. 1.
16. Davis 2010, p. 89.
17. Ibid., p. 90.
18. Ibid., p. 91.
19. Jaffe 1994, p. 148.
20. Clough 2014 [1992], back cover.
21. Doran 2012, p. 4.
22. Tichelman 1998, p. 101.
23. Ibid., p. 103.
24. Sassoon 1996, p. 167.
25. Ibid., p. 179.
26. Ibid., p. 181.
27. According to the Encyclopaedia Britannica, in 1945 the French Communist Party (PCF) won 25 per cent of the vote in France's first post-Second World War election, and in 1946 it took part in the Fourth Republic's first government. After May 1947, when the communists were dismissed from the cabinet as a result of hardening political attitudes, the PCF did not participate in any Fourth Republic administration, though it won an average of more than 22 per cent of the vote in the six general elections from June 1951 to June 1968 and won a large number of seats in the National Assembly (www.britannica.com/topic/French-Communist-Party, accessed 18 November 2018).
28. Sassoon 1996, p. 179.
29. Clough 2014 [1992], p. 61.
30. Sassoon 1996, p. 179.
31. Clough 2014 [1992], pp. 94–5.
32. Sassoon 1996, p. 179.
33. Fieldhouse 1984, pp. 96–9.
34. Curtis 2003, p. 335.
35. As the national liberation struggle against French colonialism in Vietnam drew to its inexorable conclusion (and around the same time that the US government seriously considered using nuclear weapons to prop up the flailing position of its French ally), an article published in US News and World Report on 4 April 1954 stated: 'One of the richest areas in the world will be open to the victor in Indochina. This is what lies behind the growing U.S. interest ... pewter, rubber, rice, strategic key primary produce are the true reasons for this war.' The U.S. considers this an area in which to maintain control – by any means necessary.' In addition, keeping open the field of investment within which superexploitation of cheap semi-colonial labour by monopoly investors was a major goal of the US imperialists in Vietnam. As Business Week reported on 20 April 1963: 'By the end of the 40s and increasingly during the 50s up until today – American corporations in one industry after another were discovering that their foreign incomes kept increasing. Their revenues were usually substantially higher abroad than in the U.S.'
36. The Fabian Society was a group of intellectuals and social reformers formed in 1884 that hugely influenced the ideology of the Independent Labour Party founded in 1893 and the Labour Party founded in 1900.
37. Sassoon 1996, pp. 180–1.
38. Frank 2010, p. 108.
39. Sassoon 1996, pp. 180–1.

40. Davis 2010, pp. 91–2.
41. Ibid., p. 95.
42. Ibid., pp. 96–7.
43. Ibid., p. 105.
44. Thompson 2005, pp. 71–4.
45. Hyslop 1999, pp. 398–9.
46. Ibid.
47. Tichelman 1998, p. 98.
48. Hyslop 1999, pp. 402–3.
49. Kirk 2003, p. 169.
50. Kaarsholm 1988, pp. 42–67.
51. Kirk 2003, p. 157.
52. Ibid., p. 159.
53. Ibid., p. 165.
54. Ibid., p. 158.
55. Ibid., p. 171.
56. Ibid., p. 178.
57. Cope 2016b.
58. Labour Party 2017, pp. 120–1.
59. Péju 1960, p. 499.
60. Senghor 1959, p. 47.
61. Buchanan 1963, pp. 22–3; cf. Moussa 1962, pp. 6–7.

14 Social-Imperialist Marxism

1. Redfern 2017, p. 50.
2. Degras 1956 [1937], p. 390; cf. ibid., p. 51.
3. Redfern 2017, p. 43. Mavrakis (1976, p. 131) writes: 'The policy of working within the Kuomintang [Nationalists] was, after all, perfectly correct in the framework of the struggle against imperialism and the militarists. It gave a colossal impetus to the mass movement in the towns and the countryside. Li Ta-chao and Mao Tse-Tung had carried out this policy enthusiastically for reasons quite independent of Comintern instructions.'
4. Redfern 2017, p. 46; cf. Pipes 1996, p. 99.
5. Redfern 2005, p. 56.
6. Claudín 1975, pp. 248–9.
7. Redfern 2005, p. 67.
8. Ibid., p. 57.
9. Ho Chi Minh 1977 [1924], pp. 64–5.
10. Barker 1968, pp. 292–3.
11. Jaffe 1990.
12. Redfern 2005, p. 58.
13. Arnot 1967, p. 171.
14. Redfern 2005, p. 59.
15. Ibid.
16. *The Communist*, 25 November 1920, quoted in Redfern 2005, p. 60.
17. Redfern 2005, p. 61 *et passim*.
18. Dutt quoted in Redfern 2005, p. 63.
19. Redfern 2005, p. 75.
20. *Workers Weekly*, 27 October 1924, quoted in Redfern 2005, p. 92.
21. According to the communist schema, the 'first period' of post-First World War history had witnessed the revolutionary rise and fall of working class power, and the 'second period', lasting up until the end of the 1920s, the consolidation of capitalist rule.
22. Degras 1956 [1937], p. 471.
23. Redfern 2005, p. 92.

24. Ibid., p. 94.
25. Ibid., p. 95.
26. Magraw 1999, p. 101.
27. Ibid., p. 100.
28. Guerin 1963, p. 15, quoted in Cohen 1972, p. 392.
29. Cohen 1972, p. 392.
30. de Beauvoir 1965, pp. 338–9; cf. Edwards 1978, p. 195.
31. Wall 1977.
32. Sartre 1970 [1959].
33. Sassoon 1996, p. 181.
34. Ibid.
35. Tichelman 1998, p. 98.
36. Wall 1984, p. 5.
37. Tichelman 1998, p. 99.
38. Mao 1965 [1963], p. 210.
39. For further information on the social-imperialist trend within the communist movement, see Biel (2015a) and Lauesen (2018). For evidence of the Eurocentrism endemic to the communist movement, see Claudín (1975, pp. 245–6, 249, 252, 258–9). For an analysis of the socialist imperialist labour movement in Germany before the Second World War, see Cope (2016a).
40. Redfern 2005, p. 8.
41. Desai 2016, p. 1383.
42. Thatcher 1991.
43. Trotsky 1974 [1928], p. 15.
44. Higginbottom 2016, p. 546.
45. Trotsky 1969a [1940], p. 25.
46. Trotsky 1969 [1939], p. 17.
47. Trotsky 1969b [1940], p. 17.

15 Conclusion: Imperialism and Anti-Imperialism Today

1. Amin 2015b.
2. King 2010, p. 63.
3. Smith 2017, p. 161.
4. Smith 2011.
5. Ibid.
6. Wolf 2009.
7. Smith 2011.
8. For analysis of dollar hegemony, and petrodollar warfare, see, for example, Clark 2005; Costigan et al. 2017; Hensman and Correggia 2005; Hudson 2003; Liu 2002; Liu and Deng 2012; Mastanduno 2009; Momani 2008; Moran 2010; Zhou 2009.
9. Smith 2002, p. 2.
10. Amin et al. 2018.
11. Petersen 2002, p. 25.
12. Ibid., p. 29.
13. Lüdtke 1992.
14. Chazan 2018.
15. Glazebrook 2017, p. 30.
16. Marx and Engels 2004 [1848], pp. 37–9.
17. Patnaik and Patnaik 2017, p. 152.

Appendix: Physical Quality of Life in Socialist and Capitalist Countries

1. Cereseto and Waitzkin 1986, p. 644.
2. Ibid., p. 648.
3. Ibid., p. 656.

Bibliography

Websites last accessed 18 November 2018.

Acemoğlu, Daron, Simon Johnson and James Robinson. 2002. The Rise of Europe: Atlantic Trade, Institutional Change and Economic Growth. Berkeley. 25 November. Online: http://scholar.harvard.edu/files/jrobinson/files/jr_AERAtlanticTrade.pdf

Addo, Herb. 1986. *Imperialism: The Permanent Stage of Capitalism*. Tokyo: United Nations University.

Aldrich, Robert. 1996. *Greater France: A History of French Overseas Expansion*. Basingstoke, Hampshire: Macmillan.

Alexander, Titus. 1996. *Unravelling Global Apartheid: An Overview of World Politics*. Cambridge: Polity Press.

ALFI (Association of the Luxembourg Fund Industry). 2015. International Investment by Pension Funds Increases Globally but is Still Restricted in Some Markets. 16 September. Online: www.alfi.lu/node/3019

Amin, Samir. 1974. *Accumulation on a World Scale*. New York: Monthly Review Press.

——1976. *Unequal Development: An Essay on the Social Formations of Peripheral Capitalism*. Brighton: Harvester Press.

——1977. *Imperialism and Unequal Development*. Brighton: Harvester Press.

——2011. *Maldevelopment: Anatomy of a Global Failure*. Cape Town: Pambazuka Press.

——2012. The Surplus in Monopoly Capitalism and the Imperialist Rent. *Monthly Review*. Vol. 64, No. 3, 78–85.

——2014. *Capitalism in the Age of Globalisation*. London: Zed Books.

——2015a. Imperialist Rent and the Challenges for the Radical Left. In Andreas Bieler, Bruno Ciccaglione, John Hilary and Ingemar Lindberg (eds), *Free Trade and Transnational Labour*. London: Routledge, pp. 11–23.

——2015b. Contemporary Imperialism. *Monthly Review*. Vol. 67, No. 3. July–August, 23–37.

——2018. *Modern Imperialism, Monopoly Finance Capital, and Marx's Law of Value*. New York: Monthly Review Press.

——, John Jipson and P. M. Jiteesh. 2018. Interview: Samir Amin. 'There is a Structural Crisis of Capitalism'. *Frontline*. 11 May. Online: www.frontline.in/other/there-is-a-structural-crisis-of-capitalism/article10107168.ece

Andersson, Jan Otto. 2006. International Trade in a Full and Unequal World. In Alf Hornborg and Andrew K. Jorgenson (eds), *International Trade and Environmental Justice: Toward a Global Political Ecology*. New York: Nova Science Publishers, pp. 113–25.

Anievas, Alexander and Kerem Nişancıoğlu. 2015. *How the West Came to Rule: The Geopolitical Origins of Capitalism*. London: Pluto Press.

Aristide, Jean-Bertand. 2001. *Eyes of the Heart: Seeking a Path for the Poor in the Age of Globalisation*. Monroe, ME: Common Courage Press.

Arnot, Robin Page. 1967. *The Impact of the Russian Revolution in Britain*. London: Lawrence and Wishart.

Avineri, Shlomo (ed.). 1968. *Karl Marx on Colonialism and Modernization*. New York: Doubleday and Co.

Bagchi, Amiya Kumar. 1972. Some International Foundations of Capitalist Growth and Underdevelopment. *Economic and Political Weekly*. Vol. 7, No. 31/33. August, 1559–70.

——1982. *The Political Economy of Underdevelopment*. Cambridge: Cambridge University Press.

Bain, G. S. and R. Price. 1980. *Profiles of Union Growth*. Oxford: Basil Blackwell.

Baker, Mark R. 2014. Did He Really Do It? Mirsaid Sultan-Galiev, Party Disloyalty, and the 1923 Affair. *Europe-Asia Studies*, Vol. 66, No. 4, 590–612.

Baker, Raymond W. 2005. *Capitalism's Achilles Heel: Dirty Money and How to Renew the Free-Market System*. Hoboken, NJ: John Wiley & Sons.

Banerji, A. K. 1982. *Aspects of Indo-British Economic Relations, 1858–1898*. Oxford: Oxford University Press.

Bank of England. 2014. Three Centuries of Data. Online: www.bankofengland.co.uk/research/Pages/onebank/threecenturies.aspx

Baran, Paul. 1957. *The Political Economy of Growth*. New York: Monthly Review Press.

——and Paul M. Sweezy. 1966. *Monopoly Capital*. New York: Monthly Review Press.

——2012. Some Theoretical Implications. *Monthly Review*. Vol. 64, No. 3, 24–59.

Barker, Arthur James. 1968. *The Civilising Mission: The Italo-Ethiopian War 1935–6*. London: Cassell.

Barnett, Richard J. and Ronald E. Müller. 1974. *Global Reach: The Power of the Multinational Corporations*. London: Cape.

Barnes, Leonard. 1939. *Empire or Democracy? A Study of the Colonial Question*. London: Victor Gollancz.

Bashear, Suliman. 1980. *Communism in the Arab East*. London: Ithaca Press.

Beckert, Sven and Seth Rockman (eds). 2016. *Slavery's Capitalism: A New History of American Economic Development*. Philadelphia, PA: University of Pennsylvania Press.

Bello, Waden, Bill Rau and Shea Cunningham. 1999. *Dark Victory: The United States and Global Poverty*. London: Pluto Press.

Bennigsen, Alexandre. 1958. Sultan Galiev: The USSR and the Colonial Revolution. In Walter Laqueur (ed.), *The Middle East in Transition*. London: Routledge and Kegan Paul, pp. 398–414.

Bennoune, Mahfoud. 1981. Origins of the Algerian Proletariat. *Middle East Research and Information Project*. Vol. 11. Online: www.merip.org/mer/mer94/origins-algerian-proletariat

BERR (Department for Business Enterprise and Regulatory Reform). 2008. *The 2008 R&D Scoreboard*. London: BERR.

Bettelheim, Charles. 1972. Appendix One: Theoretical Comments. In Arghiri Emmanuel (ed.), *Unequal Exchange: A Study of the Imperialism of Trade*. London: New Left Books, pp. 271–323.

Biel, Robert. 2015. *Eurocentrism and the Communist Movement*. Montréal, Quebec: Kersplebedeb.

Bieler, Andreas, John Hilary and Ingemar Lindberg. 2015. Trade Unions, 'Free Trade', and the Problem of Transnational Solidarity: An Introduction. In Andreas Bieler, Bruno Ciccaglione, John Hilary and Ingemar Lindberg (eds). *Free Trade and Transnational Labour*. London: Routledge, pp. 1–11.

Birdsall, Nancy. 2010. The (Indispensable) Middle Class in Developing Countries. In Ravi Kanbur andMichael Spence (eds), *Equity and Growth in a Globalizing World*. Washington, DC: The International Bank for Reconstruction and Development/The World Bank, pp. 157–87.

Blackburn, Robin. 2011. *The American Crucible: Slavery, Emancipation and Human Rights*. London: Verso.

Blaut, James M. 1987. *The National Question: Decolonizing the Theory of Nationalism*. London: Zed Books.

Bober, M. M. 1950. *Karl Marx's Interpretation of History*. Cambridge, MA: Harvard University Press.

Boggs, James. 2011 [1967]. Black Power: A Scientific Concept Whose Time Has Come. In Stephen M. Ward (ed.), *Pages from a Black Radical's Notebook: A James Boggs Reader*. Detroit, MI: Wayne State University Press, pp. 171–80.

Bonacich, Edna. 1972. A Theory of Ethnic Antagonism: The Split Labor Market. *American Sociological Review*. Vol. 37, No. 5, 547–59.

Böröcz, J. 2016. Global Inequality in Redistribution: For a World-Historical Sociology of (Not) Caring. In *Intersections. East European Journal of Society and Politics*. Vol. 2, No. 2, 57–83.

Braudel, Fernand. 1982. *Civilization and Capitalism, 15th–18th Century, Vol. II: The Wheels of Commerce*. California: University of California Press.

Braun, G. and A. Topan. 1998. *Internationale Migragtion: Ihre Folgen fuer die Ursprungslaender und Ansaetze eines Migrationsregimes* (*International Migration: Its Consequences for the Country of Origin and for International Migration Regimes*). Sankt Augustin: Interne Studien, 153, Konrad Adenauer Stiftung.

Braun, Oscar. 1977. *Comercio Internacional e Imperialismo* (*International Trade and Imperialism*). Mexico: Siglo Veintiuno.

Brenner, Robert. 1977. The Origins of Capitalist Development: A Critique of Neo-Smithian Marxism. *New Left Review*. No. 104. July–August, 25–92.

Brolin, John. 2007. *The Bias of the World: Theories of Unequal Exchange in History*. Human Ecology Division, Lund University. Online: https://lucris.lub.lu.se/ws/files/4378178/26725.pdf

Brown, N. 2012. A Model for How First World Wages are Based on Third World Exploitation. Online: https://anti-imperialism.org/2012/05/31/a-model-for-how-first-world-wages-are-based-on-third-world-exploitation/

Brun, Ellen and Jacques Hersh. 1990. *Soviet-Third World Relations in a Capitalist World: The Political Economy of Broken Promises*. New York: Springer.

Buchanan, Keith. 1963. The Third World – Its Emergence and Contours. *New Left Review*. Vol. 1, No. 18. January–February, 5–23.

Bukharin, Nikolai. 1973 [1915 and 1917]. *Imperialism and World Economy*. New York: Monthly Review Press.

Burleigh, Michael and Wolfgang Wippermann. 2011 [1991]. *The Racial State: Germany 1933–1945*. Cambridge: Cambridge University Press.

Campbell, John. 2016. Nipsa: Tribunal Criticises Union in 'Communist' Dispute. BBC News. 14 July. Online: www.bbc.co.uk/news/uk-northern-ireland-36791688

Cardoso, Fernando Henrique and Enzo Faletto. 1979. *Dependency and Development in Latin America*. California: University of California Press.

Castles, Stephen. 2005. Changing Citizenship: Theory and Practice. *PS: Political Science and Politics*. Vol. 38, No. 4, 667–99.

——2016. Unfree Labour and Social Transformation in Neoliberal Capitalism. Chapter for book edited by Dr Mahua Sarkar. Draft 1, 15 June 2016.

——and Godula Kosack. 1972. The Function of Labour Immigration in Western European Capitalism. *New Left Review*. No. 73. May–June, 3–21.

——and Mark J. Miller. 2003 [1993]. *The Age of Migration: International Population Movements in the Modern World*. Basingstoke, Hampshire: Palgrave Macmillan.

——, H. de Haas and M. J. Miller. 2014. *The Age of Migration: International Population Movements in the Modern World*. Basingstoke, Hampshire: Palgrave Macmillan.

Cave Brown, Anthony and Charles B. Macdonald. 1981. *On a Field of Red: The Communist International and the Coming of World War II*. New York: G. P. Putnam's Sons.

Çelik, Ercüment. 2017. The 'Labour Aristocracy' in the Early 20th-Century South Africa: An Analysis beyond Traditional Conceptual and Territorial Boundaries. *Chinese Sociological Dialogue*. Vol. 2, No. 1–2, 18–34.

Cereseto, Shirley and Howard Waitzkin. 1986. Capitalism, Socialism, and the Physical Quality of Life. *International Journal of Health Services*. Vol. 16, No. 4, 643–58.

Chandra, N. K. 1974. Farm Efficiency under Semi-Feudalism: A Critique of Marginalist Theories and Some Marxist Formulations. *Economic and Political Weekly*. Vol. 9, No. 32/34, 1309–32.

Chang, Ha-Joon. 2006. Trade and Industrial Policies During the Age of Imperialism. In K. S. Jomo (ed.), *Globalization under Hegemony: The Changing World Economy*. Delhi: Oxford University Press, pp. 278–99.

Chazan, Guy. 2018. Right Establishes Foothold in Germany's Work Councils. *Financial Times*. 9 April. Online: www.ft.com/content/012acf34-3714-11e8-8eee-e06bdeo1c544

Chossudovsky, Michel. 2003. *The Globalization of Poverty and the New World Order*. Montreal: Global Research.

Christian Aid. 2009. *False Profits: Robbing the Poor to Keep the Rich Tax Free*. London: Christian Aid.

CIA World Factbook. 2018. Labor Force by Occupation. Online: www.cia.gov/library/publications/the-world-factbook/fields/2048.html

Clark, John Bates. 1899. *The Distribution of Wealth*. London: Macmillan and Co.

Clark, William R. 2005. *Petrodollar Warfare: Oil, Iraq and the Future of the Dollar*. British Columbia, Canada: New Society Publishers.

Claudín, Fernando. 1975. *The Communist Movement: From Comintern to Cominform*. New York: Monthly Review Press.

Clayton, Pamela. 1996. *Enemies and Passing Friends: Settler Ideologies in Twentieth Century Ulster*. London: Pluto Press.

Clegg, H., A. Fox and A. F. Thompson. 1964. *A History of British Trade Unions since 1889*. Vol. 1. Oxford: Oxford University Press.

Clelland, Donald. 2016. Global Value Transfers and Imperialism. In Immanuel Ness and Zak Cope (eds), *The Palgrave Encyclopedia of Imperialism and Anti-Imperialism*. Basingstoke, Hampshire: Palgrave Macmillan, pp. 1028–40.

Clemens, Michael, Claudio Montenegro and Lant Pritchett. 2009. The Place Premium: Wage Differences for Identical Workers across the US Border. HKS Faculty Research Working Paper Series. RWP09-004. John F. Kennedy School of Government, Harvard University.

Clough, Robert. 1993. Haunted by the Labour Aristocracy. Part 1: Marx and Engels on the Split in the Working Class. In *Fight Racism! Fight Imperialism!* No. 115. October/November.

——2014 [1992]. *Labour: A Party Fit for Imperialism*. London: Larkin Publications.

Cohen, William B. 1972. The Colonial Policy of the Popular Front. *French Historical Studies*. Vol. 7, No. 3. Spring, 368–93.

Cole, G. D. H. 1958. *A History of Socialist Thought: Communism and Social Democracy*. Vol. 4, Part I. London: Macmillan and Co.

——and Raymond Postgate. 1949. *The Common People, 1746–1946*. London: Methuen and Co.

Cope, Zak. 2013. Global Wage Scaling and Left Ideology: A Critique of Charles Post on the 'Labour Aristocracy'. In Paul Zarembka (ed.), *Contradictions: Finance, Greed, and Labor Unequally Paid. Research in Political Economy*. Vol. 28. Bingley, UK: Emerald Group Publishing, pp. 89–129.

——2014. Final Comments on Charles Post's Critique of the Theory of the Labour Aristocracy. In Paul Zarembka (ed.), *Sraffa and Althusser Reconsidered; Neoliberalism Advancing in South Africa, England, and Greece (Research in Political Economy*, Vol. 29). Bingley, UK: Emerald Group Publishing, pp. 275–86.

——2015. *Divided World Divided Class: Global Political Economy and the Stratification of Labour under Capitalism*. Second edition. Montréal, Quebec: Kersplebedeb.

——2016a. German Imperialism and Social Imperialism, 1871–1933. In Immanuel Ness and Zak Cope (eds), *The Palgrave Encyclopedia of Imperialism and Anti-Imperialism*. Basingstoke, Hampshire: Palgrave Macmillan, pp. 652–66.

——2016b. Zwei Formen des Imperialismus prallen aufeinander: Warum weite Teile der Arbeiterklasse für den Brexit stimmten. (Two Forms of Imperialism Collide: Why Large Sections of the Working Class Voted for Brexit). *AK – Analyse & Kritik: Zeitung für linke Debatte und Praxis*. No. 618. 16 August. Online: www.akweb.de/ak_s/ak618/07.htm

Costigan, Thomas, Drew Cottle and Angela Keys. 2017. The US Dollar as the Global Reserve Currency: Implications for US Hegemony. *World Review of Political Economy*. Vol. 8, No. 1, 104–22.

Crooks, Jack. 2004. Dollar Drops: Good News and Bad. *Asia Times*. 25 November. Online: www.atimes.com/atimes/Global_Economy/FK25Djo2.html

Curtis, Mark. 2003. *Web of Deceit: Britain's Real Role in the World*. London: Vintage.

Davies, Robert H. 1973. The White Working Class in South Africa. *New Left Review*. Vol. 1. No. 82. November–December.

——1979. *Capital, State and White Labor in South Africa in 1900–1960: An Historical Materialist Analysis of Class Formation and Class Relations*. Brighton: Harvester Press.

Davis, John A. 1989. Socialism and the Working Classes in Italy before 1914. In Dick Geary (ed.), *Labour and Socialist Movements in Europe before 1914*. Oxford: Berg, pp. 182–230.

Davis, Mary. 2010. Labour, Race and Empire: The Trades Union Congress and Colonial Policy, 1945–51. In Billy Frank, Craig Horner and David Stewart (eds), *The British Labour Movement and Imperialism*. Cambridge: Cambridge Scholars Publishing, pp. 89–105.

Davis, Ralph. 1979. *The Industrial Revolution and British Overseas Trade*. Leicester: Leicester University Press.

Day, Richard B. 1981. *The 'Crisis' and the 'Crash': Soviet Studies of the West, 1917–1939*. London: New Left Books.

De Beauvoir, Simone. 1965. *Force of Circumstance*. Trans. Richard Howard. New York: Putnam.

Deane, Phyllis. 1965. *The First Industrial Revolution*. Cambridge: Cambridge University Press.

Degras, Jane (ed.). 1956 [1919]. Platform of the Communist International Adopted by the First Congress. In *The Communist International, 1919–1943: Selected Documents. Vol. 1, 1919–1922*. Oxford: Oxford University Press.

——1956 [1937]. Executive Committee of the Communist International (ECCI) Manifesto on the Twentieth Anniversary of the Russian Revolution. In *The Communist International, 1919–1943: Selected Documents. Vol. 3, 1929–1943*. Oxford: Oxford University Press.

Derrick, Jonathan. 2008. *Africa's 'Agitators': Militant Anti-Colonialism in Africa and the West, 1918–1939*. New York: Columbia University Press.

Desai, Radhika. 2016. South-South Cooperation. In Immanuel Ness and Zak Cope (eds), *The Palgrave Encyclopedia of Imperialism and Anti-Imperialism*. Basingstoke, Hampshire: Palgrave Macmillan, pp. 1381–92.

Doran, Christopher. 2012. *Making the World Safe for Capitalism: How Iraq Threatened the US Economic Empire and Had to be Destroyed*. London: Pluto Press.

Dos Santos, Theotonio. 1970. The Structure of Dependence. *American Economic Review*. Vol. 60, No. 2, 231–6.

Duke, Shaul. 2018. *The Stratifying Trade Union: The Case of Ethnic and Gender Inequality in Palestine, 1920–1948*. Basingstoke, Hampshire: Palgrave Macmillan.

Eaton, John. 1949. *Political Economy: A Marxist Textbook*. London, Lawrence and Wishart.

EcoNexus and Berne Declaration. 2013. Agropoly: A Handful of Corporations Control World Food Production. September. Online: www.econexus.info/sites/econexus/files/Agropoly_Econexus_BerneDeclaration_wide-format.pdf

Edelstein, Michael. 1994. Imperialism: Cost and Benefit. In Roderick Floud and Donald McCloskey (eds), *The Economic History of Britain since 1700*. Second edition. Vol. 2: 1860–1939. Cambridge: Cambridge University Press, pp. 197–217.

Edwards, H. W. 1978. *Labor Aristocracy: Mass Base of Social Democracy*. Stockholm: Aurora Press.

Eley, Geoff. 2015. Germany, the Fischer Controversy, and the Context of War: Rethinking German Imperialism, 1880–1914. In Alexander Anievas (ed.), *Cataclysm 1914: The First World War and the Making of Modern World Politics*. Leiden: Brill, pp. 23–46.

Emmanuel, Arghiri. 1972. *Unequal Exchange: A Study of the Imperialism of Trade*. London: New Left Books.

——1975. Unequal Exchange Revisited. IDS Discussion Paper. No. 77. August.

Emmanuel, Arghiri and Charles Bettelheim. 1970. International Solidarity of Workers: Two Views: The Delusions of Internationalism; Economic Inequality between Nations and International Solidarity. *Monthly Review*. Vol. 22, No. 2. June, 13–19.

Engels, Friedrich. 1962 [1858]. Letter from Engels to Marx. Manchester, 7 October. In Karl Marx and Friedrich Engels, *On Britain*. Moscow: Foreign Languages Publishing House, p. 537.

——1962 [1885]. England in 1845 and in 1885. In Karl Marx and Friedrich Engels, *On Britain*. Moscow: Foreign Languages Publishing House, pp. 24–31.

——1965 [1882]. Letter from Engels to Kautsky. London. 12 September. In *Karl Marx and Friedrich Engels: Selected Correspondence*. Moscow: Progress Publishers, p. 351.

——1978 [1872]. Relations between the Irish Sections and the British Federal Council. In *Marx and Engels on Ireland*. Moscow: Progress Publishers.

——2010 [1884]. Engels to Paul Lafargue. About 11 August. In *Marx and Engels: Collected Works*. Vol. 47. London: Lawrence and Wishart, pp. 179–84.

Engerman, Stanley. 1972. The Slave Trade and British Capital Formation in the Eighteenth Century. *Business History Review*. Vol. 46, 430–43.

FAO (Food and Agriculture Organization). 2004. *The State of Agricultural Commodity Markets*. Rome: United Nations.

Ferry, Jules François Camille. 1897 [1884]. Speech before the French Chamber of Deputies. 28 March 1884. In Paul Robiquet (ed.), *Discours et Opinions de Jules Ferry*. Paris: Armand Colin & Cie, pp. 199–201.

Fieldhouse, David Kenneth. 1982. *The Colonial Empires: A Comparative Survey from the Eighteenth Century*. London: Macmillan.

——1984. The Labour Governments and the Empire-Commonwealth, 1945–51. In Ritchie Ovendale (ed.), *The Foreign Policy of the British Labour Governments, 1945–1951*. Leicester: Leicester University Press, pp. 83–120.

Finger, Barry. 2017. Unequal Exchange: Dependency Theory and the Exploitation of Nations. *International Socialist Review*. No. 107. Winter 2017–2018, 122–41.

Folfas, Pawel. 2009. Intra-Firm Trade and Non-Trade Intercompany Transactions: Changes in Volume and Structure During 1990–2007. Working Paper. Online: www.etsg.org/ETSG2009/papers/folfas.pdf

Foster, John. 1974. *Class Struggle and the Industrial Revolution: Early Industrial Capitalism in Three English Towns*. London: Weidenfeld and Nicolson.

——1976. British Imperialism and the Labour Aristocracy. In Jeffrey Skelley (ed.), *The General Strike 1926*. London: Lawrence and Wishart, pp. 3–58.

Foster, John Bellamy, Robert W. McChesney and R. Jamil Jonna. 2011. The Global Reserve Army of Labor and the New Imperialism. *Monthly Review*. Vol. 63, No. 6. November, 1–31.

Frank, Billy. 2010. Labour's 'New Imperialist' Attitude: State-Sponsored Colonial Development in Africa, 1940–51. In Billy Frank, Craig Horner and David Stewart (eds), *The British Labour Movement and Imperialism*. Cambridge: Cambridge Scholars Publishing, pp. 107–31.

Frank, Andre Gunder. 1966. The Development of Underdevelopment. *Monthly Review*. Vol. 18, No. 4, 17–31.

——1978. *World Accumulation, 1492–1789*. London: Macmillan.

Freeman, Alan. 1998. The Material Roots of Western Racism. MPRA Paper No. 2216. Online: http://mpra.ub.uni-muenchen.de/2216/

Freund, Bill. 2013. Labour Studies and Labour History in South Africa: Perspectives from the Apartheid Era and After. *International Review of Social History*. Vol. 58, No. 3. December, 493–519.

Fröbel, Folker, Jurgen Heinrichs and Otto Kreye. 1980. *The New International Division of Labour: Structural Unemployment in Industrialised Countries and Industrialisation in Developing Countries*. Cambridge: Cambridge University Press.

Gallagher, John and Ronald Robinson. 1953. The Imperialism of Free Trade. *Economic History Review*. Vol. 6, No. 1, 1–15.

Geetha, S. 2008. Society and Politics in French India: Merger and Anti-Merger Alignments in the Mid-Twentieth Century. PhD Thesis. Department of History, Pondicherry University.

Gelb, Alan. 1999. Where are We Now? Reforms, Performance and Country Groups in Africa. Paper presented at the workshop on 'Can Africa Claim the 21st Century?' African Development Bank, Abidjan, 6–11 July.

Gereffi, G., J. Humphrey and T. Sturgeon. 2005. The Governance of Global Value Chains. *Review of International Political Economy*. Vol. 12, 78–104.

Gilroy, Paul. 1992. *There Ain't No Black in the Union Jack*. London: Routledge.

Glazebrook, Dan. 2017. 21st Century Fascism. *Counterpunch*. Vol. 24, No. 3, 30–3.

Global Financial Integrity. 2016. *Financial Flows and Tax Havens: Combining to Limit the Lives of Billions of People*. Washington, DC: Global Financial Integrity.

——2017. *Illicit Financial Flows to and from Developing Countries: 2005–2014*. Washington, DC: Global Financial Integrity.

Gowan, Peter. 1999. *The Global Gamble: Washington's Faustian Bid for World Dominance*. London: Verso.

Gray, Robert Q. 1976. *The Labour Aristocracy in Victorian Edinburgh*. Oxford: Clarendon Press.

Green, Francis and Bob Sutcliffe. 1987. *The Profit System: The Economics of Capitalism*. London: Penguin.

Greenberg, Stanley. 1980. *Race and State in Capitalist Development: Comparative Perspectives*. New Haven, CT and London: Yale University Press.

Guerin, Daniel. 1963. Le Front Populaire et la Decolonisation. *France-Observateur*. 30 May.

Habib, Irfan. 2002. *Essays in Indian History: Towards a Marxist Perception*. London: Anthem Press.

Hadjimichalis, C. 1984. The Geographical Transfer of Value: Notes on the Spatiality of Capitalism. *Environment and Planning D: Society and Space*. Vol. 2, 329–45.

Hall, Catherine, Keith McClelland, Nick Draper, Kate Donington and Rachel Lang. 2014. *Legacies of British Slave-Ownership: Colonial Slavery and the Formation of Victorian Britain*. Cambridge: Cambridge University Press.

Hampshire, James. 2008. Disembedding Liberalism? Immigration Politics and Security in Britain since 9/11. In Terry Givens, Garry P. Freeman and David L. Leal (eds), *Immigration Policy and Security: U.S., European, and Commonwealth Perspectives*. New York and London: Routledge, pp. 109–29.

——2013. *The Politics of Immigration: Contradictions of the Liberal State*. Cambridge: Polity Press.

Harvey, David. 1989. *The Urban Experience*. Baltimore, MD: Johns Hopkins University Press.

——2004. The 'New' Imperialism: Accumulation by Dispossession. In Leo Panitch and Colin Leys (eds), *Socialist Register 2004: The New Imperial Challenge*. London: Merlin Press, pp. 63–87.

Harvie, David. 2005. All Labour Produces Value and We All Struggle Against Value. *The Commoner*, Vol. 10. Online: https://lra.le.ac.uk/bitstream/2381/3289/1/Harvie%20All%20labour%20produces%20value...%20%5bCommoner%202005%5d.pdf

——and Massimo de Angelis. 2008. Globalization? No Question! Foreign Direct Investment and Labor Commanded. *Review of Radical Political Economics*. Vol. 40, 429–44. Online: www2.le.ac.uk/departments/management/documents/people/david-harvie/HARVIE-David-GlobalizationNoQuestion.pdf

Hatton, T. J., G. R. Boyer and R. E. Bailey. 1994. The Union Wage Effect in Late Nineteenth Century Britain. Online: http://digitalcommons.ilr.cornell.edu/articles/537/

Haupt, G. and M. Rebérioux. 1967. L'Internationale et le Probléme Colonial (The International and the Colonial Problem). In G. Haupt and M. Réberioux (eds), *La Deuxieme Internationale et l'Orient*. Paris, pp. 2–48.

Heintz, James. 2003. The New Face of Unequal Exchange: Low-Wage Manufacturing, Commodity Chains, and Global Inequality. Working Paper Series. No. 59. Political Economy Research Institute, University of Massachusetts, Amherst. Online: https://papers.ssrn.com/sol3/papers.cfm?abstract_id=427680

Hensman, Rohini and Marinella Correggia. 2005. The Soft Underbelly of Empire. *Economic and Political Weekly*. Vol. 40, No. 12. March, 19–25.

Hersh, Jonathan and Hans-Joachim Voth. 2009. Sweet Diversity: Colonial Goods and the Rise of European Living Standards after 1492. 17 July. Online: www.princeton.edu/rpds/seminars/Voth102809.pdf

Hickel, Jason. 2017. *The Divide: A Brief Guide to Global Inequality and Its Solutions*. London: Heinemann.

Higginbottom, Andy. 2015. 'Imperialist Rent' in Theory and Practice. In Andreas Bieler, Bruno Ciccaglione, John Hilary and Ingemar Lindberg (eds), *Free Trade and Transnational Labour*. London: Routledge, pp. 23–33.

——2016. Anti-Apartheid, Anti-Capitalism, and Anti-Imperialism: Liberation in South Africa. In Immanuel Ness and Zak Cope (eds), *The Palgrave Encyclopedia of Imperialism and Anti-Imperialism*. Basingstoke, Hampshire: Palgrave Macmillan, pp. 544–69.

Hira, Sandew. 2014. *20 Questions and Answers about Reparations for Colonialism*. The Hague: Amrit Publisher.

Hitler, Adolf. 1939 [1925]. *Mein Kampf*. London: Hurst and Blackett.

Ho Chi Minh. 1977 [1924]. Report on the National and Colonial Questions at the Fifth Congress of the Communist International. In *Selected Works of Ho Chi Minh*. Vol. 1. Hanoi: Foreign Languages Publishing House, pp. 63–73.

Hobsbawm, Eric. 1964. *Labouring Men*. London: Penguin.

——1970. Lenin and the Aristocracy of Labour. *Marxism Today*. Vol. 14, No. 7, 207–10.

——1994 [1987]. *The Age of Empire, 1875–1914*. London: Abacus.

——1999. *The Age of Capital, 1848–1876*. London: Abacus.

Hobson, John A. 1968 [1902]. *Imperialism: A Study*. London: George Allen and Unwin.

Hoffman, Elizabeth Cobbs. 2001. Decolonization, the Cold War, and the Foreign Policy of the Peace Corps. In Peter L. Hahn and Mary Ann Heiss (eds), *Empire and Revolution: The United States and the Third World since 1945*. Columbus, OH: Ohio State University Press, pp. 123–54.

Holton, Bob. 1976. *British Syndicalism, 1900–1914: Myth and Realities*. London: Pluto Press.

Homze, Edward L. 1967. *Foreign Labor in Nazi Germany*. Princeton, NJ: Princeton University Press.

Howard, Marc Morjé. 2006. Comparative Citizenship: An Agenda for Cross-National Research. *Perspectives on Politics*. Vol. 4, No. 3, 443–55.

Hudson, Michael. 2003. *Super Imperialism: The Origin and Fundamentals of U.S. World Dominance*. London: Pluto Press.

Hutt, Allen. 1975. *British Trade Unionism: A Short History*. London: Lawrence and Wishart.

Hyslop, J. 1999. The Imperial Working Class Makes Itself 'White': White Labourism in Britain, Australia, and South Africa before the First World War. *Journal of Historical Sociology*. Vol. 12, No. 4, 398–421.

ILO (International Labour Organization). 2011a. *Global Employment Trends 2011: The Challenge of a Jobs Recovery*. Geneva: United Nations.

——2011b. *World of Work Report 2011: Making Markets Work for Jobs*. Geneva: United Nations.

——2014. The Meanings of Forced Labor. 10 March. Online: www.ilo.org/global/topics/forced-labour/news/WCMS_237569/lang--en/index.htm

——2017. Average Monthly Earnings of Employees. Online: www.ilo.org/ilostat/faces/oracle/webcenter/portalapp/pagehierarchy/Page3.jspx?MBI_ID=435

IMF (International Monetary Fund). 2000. *World Economic Outlook October 2000*. Washington, DC: International Monetary Fund, Table 42: Developing Countries: Debt-Service Ratios.

Jaffe, Hosea. 1980. *The Pyramid of Nations*. Milan: Victor.

——1985. *A History of Africa*. London: Zed Books.

——1990. *Progresso e Nazione: Economia ed Ecologia* (*Progress and Nationality: Economy and Ecology*). Milan: Jaca Books.

——1994. *European Colonial Despotism: A History of Oppression and Resistance in South Africa*. London: Karnak House.

Jedlicki, Claudio. 2007. Unequal Exchange. The Jus Semper Global Alliance: Living Wages North and South. Online: www.jussemper.org/Resources/Labour%20Resources/Resources/Jedlicki_UnequalExchange.pdf

Johnston, R. J., J. O'Loughlin and P. J. Taylor. 1987. The Geography of Violence and Premature Death: A World-Systems Approach. In Raimo Väyrynen (ed.), *The Quest for Peace: Transcending Collective Violence and War among Societies, Cultures and States*. London: Sage Publications, pp. 241–59.

Jones, E. L. 1981. Agriculture, 1700–1800. In Roderick Floud and Donald McCloskey (eds), *The Economic History of Britain since 1700, Volume I, 1700–1860*. Cambridge: Cambridge University Press, pp. 66–86.

Jones, Richard Benjamin. 1974. *Economic and Social History of England, 1770–1970*. London: Longman.

Joppke, Christian. 2010. *Citizenship and Immigration*. Cambridge: Polity Press.

Kaarsholm, Preben. 1988. The South African War and the Response of the International Socialist Community to Imperialism between 1896 and 1908. In F. van Holthoon and M. van der Linden (eds), *Internationalism in the Labour Movement, 1830–1940*. Leiden: Brill, pp. 42–67.

Kadri, Ali. 2015. *Arab Development Denied: Dynamics of Accumulation by Wars of Encroachment*. London: Anthem Press.

Kagarlitsky, Boris. 2007. *Empire of the Periphery: Russia and the World System*. London: Pluto Press.

Kalecki, Michal. 2008 [1935]. *Theory of Economic Dynamics*. New York: Monthly Review Press.

Karmakar, Asim K. 2001. Dadhabai Naoroji, Drain Theory and Poverty: Towards a Discourse in Political Economy. In P. D. Hajela (ed.), *Economic Thoughts of Dadabhai Naoroji*. New Delhi: Deep and Deep Publications, pp. 65–77.

Kautsky, Karl. 2009 [1906]. The American Worker. In Richard B. Day and Daniel Gaido (trans. and eds), *Witnesses to Permanent Revolution: The Documentary Record*. Lieden: Brill.

Kennedy, Paul. 1989. *The Rise and Fall of the Great Powers: Economic Change and Military Conflict from 1500 to 2000*. New York: Random House.

Kerswell, Timothy. 2012. Consuming Value: The Politics of Production and Consumption. *Economic Affairs*. Vol. 57, No. 3. September, 213–20.

Kiely, Ray. 2009. The Globalization of Manufacturing Production: Warrenite Fantasies and Uneven and Unequal Realities. In A. Haroon Akram-Lodhi and Cristóbal Kay (eds), *Peasants and Globalization: Political Economy, Rural Transformation and the Agrarian Question*. London: Routledge, pp. 169–89.

King, Samuel T. 2018. China and the Third World are not "Catching Up" to the Rich Countries. *Labor and Society*. Vol. 21. 447–470.

King, Stephen D. 2010. *Losing Control: The Emerging Threats to Western Prosperity*. New Haven, CT: Yale University Press.

Kirk, Neville. 1985. *The Growth of Working-Class Reformism in Mid-Victorian England*. London: Croom Helm.

——2003. *Comrades and Cousins: Globalization, Workers and Labour Movements in Britain, the USA and Australia from the 1880s to 1914*. London: Merlin Press.

Kittrell, Edward R. 1970 [1965]. The Development of the Theory of Colonization in English Classical Political Economy. In A. G. L. Shaw (ed.), *Great Britain and the Colonies, 1815–1865*. London: Methuen & Co. Originally published in *Southern Economic Journal*. Vol. XXXI, pp. 46–77.

Knauss, Steve. 2015. The Myth of the Global Middle Class. *Potemkin Review*. December. Online: www.potemkinreview.com/the-myth-of-the-global-middle-class.html

Knowles, Louis L. and Kenneth Prewitt (eds). 1970. *Institutional Racism in America*. Englewood Cliffs, NJ: Prentice-Hall.

Köhler, Gernot. 2002. The Structure of Global Money. In Gernot Köhler and Arno Tausch, *Global Keynesianism: Unequal Exchange and Global Exploitation*. New York: Nova Science Publishers, pp. 1–43.

——2005. The Global Stratification of Unemployment and Underemployment. Online: http://s3.amazonaws.com/zanran_storage/www.caei.com.ar/ContentPages/394534208.pdf

——2007. *Global Economics: An Introductory Course*. New York: Nova Science Publishers.

Kohlmey, Gunther. 1962. 'Karl Marx' Theorie von den internationalen Werten mit einigen Schlussfolgerungen für die Preisbildung im Aussenhandel zwischen den sozialistischen Staaten (Karl Marx's Theory of International Values With Some Conclusions for Pricing in Foreign Trade between the Socialist States). In Deutsche Akademie der Wissenschaften zu Berlin. *Jahrbuch des Instituts für Wirtschaftswissenschaften*. Vol. 5. Berlin, GDR, pp. 18–22.

Krooth, Richard. 1980. *Arms and Empire: Imperial Patterns before World War II*. California: Harvest Press.

Kyriakides, Christopher and Satnam Virdee. 2003. Migrant Labour, Racism and the British National Health Service. *Ethnicity & Health*. Vol. 8, No. 4, 283–305.

Labour Party. 2017. For the Many Not the Few. The Labour Party Manifesto 2017. Online: https://labour.org.uk/wp-content/uploads/2017/10/labour-manifesto-2017.pdf

Lane, Tony. 1987. *Liverpool: Gateway of Empire*. London: Lawrence and Wishart.

Lauesen, Torkil. 2018. *The Global Perspective*. Montréal, Quebec: Kersplebedeb.

——and Zak Cope. 2015. Imperialism and the Transformation of Values into Prices. *Monthly Review*. Vol. 67, No. 3. July, 54–68.

Lenin, V. I. 1964 [1916]. Imperialism and the Split in Socialism. In *Collected Works*. Vol. 23. Moscow: Progress Publishers, pp. 105–20.

——1968 [1915–16]. Notebooks on Imperialism. In *Collected Works*. Vol. 39. Moscow: Progress Publishers.

——1969. *British Labour and British Imperialism: A Collection of Writings by Lenin on Britain*. London: Lawrence and Wishart.

——1970 [1916]. *Imperialism: The Highest Stage of Capitalism*. Peking: Foreign Languages Press.

——1971 [1921]. Letter to the Propaganda and Action Council of the Peoples of the East. Dictated by telephone not before December 17, 1921. In *Collected Works*. Vol. 42. Moscow: Progress Publishers, p. 369.

——1974a [1915]. Letter to the Secretary of the Socialist Propaganda League. Written in English before November 9 (23), 1915. In *Collected Works*. Vol. 21. Moscow: Progress Publishers, pp. 423–8.

——1974b [1915]. The Collapse of the Second International. In *Collected Works*. Vol. 21. Moscow: Progress Publishers, pp. 205–59. Originally published in the journal *Kommunist*, No. 1–2.

——, Christian Rakovsky, Gregory Zinoviev, Leon Trotsky and Fritz Platten. 1980 [1919]. Manifesto of the First Congress of the Comintern. 6th March. In Alix Holt, Barbara Holland, Bertil Hessel and Alan Adler (eds), *Theses, Resolutions and Manifestos of the First Four Congresses of the Third International*. New Jersey: Humanities Press.

Lensch, Paul. 2013 [1918]. *Three Years of World-Revolution*. Reprint. London: Forgotten Books.

Li, Minqi. 2016. *China and the 21st Century Crisis*. London: Pluto Press.

Liberti, Stefano. 2011. *Land Grabbing: Journeys in the New Colonialism*. London: Verso.

Lin Biao. 1965. *Long Live the Victory of People's War!* Peking: Foreign Languages Press.

Linder, Marc. 1985. *European Labor Aristocracies: Trade Unionism, the Hierarchy of Skill, and the Stratification of the Manual Working Class before the First World War*. Frankfurt: Campus.

Liu, Henry C. K. 2002. US Dollar Hegemony Has Got to Go. *Asia Times*. 11 April. Online: www.atimes.com/global-econ/DD11Djo1.html

Liu, Wei and Libing Deng. 2012. Who Is the Exchange Rate Manipulator: China or America? *World Review of Political Economy*. Vol. 3, No. 3, 344–53.

Losurdo, Domenico. 2011. *Liberalism: A Counter-History*. London: Verso.

——2013. *La Lotta di Classe: Una Storia Politica e Filosofica* (*Class Struggle: A Political and Philosophical History*). Roma-Bari: Laterza.

Ludlow, J. M. and Lloyd Jones. 1867. *The Progress of the Working Class, 1832–1867*. London: Alexander Strahan.

Lüdtke, Alf. 1992. Perpetrators, Accomplices, Victims: Further Reflections of Domination as Social Practice. CSST Working Paper No. 85. CRSO Working Paper No. 481. Online: http://deepblue.lib.umich.edu/bitstream/2027.42/51247/1/481.pdf

Lynch, Michael. 1997. Benjamin Disraeli. In Richard N. Kelly and John Cantrell (eds), *Modern British Statesmen, 1867–1945*. Manchester: Manchester University Press, pp. 16–30.

Macdonagh, Oliver. 1962. The Anti-Imperialism of Free Trade. *Economic History Review*. Vol. 14, No. 3, 489–501.

Macheda, Francesco and Nadalini Roberto. 2018. The Political Economy of Nationalism and Racial Discrimination. *Labor and Society*. Vol. 21. 337–48.

Maddison, Angus. 1994. Explaining the Economic Performance of Nations, 1820–1989. In William J. Baumol, Richard R. Nelson and Edward N. Wolff (eds), *Convergence of Productivity: Cross-National Studies and Historical Evidence*. Oxford: Oxford University Press, pp. 20–61.

Magraw, Roger. 1999. Appropriating the Symbols of the *Patrie*? Jacobin Nationalism and its Rivals in the French Third Republic. In Angel Smith and Stefan Berger (eds), *Nationalism, Labour and Ethnicity, 1870–1939*. Manchester: Manchester University Press, pp. 93–121.

252 THE WEALTH OF (SOME) NATIONS

Makhijani, Arjun. 1992. *From Global Capitalism to Economic Justice: An Inquiry into the Elimination of Systemic Poverty, Violence and Environmental Destruction in the World*. New York: Apex Press.

Mangum, Garth L. and Peter Philips. 1988. Introduction. In Garth Mangum and Peter Philips (eds), *Three Worlds of Labor Economics*. London: Routledge, pp. 3–18.

Mao Zedong. 1965 [1963]. Apologists of Neo-Colonialism. Comment on the Open Letter of the Central Committee of the CPSU (IV). In *The Polemic on the General Line of the International Communist Movement*. Peking: Foreign Languages Press, pp. 185–219. Originally published in *Hongqi (Red Flag)*. 22 October 1963.

Martin, Terry. 2001. *The Affirmative Action Empire: Nations and Nationalism in the Soviet Union, 1923–1939*. Ithaca, NY: Cornell University Press.

Martinez-Alier, J. 2002. *The Environmentalism of the Poor: A Study of Ecological Conflicts and Valuation*. Cheltenham: Edward Elgar.

Marx, Karl 1962 [1862]. Letter from Marx to Engels. London, 17 November. In Karl Marx and Frierich Engels. *On Britain*. Moscow: Foreign Languages Publishing House, p. 538.

—— 1963 [1863]. *Theories of Surplus Value*. Moscow: Progress Publishers.

—— 1977 [1867]. *Capital: A Critique of Political Economy*. Vol. I. London: Lawrence and Wishart.

—— 1977 [1885]. *Capital: A Critique of Political Economy*. Vol. II. London: Lawrence and Wishart.

—— 1977 [1894]. *Capital: A Critique of Political Economy*. Vol. III. London: Lawrence and Wishart.

—— and Friedrich Engels. 2004 [1848]. *The Communist Manifesto*. London: Penguin.

Mastanduno, M. 2009. System Maker and Privilege Taker: U.S. Power and the International Political Economy. *World Politics*. Vol. 61, No. 1, 121–54.

Mavrakis, Kostas. 1976. *On Trotskyism*. Trans. John McGreal. London: Routledge and Kegan Paul.

McCants, Anne E. C. 2007. Exotic Goods, Popular Consumption, and the Standard of Living: Thinking About Globalization in the Early Modern World. *Journal of World History*. Vol. 18, No. 4, 433–62.

McClelland, Keith. 2000. England's Greatness, the Working Man. In Catherine Hall, Keith McClelland and Jane Rendall (eds), *Defining the Victoria Nation: Race, Gender and the British Reform Act of 1867*. Cambridge: Cambridge University Press, pp. 71–119.

Meisner, Maurice. 1970. *Li Ta-chao and the Origins of Chinese Marxism*. New York: Atheneum.

Menon, Kitti. 1982. Imperialism and the Export of Capital in the Contemporary Period. *Social Scientist*. Vol. 10, No. 3. March, 4–24.

Mill, John Stuart. 1963–91. *Collected Works*. 33 volumes. Vol. 2. Ed. John M. Robson. Toronto and London: University of Toronto Press and Routledge and Kegan Paul.

—— 1972 [1861]. *Utilitarianism, Liberty, Representative Government*. Ed. Harry B. Acton. London: Dent.

Milkman, Ruth. 2015. Immigrant Workers and the Labour Movement in the USA. In C.-U. Schierup, R. Munck, B. Likic-Brboric and A. Neergaard (eds), *Migration, Precarity and Global Governance*. Oxford: Oxford University Press, pp. 160–76.

Mitchell, B. R. 1988. *British Historical Statistics*. Cambridge: Cambridge University Press.

Momani, B. 2008. Gulf Cooperation Council Oil Exporters and the Future of the Dollar. *New Political Economy*. Vol. 13, No. 3, 293–314.

Moore, Carlos. 1977. *Were Marx and Engels White Racists? The Prolet-Aryan Outlook of Marx and Engels*. Chicago, IL: Institute of Positive Education.

Moran, Andrew. 2010. Ahmadinejad: U.S. Biggest Thief in the History of Mankind. 3 March. Online: www.digitaljournal.com/article/288482

Morris, Lydia. 2002. *Managing Migration: Civic Stratification and Migrants Rights*. London: Routledge.

Moussa, Pierre. 1962. *The Underprivileged Nations*. London: Sidgwick and Jackson.

Moyo, Sam and Paris Yeros. 2007. The Zimbabwe Question and the Two Lefts. *Historical Materialism*. Vol. 15, 171–204.

Neilson, David and Thomas Stubbs. 2011. Relative Surplus Population and Uneven Development in the Neoliberal Era: Theory and Empirical Application. *Capital and Class*. Vol. 35, No. 3, 435–53.

Newsinger, John. 2010. *The Blood Never Dried: A People's History of the British Empire*. London: Bookmarks.

Niño-Zarazúa, Miguel, Laurence Roope and Finn Tarp. 2017. Global Inequality: Relatively Lower, Absolutely Higher. *Review of Income and Wealth*. Vol. 63, No. 4. December, 661–84.

Nolan, Peter. 2012. *Is China Buying the World?* Cambridge: Polity Press.

Norfield, Tony. 2016. *The City: London and the Global Power of Finance*. London: Verso.

OECD (Organisation for Economic Co-operation and Development). 2014. Social Expenditure Update. Social Spending is Falling in Some Countries, but in Many Others it Remains at Historically High Levels. November. Online: www.oecd.org/els/soc/OECD2014-Social-Expenditure-Update-Nov2014-8pages.pdf

——2016. Development Aid in 2015 Continues to Grow Despite Costs for In-Donor Refugees. Paris. 13 April. Online: www.oecd.org/dac/stats/ODA-2015-detailed-summary.pdf

——2017. Import Content of Exports. Online: https://data.oecd.org/trade/import-content-of-exports.htm

Olivesi, A. 1964. Les Socialistes Marseillais et le Problème Colonial (The Marseilles Socialists and the Colonial Problem). *Mouvement Social*. Vol. 46, 27–65.

Orrenius, Pia M. and Madeline Zavodny. 2009. Do Immigrants Work in Riskier Jobs? *Demography*. Vol. 46, No. 3, 535–51.

Orwell, George. 1958 [1937]. *The Road to Wigan Pier*. New York: Harcourt.

——1970 [1941]. The Lion and the Unicorn: Socialism and the English Genius. In S. Orwell and I. Angus (eds), *The Collected Essays, Journalism and Letters of George Orwell*. Vol. II. London: Harmondsworth, pp. 74–134.

Owen, Nicholas. 2007. *The British Left and India: Metropolitan Anti-Imperialism, 1885–1947*. Oxford: Oxford University Press.

Pal, Saroj Kumar. 2005. *Lexicon on Geography of Development*. New Delhi: Concept Publishing.

Pallares-Miralles, Montserrat, Carolina Romero and Edward Whitehouse. 2012. International Patterns of Pension Provision II: A Worldwide Overview of Facts and Figures. Social Protection and Labor Discussion Paper No. 1211. World Bank, Washington, DC. Online: http://documents.worldbank.org/curated/en/143611468168560687/pdf/703190NWP0SPL000Box370035B00PUBLICo.pdf

Patnaik, Prabhat. 2011. The Myths of Capitalism. *People's Democracy*. 3 July. Online: http://pd.cpim.org/2011/0703_pd/07032011_7.html

Patnaik, Utsa. 1995. On Capitalism and Agrestic Unfreedom. *International Review of Social History*. Vol. 40, 77–92.

——2006. The Free Lunch: Transfers from the Tropical Colonies and Their Role in Capital Formation in Britain during the Industrial Revolution. In K. S. Jomo (ed.), *Globalisation under Hegemony: The Changing World Economy*. Oxford: Oxford University Press, pp. 30–71.

—— 2007 [2000]. The Costs of Free Trade. The WTO Regime and the Indian Economy. The First EMS Namboodiripad Memorial Lecture Organised by the Students Federation of India. Delivered on 16 February 2000. In *The Republic of Hunger and Other Essays*. Monmouth, Wales: Merlin Press, pp. 17–51.

——and Prabhat Patnaik. 2017. *A Theory of Imperialism*. With a Commentary by David Harvey. New York: Columbia University Press.

Pauwels, Jacques. 2016. *The Great Class War 1914–1918*. Toronto: Lorimer.

Péju, Marcel. 1960. Mourir pour de Gaulle? *Les Temps Modernes*. No. 175–6. October–November, 481–502.

Petersen, Roger D. 2002. *Understanding Ethnic Violence: Fear, Hatred, and Resentment in Twentieth Century Eastern Europe*. Cambridge: Cambridge University Press.

Phizacklea, Annie and Robert Miles. 1980, *Labour and Racism*. London: Routledge and Kegan Paul.

Piketty, Thomas and Emmanuel Saez. 2004. Income Inequality in the United States, 1913–2002. Online: http://elsa.berkeley.edu/~saez/piketty-saezOUP04US.pdf

Pipes Richard (ed.). 1996. *The Unknown Lenin: From the Secret Archives*. New Haven, CT: Yale University Press.

Polan, A. J. 1984. *Lenin and the End of Politics*. Berkeley, CA: University of California Press.

Porter, Bernard. 1984. *The Lion's Share: A Short History of British Imperialism, 1850–1983*. London: Longman.

Prandy, K., A. Stewart and R. M. Blackburn. 1983. *White Collar Unionism*. London: Macmillan.

Prebisch, Raúl. 1950. The Economic Development of Latin America and its Principal Problems. United Nations Economic Commission for Latin America. Vol. 7, No. 1.

Quinoa, Michael Garry. 1982. Immigrant Workers, Trade Union Organization and Industrial Strategy. A Thesis submitted for the Degree of Doctor of Philosophy in the Department of Industrial Relations, Faculty of Economics, University of Sydney. May, p. 18. Online: https:// ses.library.usyd.edu.au/bitstream/2123/6412/1/Quinlan_M_thesis_1982.pdf

Raffer, Kunibert. 1987. *Unequal Exchange and the Evolution of the World System: Reconsidering the Impact of Trade on North-South Relations*. New York: St. Martin's Press.

Raman, Meena. 2005. WIPO Seminar Debates Intellectual Property and Development. TWN Info Service on WTO and Trade Issues. 3 May. Online: www.twn.my/title2/twninfo214.htm

Read, Anthony. 2009. *The World on Fire: 1919 and the Battle with Bolshevism*. New York: Random House.

Redfern, Neil. 2005. *Class or Nation: Communists, Imperialism and Two World Wars*. London: Tauris Academic Studies.

——2017. The Comintern and Imperialism: A Balance Sheet. *Journal of Labor and Society*. Vol. 20, No. 1, 43–60.

Renan, Ernest. 1947–1961. *Ouevres Completes*. 10 volumes. Paris: Calmann-Lévy.

Renault, Matthieu. 2015. The Idea of Muslim National Communism: On Mirsaid Sultan-Galiev. *Viewpoint Magazine*, 23 March. Online: https://viewpointmag.com/2015/03/23/ the-idea-of-muslim-national-communism-on-mirsaid-sultan-galiev/

Resnick, Stephen A. and Richard D. Wolff. 2006. *New Departures in Marxian Theory*. London: Routledge.

Rist, Gilbert. 2002. *The History of Development: From Western Origins to Global Faith*. New York: Zed Books.

Roberts, David D. 1979. *The Syndicalist Tradition and Italian Fascism*. Manchester: Manchester University Press.

Roberts, Glenn L. 2007. *Commissar and Mullah: Soviet-Muslim Policy from 1917 to 1924*. California: Universal Publishers.

Roberts, Michael. 2017. Market Power Again. 21 November. Online: https://thenextrecession. wordpress.com/2017/11/21/market-power-again/

Robinson, Joan. 1970. *Freedom and Necessity: An Introduction to the Study of Society*. London: George Allen and Unwin.

Robinson, William I. and Xuan Santos. 2014. Global Capitalism, Immigrant Labor, and the Struggle for Justice. *Class, Race and Corporate Power*. Vol. 2, No. 3, 1–16.

Rodney, Walter. 1989 [1972]. *How Europe Underdeveloped Africa*. Nairobi: East African Educational Publishers.

Rodrik, Dani. 2001. The Global Governance of Trade – as if Development Really Mattered. United Nations Development Programme Background Paper. Online: https://wcfia.harvard. edu/publications/global-governance-trade-if-development-really-matteredbra-undp-background-paper

Rosenthal, Elisabeth and Andrew Martin. 2008. UN Says Solving Food Crisis Could Cost $30 Billion. *New York Times*. 4 June. Online: www.nytimes.com/2008/06/04/news/04iht-04food.13446176.html

Roxborough, Ian. 1979. *Theories of Underdevelopment*. London: Macmillan.

Roy, M. N. 1984. Supplementary Theses on the National and Colonial Questions. In John Riddell (ed.), *The Communist International in Lenin's Time: Workers of the World and Oppressed*

Peoples, Unite! Proceedings and Documents of the Second Congress, 1920. Vol. I. New York: Pathfinder Press, pp. 245–51.

Rubin, Lyle Jeremy. 2018. The Left's Embrace of Empire. *The Nation*. 28 March. Online: www. thenation.com/article/the-lefts-embrace-of-empire/

Russell, Bertrand. 2013 [1966]. Peace through Resistance to US Imperialism. In Barry Feinberg and Ronald Kasril (eds), *Russell's America: His Transatlantic Travels and Writings, a Documented Account. Vol. 2, 1945–1970*. London: Routledge, pp. 394–9.

Sakai, J. 2014 [1983]. *Settlers: The Mythology of the White Proletariat from Mayflower to Modern*. Montréal, Quebec: Kersplebedeb.

Sartre, Jean-Paul. 1970 [1959]. Interview de Sartre. *Vérités*. No. 9, 2 June, 1959, 14–17. In M. Contat and M. Rybalka, *Les Ecrits de Sartre*. Paris: Gallimard, pp. 723–9.

Sassoon, Donald. 1996. *One Hundred Years of Socialism: The West European Left in the Twentieth Century*. London: Fontana Press.

Sau, Ranjit. 1978. *Unequal Exchange, Imperialism and Underdevelopment: An Essay on the Political Economy of World Capitalism*. Calcutta: Oxford University Press.

——1982. *Trade, Capital and Underdevelopment: Towards a Marxist Theory*. Calcutta: Oxford University Press.

Schierup, Carl-Ulrik and Stephen Castles. 2011. Migration, Minorities, and Welfare States. In Nicola Phillips (ed.), *Migration in the Global Political Economy*. Boulder,CO: Lynne Rienner, pp. 15–40.

Schlesinger, Rudolf (ed.). 1956. *The Nationalities Problem and Soviet Administration: Selected Readings on the Development of Soviet Nationalities Policies*. London: Routledge and Kegan Paul.

Schrevel, Margreet and Emile Schwidder. 2009. A Socialist in the Dutch East Indies. International Institute of Social History. Online: www.iisg.nl/collections/vankol/intro.php

Schumpeter, Joseph A. 1951. *Imperialism and Social Classes*. New York: Augustus M. Kelley, Inc.

——1991. *The Economics and Sociology of Capitalism*. Ed. Richard Swedberg. Princeton, NJ: Princeton University Press, pp. 201–2.

Schumpeter, Elizabeth. 1960. *English Overseas Trade, 1697–1808*. Oxford: Oxford University Press.

Semmel, Bernard. 1968 [1960]. *Imperialism and Social Reform: English Social-Imperial Thought, 1895–1914*. London: George Allen and Unwin.

Senghor, Léopold Sédar. 1959. Congrès Constitutif du P.F.A.: Rapport Sur La Doctrine et le Programme Du Parti (Constitutive Congress of the PFA: Report on the Doctrine and the Program of the Party). Dakar, 1st, 2nd and 3rd July. Pairs: Présence Africaine.

Shachar, Ayelet. 2009. *The Birthright Lottery*. Harvard, MA: Harvard University Press.

Shaikh, Anwar. 1979. Foreign Trade and the Law of Value: Part I. *Science & Society*. Vol. 43, No. 3. Contemporary Issues in Marxist Political Economy. Fall, 281–302.

——and A. E. Tonak. 1994. *Measuring the Wealth of Nations: The Political Economy of National Accounts*. Cambridge: Cambridge University Press.

Shulman, S. 1990. Racial Inequality and White Employment: An Interpretation and Test of the Bargaining Power Hypothesis. *Review of Black Political Economy*. Vol. 18, No. 3, 5–20.

Sikka, Prem and Hugh Willmott. 2010. *The Dark Side of Transfer Pricing: Its Role in Tax Avoidance and Wealth Retentiveness*. University of Essex. Online: http://repository.essex. ac.uk/8098/1/WP2010-1%20-%

Sinclair, Upton. 1994 [1935]. *I, Candidate for Governor: and How I Got Licked*. Berkeley, CA: University of California Press.

Singer, Hans W. 1950. The Distribution of Gains between Investing and Borrowing Countries. *American Economic Review*. Vol. 40, No. 2, 473–85.

Slaughter, Matthew J. 2001. Trade Liberalization and Per Capita Income Convergence: A Difference-in-Differences Analysis. *Journal of International Economics*. No. 55, 203–28.

Slavin, D. 1991. The French Left and the Rif War: Racism and the Limits of Internationalism. *Journal of Contemporary History*. Vol. 26, 5–32.

Smith, Adam. 1976 [1776]. *An Inquiry into the Nature and Causes of the Wealth of Nations.* Oxford: Oxford University Press.

Smith, J. W. 2002. *Economic Democracy: The Political Struggle of the Twenty-First Century.* Indiana: First Books Library.

Smith, John. 2010. Imperialism and the Globalisation of Production. PhD Thesis. University of Sheffield. Online: www.mediafire.com/?5r339mnn4zmubq7

——2011. Imperialism and the Law of Value. *Global Discourse.* Vol. 2, No. 1. Online: https://globaldiscourse.files.wordpress.com/2011/05/john-smith.pdf

——2013. Southern Labour – 'Peripheral' No Longer: A reply to Jane Hardy. *International Socialist Review.* No. 140. Online: http://isj.org.uk/southern-labour-peripheral-no-longer/

——2016. *Imperialism in the Twenty-First Century: Globalization, Super-Exploitation and Capitalism's Final Crisis.* New York: Monthly Review Press.

——2017. The Global South in the Global Crisis. *Journal of Labor and Society.* Vol. 20, No. 2, 161–84.

Sogge, David. 2002. *Give and Take: What's the Matter with Foreign Aid?* London: Zed Books.

Soysal, Yasemin Nuhoglu. 1994. *Limits of Citizenship: Migrants and Postnational Membership in Europe.* Chicago, IL: University of Chicago Press.

Stavrianos, L. S. 1981. *Global Rift: The Third World Comes of Age.* New York: William Morrow and Company.

Stedman Jones, Gareth. 1971. *Outcast London: A Study in the Relationship between Classes in Victorian Society.* Oxford: Oxford University Press.

Sternberg, Fritz. 1951. *Capitalism and Socialism on Trial.* London: Victor Gollancz.

Stråth, Bo. 2016. *Europe's Utopias of Peace: 1815, 1919, 1951.* London: Bloomsbury.

Strikwerda, Carl and Camille Guerin-Gonzales. 1998. Labor, Migration and Politics. In Camille Guerin-Gonzales and Carl Strikwerda (eds), *The Politics of Immigrant Workers: Labor Activism and Migration in the World Economy since 1830.* Teaneck, NJ: Holmes & Meier.

Sultan-Galiev, Mirsaid. 1979 [1919]. The Social Revolution and the East. In Alexandre Bennigsen and S. Enders Wimbush. *Muslim National Communism in the Soviet Union.* Chicago, IL: University of Chicago Press, pp. 131–7. Originally published in *Zizn' nacional'nostej.* Vol. 38, No. 46.

Sutcliffe, Bob. 1980. Conclusion. In Roger Owen and Bob Sutcliffe (eds), *Studies in the Theory of Imperialism.* London: Longman, pp. 312–31.

Suwandi, Intan. 2015. Behind the Veil of Globalization. *Monthly Review.* Vol. 67, No. 3. July/August, 37–54.

Swanson, David. 2017. The Fog Machines. US War Justification is in the Eye of the Beholder. *Counterpunch.* Vol. 24, No. 3, 23–7.

Sweezy, Paul. 1949. *The Theory of Capitalist Development: Principles of Marxian Political Economy.* London: Dennis Dobson.

Szymanski, Albert. 1981. *The Logic of Imperialism.* New York: Praeger.

Tausch, Arno. 2002. Migration and Unequal Exchange. In Gernot Köhler and Arno Tausch, *Global Keynesianism: Unequal Exchange and Global Exploitation.* New York: Nova Science Publishers, pp. 233–77.

Tharoor, Shashi. 2017. *Inglorious Empire: What the British Did to India.* London: Hurst.

Thatcher, Ian D. 1991. Uneven and Combined Development. *Revolutionary Russia.* Vol. 4, No. 2, 235–58.

Thomas, R. P. and D. N. McCloskey. 1981. Overseas Trade and Empire, 1700–1860. In Roderick Floud and Donald McCloskey (eds), *The Economic History of Britain since 1700. Volume I: 1700–1860.* Cambridge: Cambridge University Press, pp. 87–102.

Thompson, Andrew. 2005. *The Empire Strikes Back? The Impact of Imperialism on Britain from the Mid-Nineteenth Century.* Harlow, UK: Pearson Education.

Tichelman, Fritjof. 1998. Socialist 'Internationalism' and the Colonial World: Practical Colonial Policies of Social Democracy in Western Europe before 1940 with Particular Reference to the Dutch SDAP. In Frits Van Holthoon and Marcel van der Linden (eds), *Internationalism in the Labour Movement, 1830–1940.* Leiden: Brill, pp. 87–109.

Towers Watson. 2015. *Pension and Insurance/Towers Watson 300 Analysis*. Total Value of Fund Assets Split by Fund Domicile. Online: www.thinkingaheadinstitute.org/-/media/Pdf/Insights/IC-Types/Survey-Research-Results/2015/09/The-worlds-300-largest-pension-funds-year-end-2014.pdf

Tripathi, Ruchi. 2000. Implications of TRIPs on Livelihoods of Poor Farmers in Developing Countries. ActionAid, Berne. 13 October. Online: www.actionaid.org.uk/content_document.asp?doc_id=240

Trotsky, Leon. 1969 [1940]. The World Situation and Perspectives. St. Louis Post Dispatch. In *Writings of Leon Trotsky*. New York: Merit Publishers.

——1969 [1939]. The Twin Stars: Hitler-Stalin. 4 December. In *Writings of Leon Trotsky*. New York: Merit Publishers.

——1969 [1940]. On the Future of Hitler's Armies. 2 August. In *Writings of Leon Trotsky*. New York: Merit Publishers.

——1974 [1928]. *The Third International after Lenin*. London: New Park Publications.

——1975 [1922]. *Social Democracy and the Wars of Intervention, 1918–1921*. London: New Park Publications.

Tucker, G. S. L. 1970 [1960]. The Application and Significance of Theories of the Effect of Economic Progress on the Rate of Profit, 1800–1850. In A. G. L. Shaw (ed.), *Great Britain and the Colonies, 1815–1865*. London: Methuen & Co, pp. 132–42. Originally edited from G. S. L. Tucker. *Progress and Profit in British Economic Thought, 1650–1850*, chapter 8. Cambridge: Cambridge University Press.

UNCTAD (United Nations Conference on Trade and Development). 2010. *Trade and Development Report 2010. Employment, Globalization and Development*. New York and Geneva: United Nations.

——2014. *World Investment Report 2014. Investing in the SDGs: An Action Plan*. Geneva: United Nations.

——2016. *Trade Misinvoicing in Primary Commodities in Developing Countries: The Cases of Chile, Côte d'Ivoire, Nigeria, South Africa and Zambia*. New York: United Nations.

UNESCO (United Nations Educational, Scientific and Cultural Organization). 2013. Education for All Global Monitoring Report – Policy Paper 06. Paris. February. Online: http://unesdoc.unesco.org/images/0021/002199/219998E.pdf

United Nations. 2012. *World Economic Situation and Prospects 2012*. New York: United Nations.

——2018. GDP/Breakdown at Constant 2010 Prices in US Dollars (All Countries). Household Consumption Expenditure. Online: unstats.un.org/unsd/snaama/dnltransfer.asp?fID=6

United Nations Development Programme. 2011. *Towards Human Resilience: Sustaining MDG Progress in an Age of Economic Uncertainty*. New York: United Nations.

Vickers, Tom. 2013. Racism and Politics in British State Welfare. Speech to Against Racism, Newcastle, 26 January. Online: https://refugeescapitalismstate.wordpress.com/2013/01/29/racism-and-politics-in-british-state-welfare-my-speech-at-against-racism-26-january-2013/

——2016. Towards a Model for the Internal Composition of Class Fractions: Applying Marx's Reserve Army of Labour to UK Immigration Controls, 1999–2015. Unpublished manuscript.

Waldinger, Roger and Michael I. Lichter. 2003. *How the Other Half Works: Immigration and the Social Organization of Labor*. Berkeley, CA: University of California Press.

Wall, Irwin, M. 1977. The French Communists and the Algerian War. *Journal of Contemporary History*. Vol. 12, No. 3, 521–43.

——1984. The PCF, the Colonial Question, and the Popular Front. Paper presented to the International Working Class Conference, Linz, Austria, September.

Wallerstein, Immanuel. 2000 [1988]. The Bourgeois(ie) as Concept and Reality. In *The Essential Wallerstein*. New York: The New Press, pp. 324–44.

——and Terence K. Hopkins. 2000 [1986]. Commodity Chains in the World-Economy Prior to 1800. In *The Essential Wallerstein*. New York: The New Press, pp. 221–34.

Warren, Bill. 1973. Myths of Underdevelopment: Imperialism and Capitalist Industrialization. *New Left Review*. Vol. 81. September–October, 3–44.

——1980. *Imperialism, Pioneer of Capitalism.* London: Verso.

Watkin, Kevin. 2001. The World Must Rein in the Wreckers Who Trade in Misery. *The Guardian.* January, 18–24.

Weber, Max. 1981 [1927]. *General Economic History.* New Brunswick, NJ: Transaction Books.

Webber, M. J. and S. P. H. Foot. 1984. The Measurement of Unequal Exchange. *Environment and Planning A.* Vol. 16, 927–47.

Weeks, John and Elizabeth Dore. 1979. International Exchange and the Causes of Backwardness. *Latin American Perspectives.* Vol. 6, No. 2, 62–87.

Wehler, Hans-Ulrich. 1970. Bismarck's Imperialism, 1862–1890. *Past and Present.* No. 48. August, 119–55.

Werlhof, Claudia von 2000, 'Globalization' and the 'Permanent' Process of 'Primitive Accumulation': The Example of the MAI, the Multilateral Agreement on Investment. *Journal of World-Systems Research.* Vol. 3, Fall/Winter. Special Issue: Festschrift for Immanuel Wallerstein – Part 2, 728–47.

Williams, Eric. 1944. *Capitalism and Slavery.* Chapel Hill, NC: University of North Carolina Press.

Wolf, Martin. 2009. Why China Must Do More to Rebalance Its Economy. *Financial Times.* 22 September. Online: www.ft.com/content/160e4cc4-a7a7-11de-boee-00144feabdco

Wong, Hannah, Sia Nassiripour, Raza Mir and William Healy. 2011. Transfer Price Setting in Multinational Corporations. *International Journal of Business and Social Science.* Vol. 2, No. 9. Special Issue, May. Online: http://ijbssnet.com/journals/Vol._2_No._9_[Special_Issue_-_May_2011]/3.pdf

Wood, Adrian. 1997. Openness and Wage Inequality in Developing Countries: The Latin American Challenge to East Asian Conventional Wisdom. *The World Bank Economic Review.* Vol. 11, No. 1, 33–57.

Wood, Ellen Meiksins. 2003. *Empire of Capital.* London: Verso.

World Bank. 2001. *Global Development Finance 2001.* Washington, DC: World Bank.

——2010. *World Development Indicators.* Washington, DC: World Bank.

——2011. *Global Development Horizons 2011: Multipolarity – The New Global Economy.* Washington, DC: World Bank.

——2017. GDP Per Person Employed (Constant 2011 PPP $). Online: https://data.worldbank. org/indicator/SL.GDP.PCAP.EM.KD

——2018. Household Final Consumption Expenditure Per Capita (Constant 2010 US$). Online: https://data.worldbank.org/indicator/NE.CON.PRVT.PC.KD

WTO (World Trade Organization). 2011. *International Trade Statistics 2011.* Online: www.wto. org/english/res_e/statis_e/its2011_e/section1_e/i04.xls

——2017. The WTO Can Cut Living Costs and Raise Living Standards. World Trade Organization, Geneva. Online: www.wto.org/english/thewto_e/whatis_e/10thi_e/10thio1_e. htm

Yoshihara, Naoki and Roberto Veneziani. 2016. Globalisation and Inequality: A Dynamic General Equilibrium Model of Unequal Exchange. Department of Economics Working Paper Series. No. 206. University of Massachusetts. Online: http://scholarworks.umass.edu/ econ_workingpaper/206

Zarembka, Paul. 2015. Materialized Composition of Capital and its Stability in the United States: Findings Stimulated by Paitaridis and Tsoulfidis (2012). *Review of Radical Political Economics.* Vol. 47, No. 1, 106–11.

Zhou, Xiaochuan. 2009. Reform the International Monetary System. *BIS Review.* Vol. 41. 23 March. Online: www.bis.org/review/r090402c.pdf

Index

Read. Debate. Organise.

Join the Left Book Club

A subscription book club for everyone on the left.

Mass membership of the LBC in the 1930s and 40s helped to turn public opinion against fascism and bring about Labour's landslide victory after WWII.

Join us today. You will receive:

• The best books from a range of publishers on politics, economics, society and culture
• Beautiful collectable editions, unique to members
• Choice of subscriptions at affordable prices
• Access to reading groups and events
• Build networks and champion political education

Become a member: www.leftbookclub.com

The Pluto Press Newsletter

Hello friend of Pluto!

Want to stay on top of the best radical books
we publish?

Then sign up to be the first to hear about our
new books, as well as special events,
podcasts and videos.

You'll also get 50% off your first order with us
when you sign up.

Come and join us!

Go to bit.ly/PlutoNewsletter

Printed and bound by CPI Group (UK) Ltd, Croydon, CR0 4YY

16/04/2025

14658482-0003